The Foundations of Worldwide Economic Integration

Power, Institutions, and Global Markets, 1850–1930

The chapters in this volume discuss the worldwide economic integration between 1850 and 1930, challenging the popular description of the period after 1918 as one of mere deglobalisation. The authors posit that markets were not only places of material exchange but also socially structured entities, shaped by the agency of individual actors and by complex structures of political and economic power. Economic transactions were supported by an array of different institutions, ranging from formalized regulations to informal relations of personal trust. They argue that these networks were strong enough to prosper even through and after World War I, in a political climate often hostile to foreign trade. *The Foundations of Worldwide Economic Integration* shows that institutionalism altered its shape in the face of circumstances that increasingly challenged international trade. By presenting case studies from various countries, this book offers a fresh perspective on crucial periods of economic globalisation.

Christof Dejung is Senior Lecturer and Researcher in the Department of History and Sociology at the University of Konstanz, Germany.

Niels P. Petersson is Senior Lecturer in History at Sheffield Hallam University, United Kingdom.

Cambridge Studies in the Emergence of Global Enterprise

Editors

Louis Galambos, *The Johns Hopkins University*
Geoffrey Jones, *Harvard Business School*

Other Books in the Series:

Global Electrification: Multinational Enterprise and International Finance in the History of Light and Power, 1878–2007, by William J. Hausman

British Business in the Formative Years of European Integration, 1945–1973, by Neil Rollings

Banking on Global Markets: Deutsche Bank and the United States, 1870 to the Present, by Christopher Kobrak

The World's Newest Profession: Management Consulting in the Twentieth Century, by Christopher D. McKenna

Global Brands: The Evolution of Multinationals in Alcoholic Beverages, by Teresa da Silva Lopes

Knowledge and Competitive Advantage: The Coevolution of Firms, Technology, and National Institutions, by Johann Peter Murmann

National Cultures and International Competition: The Experience of Schering AC, 1851–1950, by Christopher Kobrak

The Foundations of Worldwide Economic Integration

Power, Institutions, and Global Markets, 1850–1930

Edited by

CHRISTOF DEJUNG
University of Konstanz

NIELS P. PETERSSON
Sheffield Hallam University

CAMBRIDGE
UNIVERSITY PRESS

Shaftesbury Road, Cambridge CB2 8EA, United Kingdom

One Liberty Plaza, 20th Floor, New York, NY 10006, USA

477 Williamstown Road, Port Melbourne, VIC 3207, Australia

314–321, 3rd Floor, Plot 3, Splendor Forum, Jasola District Centre, New Delhi – 110025, India

103 Penang Road, #05–06/07, Visioncrest Commercial, Singapore 238467

Cambridge University Press is part of Cambridge University Press & Assessment, a department of the University of Cambridge.

We share the University's mission to contribute to society through the pursuit of education, learning and research at the highest international levels of excellence.

www.cambridge.org
Information on this title: www.cambridge.org/9781107030152

© Cambridge University Press & Assessment 2013

First published 2013
First paperback edition 2014

A catalogue record for this publication is available from the British Library

Library of Congress Cataloging-in-Publication data
The foundations of worldwide economic integration : power, institutions, and global markets, 1850–1930 / [edited by] Christof Dejung, University of Konstanz, Niels P. Petersson, Sheffield Hallam University.
pages cm. – (Cambridge studies in the emergence of global enterprise)
Includes bibliographical references and index.
ISBN 978-1-107-03015-2 (hardback)
1. International economic integration – History.   2. International trade – History.
3. International finance – History.   4. International economic relations – History.
5. Globalization – Economic aspects – History.   I. Dejung, Christof, editor of compilation.   II. Petersson, Niels P. editor of compilation.
HF1418.5.F68   2012
337.09′034–dc23   2012021038

ISBN   978-1-107-03015-2   Hardback
ISBN   978-1-107-43697-8   Paperback

Contents

viii   *Contents*

Tables and Figures

Tables

Figures

Contributors

Bernard Attard is Lecturer in Economic History in the School of Historical Studies at the University of Leicester. He is particularly interested in international investment before the Great Depression, the political economy of British overseas expansion, and the development of British settler societies. He has published several book chapters and articles on these subjects, most recently 'Making the Colonial State: Development, Debt and Warfare in New Zealand, 1853–78', *Australian Economic History Review* (2012). He is co-editor of a forthcoming special issue of the *Journal of Imperial and Commonwealth History* on Finance, Empire, and the British World, and is currently writing a study of indebtedness and imperialism in Queensland before 1930.

Michele d'Alessandro teaches Economic History at Bocconi University, Milan. He has published two company history books and written about the multinational operations of leading Italian banks in the first half of the twentieth century. He is currently in the process of publishing his PhD dissertation on the governance of international markets through the League of Nations in the late 1920s and early 1930s.

Phillip Dehne is Professor of History at St. Joseph's College, New York. His book *On the Far Western Front: Britain's First World War in South America* (Manchester, 2010), the first history of this conflict zone far from the European battlefields, expands the geographic parameters of First World War studies and explains how early twentieth-century globalisation could both intensify and mitigate Britain's total warfare. He is presently working on a book that uncovers the activities of Lord Robert Cecil at the Paris Peace Conference in 1919.

Christof Dejung is Senior Lecturer and Researcher in the Department of History and Sociology at the University of Konstanz, Germany. Recent publications include 'British Wartime Protectionism and Swiss Trading Firms in Asia during the First World War', *Past & Present* (2010), with Andreas Zangger; 'Bridges to the East: European Merchants and Business Practices in India and China', in Robert Lee (ed.); *Commerce and Culture: Nineteenth-Century Business Elites* (Farnham, 2011) and *Die Fäden des globalen Marktes: Eine Sozial- und Kulturgeschichte des Welthandels am Beispiel der Handelsfirma Gebrüder Volkart 1851–1999* (Cologne, forthcoming).

Pierre-Yves Donzé is Associate Professor at Kyoto University. He was born in Switzerland and studied history at the University of Neuchâtel, where he obtained his PhD in 2005, before studying as a postdoctoral Fellow in Japan and in the United States. He co-organised the session 'Technology Transfer in the 20th Century: Institutions and Actors' at the XVth World Economic History Congress at Utrecht (2009) and has recently published *History of the Swiss Watch Industry from Jacques David to Nicolas Hayek* (Peter Lang, 2011). He is currently working on an economic and business history of medical technologies in Japan from a global perspective.

Bernd-Stefan Grewe is Professor of Modern History at the University of Education in Freiburg, Germany. His research interests include environmental history (*Der versperrte Wald*, Köln, 2004), global and international history (Project: The Global History of Gold in the Twentieth Century), material culture (*Luxury in Global Perspective: Objects and practices*, edited with Karin Hofmeester, Oxford, forthcoming) and didactics of history.

Harold James is Professor of History and International Affairs in the Woodrow Wilson School, Princeton University. His most recent works are *The End of Globalization: Lessons from the Great Depression* (Cambridge, MA, 2001, which is also available in Chinese, German, Greek, Japanese, Korean and Spanish); *Europe Reborn: A History 1914–2000* (Harlow, 2003); and *The Roman Predicament: How the Rules of International Order Create the Politics of Empire* (Princeton, 2006). In 2004 he was awarded the Helmut Schmid Prize for Economic History, and in 2005 the Ludwig Erhard Prize for writing about economics. Professor James is currently working on a book on the history of the corporation in modern Europe, a study of the 1929 crash and a study of the history of European monetary integration.

Isabella Löhr is Research and Teaching Assistant in the Department of History at the University of Heidelberg. Her areas of research include the history of intellectual property rights, the history of international organisations and processes of globalisation and transnationalisation in the nineteenth and twentieth centuries. Recent publications include *Die Globalisierung geistiger Eigentumsrechte. Neue Strukturen internationaler Zusammenarbeit, 1886–1952* (Göttingen, 2010) and, forthcoming, *The Propertization of Culture and Knowledge: Global Governance of Intellectual Property Rights*, a special issue of the journal *Comparativ*, co-edited with Hannes Siegrist.

Claude Markovits is Emeritus Senior Research Fellow at the Centre for Indian and South Asian Studies, Ecole des Hautes Etudes en Sciences Sociales, CNRS, Paris. His publications include *The Global World of Indian Merchants, 1750–1947: Traders of Sind from Bukhara to Panama* (Cambridge, 2000); *Merchants, Traders, Entrepreneurs: Indian Business in the Colonial Era* (Basingstoke, 2008); and 'La circulation de la main d'œuvre commerciale dans le cadre d'un réseau marchand indien international au début du XXe siècle', in A. Stanziani (ed.), *Le travail contraint en Asie et en Europe XVIIe-XXe siècles* (Paris, 2010), 197–211.

Rowena Olegario is a Senior Research Fellow and Case Study Editor at Said Business School, University of Oxford. She is the author of *A Culture of Credit: Embedding Trust and Transparency in American Business* (Cambridge, MA, 2006). She is currently writing a history of credit in America.

Niels P. Petersson is Senior Lecturer in history at Sheffield Hallam University. His research interests include imperialism, globalisation and more recently, transnational social history. Selected publications include *Anarchie und Weltrecht. Das Deutsche Reich und die Institutionen der Weltwirtschaft, 1890–1930* (Göttingen, 2009) and, with Jürgen Osterhammel, *Globalization: A Short History* (Princeton, 2005).

Jérôme Sgard holds a PhD in Economics from Université de Paris-X-Nanterre. He is a Professor of Political Economy at Science-Po, affiliated to the Centre d'Etudes et de Recherches Internationales (CERI). Before that he was a senior researcher at CEPII, also in Paris, and an Associate Professor in Economics at Université de Paris-IX-Dauphine. During the 1990s he worked on economic reforms in Eastern Europe and Russia (*Europe de l'Est, la transition économique*, 1997), and on financial crises in emerging economies (see *L'Economie de la Panique*, 2002).

Since then his research interests have focussed on the architecture and crisis of markets as seen from the perspective of their microregulators: judges, arbiters and bureaucrats. This covers, for instance, the case of IMF policies vis-à-vis sovereign debts; private bankruptcies in nineteenth-century France; or the development of early industrial policy in eighteenth-century France.

Foreword

Harold James

Describing the very dynamic global trade of the second half of the nineteenth century and the early twentieth century has become a standard part of the repertoire of economic historians. I like to think in terms of globalisation cycles, with long periods of increased interchange of goods and flows of people, capital and ideas. But then something happens, and globalisation is interrupted. Many people feel that there has been too much interaction, and they draw back from the global setting and look instead for protected areas in which they can be safe from global threat and global devastation. Politics looks for national rather than international solutions to pressing problems and concerns, and international cooperation becomes tense and difficult, if not impossible. At each stage in the globalisation cycle, we tend to extrapolate and to think that this particular phase will last forever: whether it is the confident upswing or the stagnation and anger of the downward movement of the cycle.

The breakdown of globalisation has often been studied, and it is usually seen as a consequence of the interplay of policy responses that seek to limit the extent of international connectedness. By contrast, many people think of the integration or upswing phases as happening automatically, as a result simply of the unplanned magic of myriad market interactions.

But are the ups and downs of globalisation as clearly separable as such a model would suggest? The reactions that bring about the downturn have their origins in the upswing phase. Globalisation is not only a process that occurs somewhere out there – in an objective and measurable world of trade and money. It also happens in everyone's minds, and that part of globalisation is often more difficult to manage. To understand both the process and our reactions to it, we need a historical sense. If we want to understand why it is sometimes threatened, we need to know what makes it work, what drives it. This is what this fine book provides.

The chapters collected here show how much the establishment of globalisation follows from choices, plans and strategies. Integration does not in fact simply come out of nothing. Complex transactions and relations in a globalised society and economy require an element of certainty that is provided by a simple capacity to make equivalences.

The most obvious form of this security is the stability that is provided by a secure monetary standard, and globalisation upswings have always had a widely recognized and shared international measure of value. The late nineteenth century was characterized by Charles de Gaulle in retrospect as the *époque du trois pour cent*, the absolute confidence that government and other high-quality bonds would produce a stable and predictable return of 3 per cent. The foundational belief is that market prices send an intelligible signal, and it has political implications. Markets limit the capacity of governments to behave badly. Yet markets are also not purely automatic mechanisms, but depend on a host of conventions and institutions. What ideas and what interests drove the participants, and what was the relationship between ideas and interests? This is the question that already fascinated Max Weber at the height of the late nineteenth-century era of globalisation.

The confidence that was at the core of the globalisation belief in universal connectedness led many people to extend credit and take larger and larger risks. In short, the expectations aroused by globalisation set off credit booms, and the downswing of deglobalisation came with the disappointment of bubbly expectations and then with financial collapse. Raised expectations produced the sense that anything and everything was possible; in other words, euphoria ensued that lacked rational foundations. The power of markets in this case meant that alternative disciplinary methods, in the form of state regulation or in the imposition of a complex nonstate system of authority in a corporation, also began to be eroded. There was then a universal questioning of every type of value.

One of the most fascinating problems occurs when trying to determine how the trust or confidence arises that allows people to undertake risky transactions over long geographical distances, often across multiple political and judicial settings. It may stem from more information about business partners, made available through new organisations, through highly complex business corporations, credit agencies or official institutions that transmit and translate market signals into usable or reliable information. Weber gave an answer in terms of religious ideas and religious communities, in particular the gathered Protestant congregations of Northern Europe and North America. How do all of these institutional ways of managing space and time reduce transaction costs? How far do public authorities shape the institutional possibilities, and what kinds of cooperation are possible among states that see themselves in competition with each other? What are states doing when they manage their relations with each other and they work on international agreements?

The chapters in this collection also raise the intriguing question of how separable the globalisation and deglobalisation phases are from each other. Can we be in a period of deglobalisation while imagining that the world is ever more globalised? Do crises also produce countervailing forces? Finally, one of the greatest paradoxes is that it is military conflict that usually ends globalisation cycles and unleashes the backlash. The globalised world of the eighteenth century broke apart with the wars of the French Revolution and Napoleon, and the First World War gave a bad shock to the assumptions of early twentieth-century globalisers. Yet military activity and the imperialism of which it is an expression are also social processes that are transnational and globalised. The authors in this volume rightly do not see the First World War and its aftermath as simply a break in globalisation but rather as a turning of its direction and even as an element of continuity. Violence, as well as economic interaction, is contagious and spills over from country to country and from continent to continent.

I

Introduction

Power, Institutions, and Global Markets – Actors, Mechanisms, and Foundations of Worldwide Economic Integration, 1850–1930

Christof Dejung and Niels P. Petersson

The rapid expansion of world trade between 1850 and 1914, its difficult reconstruction during the 1920s and its subsequent decline during the Great Depression are key themes in the current historiography of economic globalisation.[1] Yet such scholarship has broadly focused on the changing volume of foreign trade between nation-states, on macroeconomic problems such as national tariff policies and on the history of the advancement of transport and communication technologies. There have been very few discussions of global trade development between the 1850s and the 1930s from the perspective of economic actors below the nation-state level, which is to say actors conducting trading operations in everyday business life. Likewise, economic and business historians have broadly neglected the institutional framework that both shapes and is shaped by the enterprises involved in such everyday trade.[2]

Through such a shift of focus, the contributions in the present volume strongly suggest that in the late nineteenth and early twentieth centuries,

[1] Among the numerous examples, it is perhaps helpful to refer to the work by the various contributors to Michael D. Bordo et al. (eds.), *Globalization in Historical Perspective* (Chicago, 2003) which in the 1990s began to complement older studies such as Albert G. Kenwood and Alan L. Lougheed, *The Growth of the International Economy 1820–2000: An Introductory Text* (4th edn. London, 1999).

[2] There are, of course, exceptions, which include, for example, Richard Tilly and Paul J. J. Welfens (eds.), *Economic Globalization, International Organizations and Crisis Management: Contemporary and Historical Perspectives on Growth, Impact and Evolutions of Major Organizations in an Interdependent World* (Berlin, 2000); Tilmann J. Röder, *Rechtsbildung im wirtschaftlichen 'Weltverkehr'. Das Erdbeben von San Francisco und die internationale Standardisierung von Vertragsbedingungen (1871–1914)* (Frankfurt a.M., 2006).

global economic integration was far more than the result of supply and
demand and ever more efficient means of transport and communications.
Rather, it was a fundamentally social process, one that would have been
impossible without rules and institutions. Long-distance trade has always
been an inherently risky business, requiring access to finance, reliable
business partners in far-away countries, and protection of property rights
under unfamiliar conditions and unforeseen circumstances. To these ends,
market participants have developed conventions, sought standardisation
and relied on mercantile law. Daniel W. Drezner has thus argued that the
global economy's regulation 'is intrinsically important. Markets rely on
rules, customs and institutions to work efficiently. Global Markets need
global rules and institutions to work efficiently'.[3]

Recent writing in business history has underscored the importance
of internationally operating firms for the establishment of global economic relations.[4] Yet for the most part such history has concentrated on
entrepreneurial decision making and foreign investments without being
very specific about either the social, cultural and political environments in
which these enterprises operated or the norms and regulations underpin-
ing their activities. In contrast, in other fields such as international history
and legal history, there has been a growing interest in how institutions –
rules, norms, regulations and organisations – evolve in settings beyond
the nation-state.[5] Such research has also pointed to the important role
played by nonstate actors in the development of institutions, these actors
including merchants, banks, interest groups and internationally organised
epistemic communities such as the community of international lawyers.[6]

[3] Daniel W. Drezner, *All Politics Is Global: Explaining International Regulatory Regimes*
(Princeton, 2007), 6.
[4] See for instance John H. Dunning, *Multinational Enterprises and the Global Economy*
(Wokingham, 1993); Geoffrey Jones, *Multinationals and Global Capitalism* (Oxford,
2005); Michael B. Miller, 'The Business Trip: Maritime Networks in the Twentieth Century', *Business History Review* 77 (2003), 1–32; Mira Wilkins, 'Multinational Enterprise
to 1930. Discontinuities and Continuities', in Alfred D. Chandler and Bruce Mazlish
(eds.), *Leviathans: Multinational Corporations and the New Global History* (Cambridge,
2005), 45–79.
[5] See, for example, Martin H. Geyer and Johannes Paulmann (eds.), *The Mechanics of
Internationalism: Culture, Society and Politics from the 1840s to the First World War*
(Oxford, 2001); Miloš Vec, *Recht und Normierung in der industriellen Revolution. Neue
Strukturen der Normsetzung in Völkerrecht, staatlicher Gesetzgebung und gesellschaftlicher Selbstnormierung* (Frankfurt a.M., 2006).
[6] For a description of the role of nongovernmental organisations in shaping international
relations in the twentieth century see Akira Iriye, *Global Community: The Role of International Organizations in the Making of the Contemporary World* (Berkeley, 2002).

The emergence of transnational institutions and organisations is complicated by the fact that they are in potential conflict with the control of states over national sovereignty and borders. In fact, international and intercontinental trade has always been a highly politicised activity. The processes of institutional development and economic integration thus need to be studied within their wider contexts. It is necessary to examine which actors have been involved and how they have contributed to the development of foreign commercial relations. Such a perspective has to take account of the interplay among state bureaucracies, internationally operating firms, stock and commodity exchanges, trade unions, peasants, and international and transnational organisations such as the League of Nations and the International Chamber of Commerce.

A focus on the creation of institutions by nongovernmental economic actors raises new questions about the periodisation of the history of economic globalisation. In particular, accounts of institutional continuity over time and the persistence of individual firms and internationally oriented institutional innovation in difficult periods of world trade may challenge the notion that we can clearly distinguish between eras of economic globalisation and deglobalisation. As a result, the First World War may appear as less of a watershed than in many historical accounts in which a period of Victorian and Edwardian globalisation is followed by deglobalisation in the interwar years.[7]

This volume addresses the question of how the rules and institutions that world markets needed to work efficiently came into being and evolved during the late nineteenth and early twentieth centuries, bringing together contributions from economic and business history, global and world history and legal history. It is informed by two sets of questions in particular. Firstly, which actors were most prominent in the creation of norms and institutions for global trade, and what were their interests, coalitions, conflicts and patterns of action? Second, how far should the First World War be seen as a turning point, dividing a period of rapid transnational

---

[7] For instance Hugo Ott, 'Kriegswirtschaft im 1. Weltkrieg – Ende der Weltwirtschaft?', in Jürgen Schneider et al. (eds.), *Wirtschaftskräfte und Wirtschaftswege. Festschrift für Herrmann Kellenbenz* (Bamberg, 1981), 505–24; Patrick Karl O'Brien, 'The Great War and the Dislocation of the International Economy 1914–1929', in Wilfried Feldenkirchen, Frauke Schönert-Röhlk and Günther Schulz (eds.), *Wirtschaft, Gesellschaft, Unternehmen. Festschrift für Hans Pohl zum 60. Geburtstag* (Stuttgart, 1995), 245–65; Eric Hobsbawm, *The Age of Extremes: The Short Twentieth Century, 1914–1991* (London, 1995); Ronald Findlay and Kevin H. O'Rourke, *Power and Plenty: Trade, War, and the World Economy in the Second Millennium* (Princeton, 2007), 429 ff.

integration from one of laborious, precarious and ultimately failed reconstruction, and to what extent or in what areas can a continuity of global
integration be discerned between the two periods? In the remainder of this
introduction, we take a closer look at the volume's three key concepts –
institutions, power and global markets – and provide some reflections on
the periodisation of economic globalisation between the 1850s and the
1930s.

The Importance of Institutions for Worldwide Economic Interaction

Intercontinental trade is an especially relevant topic for research on internationalism because it is associated with particularly high transaction
and information costs; as institutional economics points out, these costs
may be reduced by institutions or organisations that make interaction
predictable and contracts enforceable. Indeed, already in the early twentieth century, the study of business organisation in international trade
led scholars such as Austria's Josef Hellauer to analyse organisational
phenomena with reference to factors such as principal-agent problems
and information and transaction costs in much the same way as did later
institutional economists.[8]

It may be useful to point out two 'structural facts' about economic
transactions. The first of these is the fundamental problem of balancing security and efficiency. To maximise security, traders would have to
deal only with known and trusted partners, directly and simultaneously
exchanging goods or services against money. However, such a way of
doing business would not be very efficient because it unduly restricts the
choice of partners and limits the scope and speed of deals, thereby diminishing profits. In the real world, traders can subsist and thrive only if
they deal with people they do not know, when for example they borrow
money to finance deals, extend credit to their customers, sell goods they
do net yet own and ship goods they have not yet sold. It is by doing just
these things that intermediaries perform a useful service for which other
people are willing to pay. Such practices increase both business volume
and the turnover of funds, which means multiplying the profit to be made
with a given amount of capital. The practices do, however, transform

---

[8] Josef Hellauer, *System der Welthandelslehre. Ein Lehr- und Handbuch des internationalen Handels. Erster Band: Allgemeine Welthandelslehre* (8th edn. Berlin, 1920, 1st
edn. 1910). Hellauer's institutional focus did not prevent him from resorting to racist and
'culturalist' explanations for the actions of non-European businesspeople.

simple individual transactions into complex and interdependent networks of contractual relationships among a great number of highly specialised parties. When something goes wrong, disturbances can spread like a chain reaction through these networks, disrupting much more than individual transactions and possibly putting the existence of an entire business at risk. Increased efficiency often means increased risk. Awareness of these basic facts is evident from the anguished musings of a nineteenth-century 'mercantile Hamlet' recently unearthed by Hartmut Berghoff:

> To sell or not to sell?
> That is the question
> Whether it is better to send the goods
> And take the risk of doubtful payment,
> Or to make sure of what is in possession
> And, by declining, hold them.
> To sell; to ship; perchance to lose –
> Aye, there's the rub!
> For when the goods are gone,
> what charm can win them back
> From slippery debtors?
> Will bills be paid when due?
> Or, will the time stretch out till crack of doom?[9]

Many nineteenth-century innovations such as the credit rating agencies studied by Rowena Olegario in her contribution to this volume were designed to deal with such risks. Another solution was to substitute intra-firm transactions governed by hierarchy for market exchanges, as Ronald Coase has argued in a seminal paper.[10] In global trade, this could mean that merchant firms chose to open up company-owned agencies in far-off trading posts, thereby reducing transaction costs by bringing transactions under the control of their representatives. The contributions by Christof Dejung and Claude Markovits provide case studies of how traders on the Indian subcontinent tried to implement this strategy.

The second structural fact is the pronounced multilateral nature of trade and finance especially but by no means exclusively before 1914. It is well known that, from a macroeconomic perspective, multilateral clearing of balances of payment was an important contributor to growth

---

[9] Undated poem quoted in Peter R. Earling, *Whom to Trust: A Practical Treatise on Mercantile Credits* (Chicago, 1890), 200, here quoted from Hartmut Berghoff, 'Civilizing Capitalism? The Beginnings of Credit Rating in the United States and Germany', *GHI Bulletin*, 45 (2009), 9–28, 13.

[10] Ronald H. Coase, 'The Nature of the Firm', *Economica New Series* 4 (1937), 386–405.

and equilibrium in the prewar world economy.[11] From a microeconomic perspective, we see that, as a matter of unquestioned routine, *each individual commercial transaction* involved merchants, producers, brokers, transporters, insurers, banks and so forth from various countries or even continents, with contractual relationships thus usually stretching over several national jurisdictions. How did those involved in international business prevent things from going wrong or protect themselves if they did? Transactions on a global scale confront trading partners with particularly severe challenges. The huge distances they cover means that for a long time, goods will be in transit, entrusted to a third party, exposed to the considerable risks of long-distance transport, and under the control of neither the buyer nor the seller. Capital will be tied up in these goods and unavailable for other uses. There are likely to be cultural differences between the trading partners, as well as different understandings of key business practices and customs. Finally, buyers and sellers are likely to be situated in different nations with different legal systems. Similar risks are faced by those investing capital in ventures abroad or in railway, municipality and government bonds in far-off countries.

'New institutional economics' has addressed the question of how problems arising from such a situation – the enforcement of contracts, information asymmetries, principal-agent problems and so on – have been solved, bringing down transaction costs to an acceptable level. Following Douglass North, we may distinguish between formal and informal types of institution.[12] For a long time, international trade was marked by an absence of strong formal institutions. In an earlier age, traders had often relied on personal networks, kinship or religion to identify business partners they could trust.[13] As Timothy Guinanne has pointed out, trust is not an *explanans* but an *explanandum*. It results, for example, from knowledge about the trading partner or from a conviction that contracts can be enforced (a point supported by Claude Markovits's discussion in this volume of the credit networks of Indian firms).[14]

[11] Kenwood and Lougheed, *Growth of the International Economy*.
[12] Douglass C. North, *Institutions, Institutional Change and Economic Performance* (Cambridge, 1991). See also Mark Casson, 'Institutional Economics and Business History: A Way Forward', in Mark Casson and Mary B. Rose (eds.), *Institutions and the Evolution of Modern Business* (London, 1998), 151–71.
[13] A highly influential study has been Avner Greif, *Institutions and the Path to the Modern Economy: Lessons from Medieval Trade* (Cambridge, 2006).
[14] Timothy W. Guinnane, 'Trust: A Concept too Many', *Jahrbuch für Wirtschaftsgeschichte* (2005), 77–92.

However, as the cultural and geographical distance between trading partners increases, the foundations of such informal institutions become weaker or else even have to be created ex nihilo. This is precisely the situation created by the expanding late nineteenth-century world trade, which was taking place in a rapidly changing legal and institutional framework. Global markets were bringing together buyers, sellers and intermediaries with widely different cultural backgrounds, experiences, expectations and allegiances, as well as very heterogeneous ideas about the nature of the market in which they were participating. It thus became more important to create explicit sets of rules, either from scratch or based on precedents.

Both formal and informal institutions can be created by a variety of actors and in a variety of ways. Individual nation-states make laws for their national territory and for their colonial dependencies (see Chapter 7);[15] international conventions create laws valid in a number of states or that harmonise national legal rules (see Chapters 2, 3, 9, and 10); particular merchants' associations draw up standard contracts and codifications of mercantile custom (see Chapter 2); individual firms make agreements with agents in other parts of the world that are reinforced by personal ties and conceptions of honour (see Chapter 8); and business information is provided on a commercial basis (as examined in Chapter 4).

Our hypothesis is that institutions developed in complex negotiations between – in each case highly specific – sets of public and private, local, national and global actors. The rules and institutions that were discussed and sometimes implemented were of various types and status, among them national and international law, customary law, local customs, informal rules of the game and privately established orders. A tension was always manifest between the tendency of individual actors or networks to organise themselves, on the one hand,[16] and the claim of states and international organisations to create generally binding rules in their jurisdiction, on the other hand.

---

[15] Wolfgang J. Mommsen and Jaap A. de Moor (eds.), *European Expansion and Law: The Encounter of European and Indigenous Law in 19th and 20th Century Africa and Asia* (Oxford, 1992); Lauren Benton, *Law and Colonial Cultures: Legal Regimes in World History, 1400–1900* (Cambridge, 2002); Helmut Janssen, *Die Übertragung von Rechtsvorstellungen auf fremde Kulturen am Beispiel des englischen Kolonialrechts. Ein Beitrag zur Rechtsvergleichung* (Tübingen, 2000).

[16] This is a point stressed by scholars influenced by Niklas Luhmann's systems theory.

Power and Economic Exchange

Power, both economic and noneconomic, inscribes itself into markets by shaping institutions. Power is thus an aspect of every market, and the institutions governing international and global markets cannot be studied without reference to it. Four aspects of power stand out in the period studied here.

First, on a global scale, we need to take account of 'the rise of the West' and the 'great divergence' around 1800 that put an end to relative parity between Europe and other advanced regions, bringing ever larger parts of the world under European dominance.[17] In their classic paper, 'Imperialism of Free Trade', John Gallagher and Ronald Robinson have argued that Europeans preferred informal influence and economic integration to colonial rule where possible.[18] Countries unwilling to integrate into the Western-dominated global economy, however, were often forced to 'open up' and accept free trade with the help of gunboats, as was the case in China and Japan. Colonial territories were developed into areas for the production of raw materials, thus securing supplies for European industry. European law was introduced to provide legal security in the colonies, thereby reducing transaction costs, and to facilitate the operation of Western merchants and plantation owners in these areas.[19] This process often amounted to economic exploitation of the conquered regions, but the exploitation did not extinguish the agency of indigenous merchants, moneylenders and peasants. Often local social and economic conditions made the objectives of colonial bureaucrats much more difficult to attain than they had assumed, as Christof Dejung argues in an analysis of the problems faced by the British when they tried to improve cotton quality on the Indian subcontinent. Furthermore, as Claude Markovits demonstrates, indigenous economic elites

---

[17] William H. McNeill, *The Rise of the West: A History of the Human Community* (Chicago, 1963); Kenneth Pomeranz, *The Great Divergence: Europe, China, and the Making of the Modern World Economy* (Princeton 2000); John Darwin, *After Tamerlane: The Global History of Empire since 1450* (London, 2007). For a critical review of these approaches see Patrick Karl O'Brien, 'The Deconstruction of Myths and Reconstruction of Metanarratives in Global Histories of Material Progress', in Benedikt Stuchtey and Eckhardt Fuchs (eds.), *Writing World History, 1800–2000* (Oxford, 2003), 67–90; Peter Kramper, 'Warum Europa? Konturen einer globalgeschichtlichen Forschungskontroverse', *Neue Politische Literatur* 54 (2009), 9–46.

[18] John Gallagher and Ronald Robinson, 'The Imperialism of Free Trade', *Economic History Review New Series* 6 (1953), 1–15.

[19] Mommsen and de Moor (eds.), *European Expansion and Law* (Berg, 1992).

were sometimes able to create their own commercial networks, functioning in parallel to the globalised infrastructure of Western business.

Second, any discussion of power would be incomplete without reference to the often overwhelming importance of the nation-state – which often was also an imperial power.[20] The same period that witnessed the establishment of a truly globalised economy and of imperial expansion also witnessed a consolidation of national identities and a reinforcement of national borders. Several scholars have claimed that, at least in the nineteenth century, globalisation and territorialisation were not diametrically opposed developments but rather were closely interrelated or dialectally intertwined.[21] After the 1870s and then particularly in the interwar years, nations aimed to consolidate their economic influence on a global scale while at the same time trying to protect their domestic markets from foreign competition. International patent law is one example of the creativity of national governments in applying international conventions for the benefit of their domestic industries. For the sake of allowing their entrepreneurs to continue copying foreign products, small European countries like Switzerland and the Netherlands delayed the adoption of patent laws despite having signed the Paris Convention. As Pierre-Yves Donzé shows in Chapter 9, Japan also promoted technology transfer through a highly selective application of such international law: on the one hand, by protecting Western intellectual property, the Japanese government sustained the cooperation between major Japanese and Western firms necessary for breaking into technologically advanced sectors; on the other, it allowed Japanese firms to copy easily reproduced low-tech consumer goods by excluding them from that law.

Third, both individual companies and company networks enjoy a certain degree of power over the market. Obviously, they influence markets by simply participating in them – that is, by providing products and services at the highest price they can obtain and buying raw materials and services at the lowest available price. Large corporations may also seek to control markets by gaining monopoly position, forming cartels or creating formal institutions for a particular segment of the market. In addition, firms may try to influence decision makers outside the market, such as governments, political parties and regulatory authorities,

---

[20] On this, see Jürgen Osterhammel, 'Globalizations', in Jeremy H. Bentley (ed.), *The Oxford Handbook of World History* (Oxford, 2011).

[21] Ian Clark, *Globalization and Fragmentation: International Relations in the Twentieth Century* (Oxford, 1997); Sebastian Conrad, *Globalisierung und Nation im Deutschen Kaiserreich* (Munich, 2006).

thus shaping the economic rules. Economic power has often been influential in shaping political decision making – an argument developed by, for instance, Peter Cain and A. G. Hopkins, who have proposed that the 'gentlemanly capitalism' of the City of London was the main force shaping the evolution of British imperialism;[22] this issue is considered by Bernard Attard in Chapter 5, with reference to the City of London's 'structural power' in the global economy after 1850. Britain may have been a special case in this respect because maintaining institutions capable of supporting London's pivotal role in the world economy was a consistent priority of British economic policy, a fact explored in the contributions of Phillip Dehne, Christof Dejung and Bernd-Stefan Grewe. The United States and Germany appear to offer a contrast: in both countries, it has been argued that, in many areas crucial for international economic integration, policy has often been shaped by those societal groups least interested in its promotion.[23] In any event, political and corporate power interpenetrate and reinforce each other, and frequently, large – especially multinational – firms are able to resist political interference with their operations.[24]

Fourth and finally, power may of course have a much more direct impact on markets than that mediated through institutions. A prime example of such direct impact is warfare. As Ronald Findlay and Kevin H. O'Rourke have shown, international trade has rarely existed in splendid isolation from the sphere of international rivalry and war.[25] In the First World War, belligerent powers were aware that economic performance and the supply of raw materials were decisive for military success and thus closed or blacklisted firms suspected of 'trading with the enemy'.[26] Yet as Phillip Dehne's contribution makes clear, neutral countries provided

---

[22] Peter J. Cain and A. G. Hopkins, *British Imperialism, 1688–2000* (Harlow, 2001).

[23] See Drezner, *All Politics Is Global*, 5, on this point, which finds general support in Niels P. Petersson's contribution to this volume.

[24] For this reason, they were depicted as modern leviathans by Alfred Chandler and Bruce Mazlish in their *Leviathans: Multinational Corporations and the New Global History* (Cambridge, MA, 2005).

[25] Findlay and O'Rourke, *Power and Plenty*.

[26] For economic warfare during the First World War, see among others Avner Offer, *The First World War: An Agrarian Interpretation* (Oxford, 1989); John McDermott, 'Trading with the Enemy: British Business and the Law during the First World War', *Canadian Journal of History* 32 (1997), 201–20; Marc Frey, 'Trade, Ships, and the Neutrality of the Netherlands in the First World War', *International History Review* 19 (1997), 541–62; Niall Ferguson, *The Pity of War: Explaining World War I* (New York, 1999), 248–81; Stephan Broadberry and Mark Harrison (eds.), *The Economics of World War I* (Cambridge, 2005); Christof Dejung and Andreas Zangger, 'British Wartime Protectionism and Swiss Trading Companies in Asia during the First World War', *Past and Present* 207 (2010), 181–213.

a space in which firms such as the important Argentine grain merchant Bunge & Born could maintain and even expand their networks in wartime. Likewise, international organisations like those established by the Berne conventions on intellectual property preserved their internationalist orientation throughout the war, as we learn from Isabella Löhr's contribution. This underlines the resilience of economic actors and international organisations even in the chauvinist climate of the wartime years.

Global Markets as Social Entities

Markets are more than abstract mechanisms equilibrating supply and demand; rather, they need to be analysed as social entities and as 'social facts' that exist, in the sense proposed by Emile Durkheim, only because they are recognised as such in social practice.[27] Historically, markets have always been characterised by highly specific rules about the forms and objects of economic transactions and who may participate in them. Such rules are part of the constitution of all markets, which can only be analysed against their social, cultural and political backgrounds. The rules themselves have both an inward and an outward dimension. The inward dimension involves their effect on market participants and the relations between them. Clearly, it is quite often the aim of powerful market participants to bend or rewrite the rules in their favour, whether through cartels, their influence in chambers of commerce and stock exchanges – a focus of Bernard Attard's contribution – or the lobbying of governments as touched on earlier.

The outward dimension involves the effect of these rules on third parties such as the state or the public. In the framework of the present financial crisis, it is no longer necessary to dwell on the facts that governance of markets is of strong interest to society as a whole and that rules for global markets produce global externalities. The rules governing market transactions are thus subject to political debate, and they are always the result of political decisions either to leave the nature and form of transactions to the discretion of market participants or restrict them in the interest of some higher good. Such an understanding of markets thus underscores the insight that even in modern capitalism they are by no means autonomous spheres that can be clearly distinguished from the rest of society.

---

[27] Emile Durkheim, *The Rules of the Sociological Method* (New York, 1982), 50–59.

Markets, then, have to be conceptualised as socially embedded entities[28] framed by cultural patterns, as has been argued recently by a number of authors.[29] They are created by specific actors acting under their own particular vision of world order,[30] regulated by various institutions, and influenced by power relations. Because they only come into being through the agency of market participants, it might be appropriate to describe them as social structures that both shape the agency of individual actors and, at the same time, are sustained and shaped by their activities. Such a view of markets may be based on theories of '*structuration*' as proposed by Max Weber, Antony Giddens and others.[31]

Periodisation

An approach aimed at investigating the creation of institutions by economic actors beyond the nation-state may also challenge the idea that we can clearly distinguish between periods of economic globalisation and deglobalisation. In light of recent research on business and colonial history, accounts of a 'globalisation backlash' in the late nineteenth century or of the 1929 stock market crash as the 'end of globalisation'[32] in fact appear to be referring more to – doubtlessly severe – episodes in the history of international economic exchange than to its actual 'end'. After the Great War, internationalism was revived through a number of conventions and organisations such as the Berne convention (see Chapter 10) and the treaty establishing the League of Nations (see Chapter 10),

---

[28] Mark Granovetter, 'Economic Action and Social Structure: The Problem of Embeddedness', *American Journal of Sociology* 91 (1985), 481–510.

[29] James G. Carrier (ed.), *Meanings of the Market: The Free Market in Western Culture* (Oxford, 1997); Thomas L. Haskell and Richard F. Teichgraeber III (eds.), *The Culture of the Market: Historical Essays* (Cambridge, 1993); Hansjörg Siegenthaler, 'Geschichte und Ökonomie nach der kulturalistischen Wende', *Geschichte und Gesellschaft* 25 (1999), 276–301; Hartmut Berghoff and Jakob Vogel (eds.), *Wirtschaftsgeschichte als Kulturgeschichte*. Dimensionen eines Perspektivenwechsels (Frankfurt a.M., 2004).

[30] Sebastian Conrad and Dominic Sachsenmaier (eds.). *Competing Visions of World Order: Global Moments and Movements, 1880s–1930s* (New York, 2007).

[31] Max Weber, *Wirtschaft und Gesellschaft. Grundriss der verstehenden Soziologie* (Tübingen, 1972; first published 1922); Anthony Giddens, *The Constitution of Society: Outline of the Theory of Structuration* (Cambridge, 1984).

[32] Kevin H. O'Rourke and Jeffrey G. Williamson, *Globalization and History: The Evolution of a Nineteenth-Century Economy* (Cambridge, MA, 1999), 93; Harold James, *The End of Globalization: Lessons from the Great Depression* (Cambridge, MA, 2001); Karl Polanyi, *The Great Transformation: The Political and Economic Origins of Our Time* (Boston, 1944).

which aimed at reconstructing institutions on a global scale or even creating new ones – although from the late 1920s onwards, the obstacles
and problems became more prominent than the success stories. Nevertheless, business historians have pointed to the fact that for many large
firms, the interwar years were a time of extensive foreign investment
and of operations on an ever more global scale. This suggests resilience, despite the indisputably more difficult business environment after
1914–18, and a measure of creative adaptation to economic policies
marked by a widespread protectionist mood.[33] Recent studies indicate
that the interwar years were the golden age for the organisation of international cartels, which gained power over markets on a global scale.[34]
This complex reality is confirmed in several of the following chapters:
taken together the contributions of Claude Markovits, Christof Dejung
and Phil Dehne underscore that, after 1918, trading firms from countries as different as Switzerland, Argentina, India, Japan and the United
States significantly extended their range of operations. Indeed, from the
perspective of many countries on the non-European 'periphery', the interwar years were a time of accelerated economic development and integration. Starting in the late nineteenth century, not only Japan but also
China and India experienced industrial development, most notably in
textiles – a process opening new markets for Western producers of
machines and power looms, while at the same time permitting non-
Western entrepreneurs to compete with Western imports, at first in
domestic and then in international markets.[35]

---

[33] Geoffrey Jones, 'The End of Nationality? Global Firms and 'Borderless Worlds', *Zeitschrift für Unternehmensgeschichte* 51 (2006), 164; Margrit Müller, 'From Protectionism to Market Liberalisation: Patterns of Internationalisation in the Main Swiss Export
Sectors', in Margrit Müller and Timo Myllyntaus (eds.), *Path Breakers: Small European
Countries Responding to Globalisation and De-Globalisation* (Bern, 2008), 113–49.

[34] Harm G. Schröter, 'Kartellierung und Dekartellierung 1890–1990', *Vierteljahrschrift
für Sozial- und Wirtschaftsgeschichte* 81 (1994), 457–93; Peter E. Fäßler, 'Internationale
Kartelle während der Deglobalisierung 1918–1939', in Rolf Walter (ed.), *Globalisierung in der Geschichte. Erträge der 23. Arbeitstagung der Gesellschaft für Sozial- und
Wirtschaftsgeschichte vom 18.–21. März 2009* (Stuttgart, 2011), 233–51.

[35] Kaoru Sugihara, 'British Imperialism, the City of London and Global Industrializa-
tion', in Shigeru Akita (ed.), *Gentlemanly Capitalism, Imperialism and Global History*,
(Basingstoke, 2002), 185–204. For Japan, see Michael Smitka (ed.), *The Interwar Eco-
nomy of Japan. Colonialism, Depression, and Recovery, 1910–1940* (New York, 1998);
David Flath, *The Japanese Economy* (Oxford, 2000). For India, see Rajat Kanta Ray,
Industrialization in India: Growth and Conflict in the Private Corporate Sector, 1919–47
(Delhi, 1979); Daniel R. Headrick, *The Tentacles of Progress: Technology Transfer in the
Age of Imperialism, 1850–1940* (Oxford, 1988), 285 ff., 361 ff.; Rajnarayan Chandav-
arkar, *The Origins of Industrial Capitalism in India: Business Strategies and the Working*

TABLE I. *Share of Global Trade According to Areas (per cent)*

Area	Import 1913	Import 1924	Export 1913	Export 1924	Total of Foreign Trade 1913	Total of Foreign Trade 1924
Europe	69.34	61.78	62.40	50.97	65.99	56.52
Northern America*	12.23	16.33	15.83	22.16	13.96	19.15
Central America**	1.54	2.04	2.10	3.64	1.82	2.83
South America	5.59	4.95	6.60	6.81	6.07	5.85
Africa	1.7	1.89	2.61	2.66	2.14	2.27
Asia	7.14	9.81	7.84	10.36	7.48	10.08
Oceania***	2.46	3.20	2.62	3.40	2.54	3.30

* Canada and United States. **From Mexico to Panama including the West Indies. ***Australia and Polynesia.
Source: Hermann Levy, 'Die Enteuropäisierung der Welthandelsbilanz', *Weltwirtschaftliches Archiv* 23 (1926), 331.

A review of statistical data confirms that – with variations depending on the measures used – the volume of international trade regained its pre-1914 level by the mid-1920s (see Figure 1). Importantly, not all parts of the globe were hit in equal measure by the dent in foreign trade after 1914 (see Table 1). Rather, this was first and foremost a European phenomenon. The share of European countries in global trade declined from more than 62 per cent in 1911–13 to below 51 percent in 1927–29 – though even with this obvious decrease Europe was still responsible for more than half of global imports and exports. Other parts of the world, in contrast, increased their share in global trade in the interwar years. The share in global trade of Canada and the United States grew from 14 to 19 per cent and that of Asian countries from 7.5 to 10 percent between 1913 and 1924. In particular, trade between North America and Asia increased remarkably in the interwar years, virtually doubling between 1913 and 1924. The crisis of the European economy becomes obvious when we consider that intra-European trade declined from 40 per cent of worldwide trade in 1911–13 to 30 per cent in 1927–29. In contrast, the part of trade between Europe and non-European countries remained

Classes in Bombay, 1900–1940 (Cambridge, 1994). For China, see Jürgen Osterhammel, 'Imperialism in Transition: British Business and the Chinese Authorities, 1931–37', *China Quarterly* 98 (1984), 260–86; Mathias Mutz, '"Ein unendlich weites Gebiet für die Ausdehnung unseres Geschäfts": Marketingstrategien des Siemens-Konzerns auf dem chinesischen Markt (1904–1937)', *Zeitschrift für Unternehmensgeschichte* 51 (2006), 93–115.

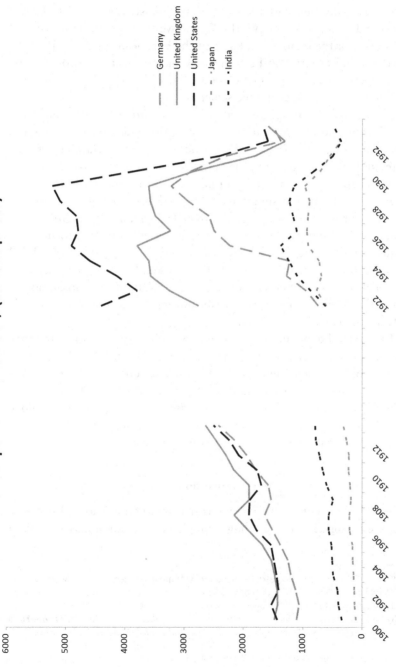

FIGURE 1. World Exports, 1900–1934. *Source:* United Nations, *International Trade Statistics 1900–1960* (New York: United Nations, 1962, available online at http://unstats.un.org/unsd/trade/imts/Historical%20data%201900–1960.pdf).

nearly constant.[36] The shift of the global economic equilibrium began as early as the late nineteenth century with the industrial boost in the United States and Japan. The First World War, however, reinforced this trend.[37] In the face of the relative weakness of the European economy, the German economist Hermann Levy in 1926 diagnosed 'a de-Europeanizing tendency in economic interactions on a global level' and the emergence of a more polycentric economic structure.[38]

Hence, from a perspective taking in international cartels, multinational firms and the non-European world, the interwar years were not a period of deglobalisation, but a period in which the relations between states and firms and between the West and the 'rest' were reordered and renegotiated. In many respects, rather than being stopped in its tracks, economic globalisation simply changed its shape, finding expression in different forms. The fact that the Great Depression was a *global* economic crisis points to the persistence of economic interdependence. Yet unquestionably, this interwar reordering and renegotiation of the global economy took place in an environment marked by increasing suspicion of global economic interdependence and by its routine subordination to other domestic concerns – as described in the contributions by Michele d'Alessandro and Niels P. Petersson.

This general dynamic supports an approach to globalisation attentive to discrepancies, asynchronies and dead ends and that does not assume the phenomenon is a teleological and homogeneous process. As Frederick Cooper has argued, we need to observe precisely in which regard – political, social, cultural or economic – and in which parts of the globe cross-border interaction was increasing or decreasing at any particular time, as well as the identity of the actors involved.[39]

Conclusion

A central argument of this volume is that international and global economic exchange is far more than a simple flow of commodities between

[36] Werner Schlote, 'Zur Frage der sogenannten "Enteuropäisierung" des Welthandels', *Weltwirtschaftliches Archiv* 37 (1933), 381–411; Hermann Levy, 'Die Enteuropäisierung der Welthandelsbilanz', *Weltwirtschaftliches Archiv* 23 (1926), 329–41.

[37] Sydney Pollard, *Peaceful Conquest: The Industrialization of Europe 1760–1970* (Oxford, 1981), 281; Christoph Nonn, *Das 19. und 20. Jahrhundert* (Paderborn, 2007), 29.

[38] Levy, 'Die Enteuropäisierung der Welthandelsbilanz', 329.

[39] Frederick Cooper, 'What is the Concept of Globalization Good For? An African Historian's Perspective', *African Affairs* 100 (2001), 189–213.

various nation-states. Long-distance trade requires complex institutional underpinnings that evolved in the – at times cooperative, but often confrontational – interplay of private actors, national governments and international bodies, with each trying to establish structures or introduce regulations to control the flow of goods and reduce uncertainty in international trade.

One general finding running through the volume's chapters is that, both before and after the First World War, the institutional underpinnings of global economic integration were only to a small extent the work of international agreements between governments, which usually were more concerned with maintaining their sovereignty. Much more frequently, these underpinnings were either the result of imperial policy, as with the British Empire – thus primarily reflecting Britain's own economic interests – or else emerged from the practical activity of individual firms and various agreements between merchants.

In tracing the nature of such dialectical processes, the following chapters seek to arrive at a better understanding of the complex relationship between economic activity, agents, institutions and power in the period beginning in the 1850s and ending in the 1930s. Within such a historical and analytic framework, the editors hope this volume will not only illuminate important aspects of the global economy before the Great Depression but also help us to better understand the premises and implications of globalisation in our own time.

The majority of the chapters in this volume were presented and discussed at a conference in Konstanz, Germany, in June 2008; two chapters, those of Claude Markovits and Isabella Löhr, were commissioned after the conference to round off the volume. We would like to thank Boris Barth, Sven Beckert, Youssef Cassis, Monika Dommann, Jan-Otmar Hesse, Harold James and Jürgen Osterhammel for their invaluable contributions to the conference as commentators. We also would like to thank Joel Golb for his work as line editor and translator of several of the chapters. We gratefully acknowledge the support we received from the Centre of Excellence 'Cultural Foundations of Integration' at the University of Konstanz for both the conference and the preparation of the present volume.

PART I

LEGAL INSTITUTIONS AND PRIVATE ACTORS

2

Legal Institutions and the World Economy, 1900–1930

Niels P. Petersson

On the eve of the First World War, a respected German economist, Bernhard Harms, founder of the Kiel Institute for the World Economy, wrote that over the last two or three decades he and his contemporaries had been witnessing the emergence of a new world-economic institutional and legal order. Pointing to the ever-expanding scope of commercial treaties and the establishment of international organisations, cartels, technical norms and so on, Harms concluded that '[w]here once was arbitrariness and often anarchy, there is now order and norm'.[1] However, even then things were much more complicated, and indeed they would soon become even more so because of the transformation of states, societies and economies brought about by the war. In this chapter, I address the following questions: What was the role of legal institutions in governing economic transactions in an international setting? Who could (and did) create such legal institutions – more specifically, what was the role of states, private actors and international bodies? What were the achievements and limitations of national, international and transnational legal institutions for international trade? Addressing these questions will yield insight into the possibility of regulating global economic activity and the dynamics of international regulation in the decades around the First World War.[2]

---

[1] 'Wo früher mehr oder weniger Willkür, ja oftmals Anarchie herrschte, da ist heute Ordnung und Norm,' in Bernhard Harms, *Volkswirtschaft und Weltwirtschaft. Versuch der Begründung einer Weltwirtschaftslehre* (Jena, 1912), 315.

[2] For an earlier study of this topic, see Wolfram Fischer, 'Die Ordnung der Weltwirtschaft vor dem Ersten Weltkrieg. Die Funktion von europäischem Recht, zwischenstaatlichen Verträgen und Goldstandard beim Ausbau des internationalen Wirtschaftsverkehrs,' *Zeitschrift für Wirtschafts- und Sozialwissenschaften*, 95 (1975), 289–304.

Trading and investing imply taking risks in the hope of earning a return. Often, a higher return may be obtained by taking greater risks. Some of these risks, including those of nature (accidents, natural disasters), can be offset by buying insurance. Gathering accurate information can at least reduce the risk of default on the part of trading partners.[3] Mostly, however, trading and investment risks are dealt with by designing, interpreting and enforcing appropriate contracts. The most important institution governing this process is law – more specifically, private law. In international trade and investment, transactions usually involve merchants, producers, brokers, transporters, insurers, banks and so forth from a number of different countries, with contractual relationships thus stretching over several national jurisdictions. This fact has relevance for the following discussion of the three possible sources of legal institutions governing international economic transactions: the law made by individual states, the law made by several states acting in cooperation and customary law made by merchants (the legal status of which has often been questioned).

National Legal Systems

The first thing that inevitably comes to mind when talking about institutions that govern commercial transactions is law. The late nineteenth century witnessed an enormous wave of legal innovation in the Western world, soon to be imitated elsewhere, which resulted in the creation of a legal framework for the many advances of the Industrial Revolution. Examples of such legal innovations include patent and copyright law, law governing both public companies and bills of exchange, insurance law and tort law. One might argue that the law that integrated and deregulated national markets was equally useful for international transactions. For instance, in the realm of technology, nineteenth-century national economic integration, achieved primarily through railway construction, can explain much of the fall in transport costs, which in turn caused globalisation to advance.[4] Similar hopes were attached to the development of systems of commercial law; after all, legal innovation and deregulation had played a crucial role in unifying and energising large

---

[3] See Chapter 4.
[4] Ronald Findlay and Kevin H. O'Rourke, *Power and Plenty: Trade, War, and the World Economy in the Second Millennium* (Princeton, 2007).

national markets on the European continent, most notably the German market.[5]

In Germany, the *Wechselordnung* (bills of exchange act), promulgated in the various German states between 1848 and 1862, and the *Allgemeine Deutsche Handelsgesetzbuch* (German trade code), promulgated between 1861 and 1865, were the first laws made by and for all the states in the German Federation – even before the country's unification in 1871.[6] Implementing such early transnational legislation was by no means a simple process, as is evident from the history of the bills of exchange act. The act did not enter into force in all states of the German Federation, although it did become law in some nonfederation states; some states erroneously promulgated the penultimate rather than the act's final version; and differences of interpretation and subsequent modifications limited its impact on legal unification. Nevertheless, scholars of the time acknowledged the role of commercial law in the unification of Germany. In 1902, a leading law professor, Karl Lehmann, pointed to a naturally 'expansionist and universalising tendency' in commercial law, confidently predicting that after having contributed to unifying Germany as a single market, such law would now develop in the direction of a universal law governing commercial transactions worldwide.[7]

However, technological and institutional instruments of economic integration seemed to develop differently: whereas the former tended to grow into more or less seamless systems crossing national borders with relative ease, the latter, at least until the late twentieth century, developed into distinct and clearly demarcated regulatory spaces.[8] As a result, the usefulness of the various bodies of commercial law as underpinnings of cross-border exchange remained very limited. Three factors in particular account for commercial law's limited usefulness. First, the late nineteenth century was a time of rapid institutional innovation. To increase the speed and efficiency of transactions (i.e., the turnover of capital),

---

[5] For example, Clemens Wischermann and Anne Nieberding, *Die institutionelle Revolution. Eine Einführung in die deutsche Wirtschaftsgeschichte des 19. und frühen 20. Jahrhunderts* (Stuttgart, 2004).

[6] See Levin Goldschmidt, *Handbuch des Handelsrechts*, 3 vols., 3rd edn. (Erlangen, 1868–91), vol. B, 73–85 for the *Wechselordnung* and 84–129 for the *Handelsgesetzbuch*.

[7] Karl Lehmann, 'Die Entwicklung des deutschen Handelsrechts', *ZHR*, 52 (1902), 1–30; 29 ('Die Richtung auf ein Weltverkehrsrecht aber wird unzweifelhaft in steigendem Maße dem Handelsrecht des 20. Jahrhunderts die Signatur aufdrücken').

[8] A good example of this is bankruptcy law, as discussed in Jérôme Sgard's contribution in this volume.

merchants, bankers and industrialists were constantly developing new ways of doing business and new documents permitting the sale or lending of money on contracts long before they were executed. The legal status of many of these innovations was doubtful and open to widely differing interpretations by the courts. At any given time, a large number of transactions making use of not yet recognised instruments were thus carried out in a legal no-man's-land – even where no crossing of borders was involved. A telling, but by no means unique, example is that of the 'delivery orders' becoming popular among wholesalers in North German ports after 1900 for sales transactions on parts of shipments that had not yet been received. The original reason for creating delivery orders was that wholesalers who bought large shipments of particular commodities and sold them on in many small batches received only one bill of lading – the officially recognised instrument for selling on goods in transit – per shipment. Soon, however, merchants endorsed and traded these privately created instruments, and banks discounted them as if they were bills of exchange, although they were not recognised by law and gave the bearer no legally enforceable rights whatsoever.[9]

Second, national legislators undertook the modernisation of law in response to problems perceived in a national context, and this process resulted in a variety of national codifications. Legal modernisation meant that the differences among national legal orders became more pronounced the more commercial law was brought into line with the changing requirements of business in the industrial age. Specific laws differed in many minor ways, despite many of the principles involved being the same the world over. (This is why Eugen Langen sees reference to transnationally recognised principles rather than to the letter of the law as a viable stop-gap solution to many problems caused by differences among legal systems.[10]) Furthermore, the scope and volume of legislation increased markedly in the second half of the nineteenth century, and stipulations that could be modified by agreement between contractual parties were increasingly replaced by binding law; in other words, law designed to make economic actors do what seemed desirable from the point of view of national interest or public policy. In short there was nationalisation

---

[9] See Deutsche Bank Hamburg to Deutsche Bank Berlin, 31.8.1908; Deutsche Bank Bremen to Deutsche Bank Berlin, 22.9.1908; Deutsche Bank Berlin to Deutsche Bank Bremen; Otto Brandis to Deutsche Bank Berlin, 3.8.1913; Bundesarchiv Lichterfelde, R 88119 / P-9322; and 'Delivery Orders', *Hamburger Fremdenblatt*, 20.8.1908 and 10.9.1908.

[10] Eugen Langen, *Transnationales Recht* (Heidelberg, 1981).

both of and within commercial law, which meant that the likelihood of different laws in different countries saying different things about one and the same international transaction was growing exponentially.

Third, the rules determining which national law was applicable to which transaction – in other words, rules of 'international private law' or 'conflict of laws' – were thus of increasing importance. Unfortunately, since this process began, each state had followed its own, often highly impractical rules to determine which state's law was to be applied to a particular case. A fairly typical court case from the 1900s illustrates the consequences of this situation.

In August 1903, a merchant from Hamburg chartered a British ship through a broker in London to transport ore from Huelva in Spain to Dunkirk in France. Had everything gone according to plan, everyone involved would have had a clear idea of their responsibilities under the various contracts concluded to ensure the purchase, sale, insurance and transport of the ore and the financing of the transaction. Unfortunately, the ship sank in the French port of Granville, where it had stopped en route. The ore was salvaged, but had become worthless. The Hamburg merchant thus refused to take delivery or pay for the ore and freight. The ship owner went to court, demanding payment of the freight for the part of the journey that had been completed.

The Hamburg *Landgericht* (district court) decided that the case had to be heard under French law, because it concerned a contract meant to be honoured in France. It interpreted the French *Code de commerce* as indicating that freight for damaged but still extant goods had to be paid. However, on appeal, the *Oberlandesgericht* (regional appeals court) used different reasoning, ruling that each party to the contract should have the rights and responsibilities determined by his or her own nation's legal system, rather than by French law, which was alien to all of them. The German law defining the merchant's responsibilities did not grant the shipper any rights to parts of freight if a voyage was not completed.[11]

The decision was then appealed again, this time before the *Reichsgericht*, Germany's final appeals court for private law disputes. In 1908, five years after the accident in Granville, the court confirmed the *Oberlandesgericht*'s ruling that the merchant did not have to pay, even though it ruled that the decision was based on faulty legal reasoning: each contract had to be placed under a single nation's law to ensure a full

---

[11] The first part of the case is documented in *Hanseatische Gerichtszeitung* 27 (1906), no. 61.

correspondence of the rights and obligations of different parties. For the *Reichsgericht*, the law to be applied was clearly neither French nor German but British, because the charter had been concluded with the help of British agents in London and on a British contract form containing clauses and expressions referring to British law. Because in this respect British and German law were the same, the merchant did not have to pay the ship owner. Finally, the court criticised the interpretation of French law advanced by the *Landgericht*: the ore needed to be regarded as lost, not damaged, and French law itself offered the shipper no right to the payment of freight.[12]

In this manner, three German courts based their decisions on three different views of which national law was to be applied to the case at hand. This explains why a Swiss authority on international private law, Adolf Schnitzer, described his field as essentially in a state of complete anarchy.[13] From this example, it is easy to see that the law of sovereign states could not in itself be the solution to the problems encountered in concluding and enforcing international contracts. There was fundamental legal insecurity – and yet profitable cross-border transactions routinely took place every day. The institutional underpinnings of these transactions must be sought elsewhere.

International Legal Unification: The Case of the Law of Bills of Exchange

One obvious solution to the problem of legal insecurity arising out of the differences among national legal systems was the international unification of laws. The most far-reaching initiative of this sort was the series of efforts to unify the law of bills of exchange that unfolded at international conferences in 1910, 1912 and 1930. A brief look at these efforts points to the basic difficulties inherent in the international unification of laws.

At least until the Second World War, bills of exchange were the most important international means of payment. However, their precise nature varied among national legal systems; their usefulness as a means of payment and credit in international transactions was largely due to banks and merchants being prepared to quietly disregard the finer legal points – of which they often were unaware anyway – and treat such bills as basically

---

[12] See *Hanseatische Gerichtszeitung* 29 (1908), no. 128 for the decision of the *Reichsgericht*.
[13] Adolf F. Schnitzer, *Handbuch des internationalen Handels-, Wechsel- und Checkrechts* (Zürich, 1938), 190, 217 f.

a form of privately created money.[14] However, since the Franco-German war of 1870–1 it was known that the smooth functioning of cross-border payments and credit involving the bills could not be taken for granted. France had declared a moratorium that effectively prohibited French drawees and endorsers from having to pay up, but Germany did not recognise the moratorium; with the French default on the internationally circulating bills, other nationalities had to step in. After the Franco-German war, both the *Deutsche Juristentag* (German Legal Association) and the Association for the Codification and Reform of International Law called for a uniform law on bills of exchange, containing one set of stipulations on how to deal with moratoriums. Later, the *Deutsche Handelstag* (German Trade Association) joined in, paying a legal expert to prepare a draft for a complete *Weltwechselrecht* – a worldwide law governing bills of exchange.[15] Eventually, Germany, Italy and the Netherlands joined forces, inviting interested powers to convene to such an end. Two conferences were held in The Hague in 1910 and 1912, and the resulting convention was signed by twenty-one countries, most of them from continental Europe and Latin America.[16]

---

[14] There is a large body of literature on the use of bills of exchange: Heinrich Biedermann, *Lehrbuch des Überseehandels. Organisation, Betrieb, Buchhaltung und Rechnungswesen des überseeischen Export- und Importgeschäftes*, 2nd edn. (Berlin, 1922), 22–28; Josef Hellauer, *System der Welthandelslehre. Ein Lehr- und Handbuch des internationalen Handels. Erster Band: Allgemeine Welthandelslehre* 8th edn. (Berlin, 1920), 372–81; Wilhelm auf der Nöllenburg, *Die Exportorganisation und ihre Technik* (Leipzig, 1925), 111–30; Klemens Ottel, *Die Technik des wirtschaftlichen Verkehrs. Ein Handbuch des internationalen Waren- und Bankgeschäftes* 2nd edn. (Wien, 1927), 46–49; Jacob Riesser, *Die deutschen Großbanken und ihre Konzentration* 4th edn. (Jena, 1912), 232 ff.; Schnitzer, *Handbuch*, 361–417; Walter Schück, *Handbuch der Exportpraxis. Betriebslehre des Exports unter besonderer Berücksichtigung der Ausfuhr deutscher Fertigwaren* (Stuttgart, 1931), 184 ff., 199 f.; Rudolf Sonndorfer, *Die Technik des Welthandels. Ein Handbuch der internationalen Handelskunde für Kaufleute, Ex- und Importeure, Spediteure, Bankiers, Industrielle, Landwirte, für Konsulate, für Eisenbahn- und Schiffahrts-Gesellschaften, für Studierende an Konsular-, Export- und Handels-Akademien u. a.*, 2 vols., 3rd edn. (Wien, 1905), 297–312; Paul Stähler, *Der Giroverkehr, seine Entwicklung und internationale Ausgestaltung* (Leipzig, 1909), 110; Friedrich v. Westphalen, *Rechtsprobleme der Exportfinanzierung* (Heidelberg, 1975), 82–95; on bills of exchange, credit and banks: Riesser, *Die deutschen Großbanken und ihre Konzentration*, 232–57; on the history of the bill of exchange: John Braithwaite and Peter Drahos, *Global Business Regulation* (Cambridge, 2000), 47–52.

[15] Felix Meyer, *Das Weltwechselrecht*, 2 vols. (Leipzig, 1909).

[16] Ministère des Affaires Etrangères, *Documents Diplomatiques: Conférence internationale de la Haye pour l'unification du droit relatif à la lettre de change et au billet à ordre, 23. juin–25 juillet 1910* (Paris, 1910); Ministère des Affaires Etrangères, *Conférence de La Haye pour l'unification du droit relatif à la lettre de change etc.: Actes*, 2 vols. (Den Haag, 1910); Ministère des Affaires Etrangères, *Deuxième conférence de La Haye*

One feature of the conferences that made their outcome less than global was a (still quite familiar) difference between continental European and Anglo-American attitudes to international economic institutions. Hence almost from the outset, Britain decided not to sign any agreement: the British government and British bankers were reluctant to consider any changes to British law, which, after all, was in force throughout most of the English-speaking world, thus governing the largest part of internationally circulating bills of exchange. There were also important differences of approach between British and continental law: the former was based on the notion 'that the substance and not the form of an instrument should be considered'; correspondingly, in Britain 'the parties are left to make their own arrangements . . . without any interference on the part of the law',[17] which, the British delegates explained, 'does but incorporate the usage of our commerce. It is not an arbitrary law imposed by the Legislature on the commercial community; the Legislature has but given the sanction of law to the usages of our commerce and trade, and in modifying that law we should upset long established customs'.[18] In this way Britain rejected the detailed formal requirements of continental law, included for reasons economic policy or the public good. Mostly ignored in mercantile practice in any case, these requirements reflected a continental view of law as a means to improve, rationalise and sometimes moralise business practices.

With Britain content to observe proceedings from the sidelines and France and Germany dominating the proceedings, it is little wonder that the new 'global' law agreed on in 1912 bore many of the features of German law, which by then had become a model towards which French legal reformers were already looking. An even more important feature of the new law was, however, the large number of exemptions that allowed states to avoid having to bring their own laws into accord with those stipulated in the treaty. Moratoriums – the question constituting the

pour l'unification du droit relatif à la lettre de change, du billet à ordre et de chèque,
1912: Actes, 2 vols. (Den Haag, 1912); C. Wieland, 'Die Haager Wechselkonferenz
von Juni-Juli 1910 und der Vorentwurf eines einheitlichen Wechselrechts', *ZHR,* 68
(1910), 345–404; C. Wieland, 'Das internationale Wechselrechtsübereinkommen vom
28. Juli 1912 und sein Geltungsbereich', *ZHR,* 74 (1913), 1–92; C. Wieland, 'Die
gegenwärtigen Aussichten eines Weltwechselrechts', *Zeitschrift für das gesamte Handels-
und Konkursrecht,* 88 (1926), 156–73.

[17] Grey to Gericke, 22.3.1910, in H.M. Stationery Office, *Correspondence Relating to the
Conference on Bills of Exchange and Cheques at The Hague, June 1910* (London, 1911).

[18] Chalmers and Jackson to Grey, 8.8.1910, ibid.

starting point of the entire unification project – were included in the exemptions: no state wished to bind itself in advance either to accept or reject moratoriums declared by other countries.

Reflecting this situation, in the autumn of 1910 *The Times* observed that the 'unification of the Law of Bills of Exchange is for some time to come a practical impossibility. That is the most striking result of the recent Conference at The Hague'.[19] The differences among various legal systems simply proved much more difficult to overcome than initially hoped: even a 'technical' matter such as bills of exchange had touched on questions of general policy, especially regarding currency and the protection of weak economic actors against stronger ones. Likewise, interdependence between the law of bills of exchange and other legislative areas turned out to be an important obstacle. No law, it was unexpectedly found, stood on its own feet; a law only made sense when understood in the context of a legal system that endowed meaning to its terms and concepts (regarding, for example, questions of legal procedure, capacity and competence). For this reason, both the geographical and legal scope of the new law were limited; rules governing international private law remained as much a necessity as before.

At the same time, the legislation had raised basic questions of international and constitutional law that neither lawyers nor diplomats had previously discussed in depth. At The Hague, long-standing confusion was evident regarding the process of treaty signing and ratification and the adaptation of a state's internal legislation to the treaty it had signed. It was nonetheless clear that national law would have to be brought into line with universal law in signatory states. The focus of French and German parliamentary criticism was in any event not so much on that development as on the generally undemocratic nature of legislation drafted via international conference: after all, the new law had been shaped by diplomats advised by professors and interest groups, leaving legislators the only option to accept or reject the results en bloc. Later revision of the law in the face of changed circumstances or a new political majority would be nigh impossible, because the law entailed an international commitment. As remains the case, such international legal unification thus strengthened both the executive and informal interest groups at the expense of democratic institutions for legislation and control. The French government was so concerned about this reality that it shelved ratification; the German

[19] 'The Bills of Exchange Conference', *The Times*, 19.10.1910.

government started the ratification process, but it got nowhere before the outbreak of the First World War.

After 1918, there were renewed attempts to create a global law regulating bills of exchange. Conditions were then both more propitious and more difficult. On the one hand, new private and public international organisations like the International Chamber of Commerce and the League of Nations with its Economic and Financial Committees provided new forums and new driving force for such unification projects. On the other hand, the war had brought with it a huge increase in public and binding law at the expense of private law. This was the result of the massive state intervention in private transactions necessary to conduct the war, distribute scarce resources and equitably share the burden of war and economic crisis. Once again, the increase in the sheer number of legal provisions meant that reaching international legal agreement had become that much more complicated.

The question that emerged was thus whether to start a new effort at global legal unification or try to conclude a treaty on specific points where differences among various legal systems were causing practical problems. The Germans, now that they could no longer hope to play an important role in the unification project and reap the diplomatic rewards, denounced its impractical, purely idealistic nature. Nevertheless, a new conference was held in 1930 at the behest of the League of Nations, leading to a new treaty for globally governing bills of exchange. Although preliminary studies had recommended harmonising only a few essential elements of the 1912 treaty, the final result looked much like it: a universal law adopted by many states, but not by the Anglo-Saxons. Even more than in 1912, states persisted in maintaining sovereignty over both relevant legislation and emergency measures for protecting their currencies and balances of payment. Hence one of the most salient features of the new law was that, although it removed some fairly minor obstacles to international transactions, it also directly affirmed the right of states to stop or regulate international payments at will.

Nevertheless, the 'global law of bills of exchange' at that time was the most ambitious piece of international legislation in any domain to have actually been ratified, its passage signalling both continuity and change. Change was most evident in the type of actors involved and in the policy environment: where before the war the only actors had been scholars, business organisations such as the *Deutsche Handelstag* and states, in the interwar years they were joined by the International Chamber of Commerce and the League of Nations. This change was accompanied by increasing state intervention and a growth in binding law in the economic sphere, especially in the matter of cross-border payments.

Continuity was evident in the problems encountered in trying to create global law. The task of reconciling legal systems aimed in British fashion at codifying actual commercial practice with those aimed, like most continental systems, at pushing economic activity in a politically desirable direction was soon seen as impossible. The tension between democracy organised within nation-states and legal rules made at international conferences persisted. Finally, it was still the case that a law only acquired meaning as part of a larger national legal system and that even a 'uniform' law meant different things in different countries.

Consistently, those who used bills of exchange preferred disregarding finer legal points to actually changing or harmonising the law. For merchants and bankers, the one issue making international legal unification attractive lay outside the scope of *commercial* law: the original proposals put forward by international lawyers and merchants from the 1870s onward aimed at limiting the intervention of *public* law in mercantile transactions, for instance in moratoriums and currency legislation; these were essentially projects of 'negative integration', as one would say today. For merchants, public law governing international payments was the real problem, not private law governing bills of exchange. They wished such bills to specify how they would be paid, whether in gold, specific coinage or currency, or according to the exchange rate between two currencies on a specific date. They hoped to evade attempts by states to prohibit payments in gold, regulate international payments, set exchange rates by fiat and so forth – all evidence of a 'mercantile internationalism' seeking to secure international business against the vagaries of national economic policies and international conflicts.

The unification of bills of exchange law was thus initiated and promoted as a project of privatisation and deterritorialisation of economic transactions. Yet international legislation could be undertaken only by sovereign states acting in concert. It is little wonder, then, that the treaties concluded in international conferences bore the mark of state interests: as suggested, they proposed a law harmonising some minor aspects of the relevant *private* law while leaving states free to interfere with cross-border payments as they pleased. This was already so before 1914 but became increasingly manifest after the First World War. Indeed, the true obstacle to international transactions after the war was not posed by accidental differences between national legal orders but by the economic and currency policies of individual states – policies designed to regulate international payments.

Private Legal Orders: Standard Contracts, Business Associations and Commercial Arbitration

This still leaves unanswered the question of which institutions were capable of framing international transactions. In the 1920s both Masaichiro Ishizaki, a Japanese scholar working in the silk-trading city of Lyons, and Hans Großmann-Doerth, a German scholar working in the port city of Hamburg, embarked on empirical studies of the effect of different legal systems on commerce. Both set out to propose ways to remove the most inconvenient differences among the systems. To their surprise, they found that merchants' and similar private associations were already in effect creating and enforcing their own transnational legal orders, without any reference to state-made law and state courts. Ishizaki, for example, noted that 'commercial corporate law . . . rises up in struggle, and generally in victorious struggle . . . against commercial law made by legislators, judges and jurists [and] in its broad lines presents itself in effect in the form of an already internationalised law'.[20]

Though it is perhaps more significant that legal scholars were surprised by mercantile self-regulation than that it actually did exist, a quick look at how it worked may be useful. Business organisations such as the London Corn Trade Association and the associations of cotton traders in Liverpool and Bremen and of silk traders in Lyon gained international importance because they represented merchants in centres of global trade in certain products. They developed standard contracts, often in negotiations with all parties interested in a particular trade – merchants, exporters, importers, shippers and insurers. These contracts contained a large amount of 'small print', the 'general terms and conditions' spelling out in great detail the rights and obligations of all contractual parties. They also referred to the particular commercial usages and customs to be used in interpreting contracts and in regulating any matters on which a contract was silent – thereby assuming the role commercial law would play in cases heard by a law court. These usages and customs were being

---

[20] Masaichiro Ishizaki, *Le droit corporatif international de la vente de soies: Les contrats-types américains et la codification lyonnaise dans leurs rapports avec les usages des autres places* (Paris, 1928), 13 f. For a synthesis of Großmann-Doerth's work see Hans Großmann-Doerth, *Das Recht des Überseekaufs* (Mannheim, 1930).

increasingly codified by merchants' associations and chambers of commerce, giving these bodies an active role in shaping the framework for concluding and interpreting contracts.[21]

Through standard contracts and codified usage, the rights and obligations of each party to the contract were clearly defined, so as to prevent interpretive conflicts arising out of differences between local customs or national legal systems. Usually, a final important point in the small print was the arbitration clause. It stipulated that all disputes arising out of the contract were to be settled out of court by arbiters named under rules established by the merchants' association. Standard contracts, the codification of mercantile custom and commercial arbitration taken together formed a privately created, transnational legal order – a system capable of producing rules, interpreting them, administering justice and enforcing judgments (for example through the threat not to trade with anyone refusing to carry out an arbitral award).[22]

In the world of commerce, arbitration was often preferred to the justice administered by ordinary law courts because it was cheaper, quicker and more likely to take into account that world's particular practices and customs. Law professors tended to assume that standard contracts

---

[21] For a highly critical view of this quasi-legislative activity of merchants' associations and chambers of commerce see Otto Schreiber, *Handelsbräuche. Studien* (Mannheim, 1922).

[22] For examples of the arbitration clause see Otto Jöhlinger and Hans Hirschstein, *Die Praxis des Getreidegeschäfts an der Berliner Börse. Ein Hand- und Lehrbuch für den Getreidehandel* 3rd edn. (Berlin, 1925), 75; Sonndorfer, *Technik des Welthandels* vol. 2, 28 f. On arbitration in general, see René David, 'The International Unification of Private Law', in René David (ed.), *International Encyclopedia of Comparative Law* (Tübingen, 1972), 61–67; Großmann-Doerth, *Recht*, 50–59; Alexander Haffner, *Das ständige kaufmännische Schiedsgericht* (Berlin, 1911); Hellauer, *Welthandelslehre*, 59, 424; Jöhlinger and Hirschstein, *Getreidegeschäft* 313–30; Otto Mathies, *Die ständigen Schiedsgerichte des Hamburger Großhandels* (Braunschweig, 1921); Otto Mathies, 'Die Entwicklung der Hamburger Arbitrage und ihre Stellung im Weltverkehr', *Zeitfragen des Wirtschaftsrechts (Beilage zum 'Wirtschaftsdienst')*, 1924; Mittelstein, 'Recht und Praxis der Schiedsgerichte in Deutschland', *Internationales Jahrbuch für Schiedsgerichtswesen*, 1 (1926), 37–53; Eduard Nelken, *Die Arbitrageklausel* (Berlin, 1912); auf der Nöllenburg, *Die Exportorganisation und ihre Technik*, 40; Arthur Nußbaum, 'Der gegenwärtige Stand der Schiedsgerichtsfrage', *Zeitschrift für das gesamte Handels- und Konkursrecht*, 83 (1920), 275–320; Arthur Nußbaum, 'Probleme des internationalen Schiedsgerichtswesens', *Internationales Jahrbuch für Schiedsgerichtswesen*, 1 (1926), 7–37. See also Niels P. Petersson, *Anarchie und Weltrecht. Das Deutsche Reich und die Institutionen der Weltwirtschaft, 1890–1930* (Göttingen, 2009), ch. II.3 and for a study of developments in Britain: Ross Cranston, 'Law through Practice: London and Liverpool Commodity Markets c. 1820–1975', *Law, Society and Economy Working Papers* 14, London, 2007.

and arbitral procedures filled gaps where state law was silent or where it explicitly left matters to the discretion of the parties. Yet mercantile self-regulation went beyond that. Often, the rules of the merchants' associations were in conflict with the law of the states where they were applied. This might simply be because the standard contracts had been drawn up with British law and British usages in mind, though they were widely used even where none of the parties was British. Yet this conflict also reflected the fact that arbiters were expected to make their judgments based on custom and equity, not on law, and were not bound to pay any attention to any state's law. Obviously, the problems of conflict of laws plaguing state courts could not arise under such circumstances.

Arbitral tribunals had to call on courts of law only when one of the parties refused to submit to an arbitral award – a rare occasion in the great trading centres, because such a refusal meant exclusion from further trading, but a problem of some significance in less tightly integrated lines of business. There was an obvious tension between self-regulation, standard contracts and arbitration on the one hand, and the ambition of states to achieve policy goals through appropriate legislation on the other hand. The various systems of law dealt with this tension in very different ways: whereas German courts ordered the execution of any judgment that had been reached in a formally correct way, French law simply regarded the arbitration clause as void. British law adopted an intermediate position, allowing courts to reexamine arbitral awards on both procedural and substantive grounds.[23]

After the war, private arbitration not only became more important but also more closely intertwined with national and international public law. Whereas before the war arbitration had worked best in well-organised business communities, located for the most part at the great raw materials exchanges, after the war it became increasingly attractive for two new constituencies. First, in a purely national context, large German interest groups and business organisations (*Verbände*) that had been able to strengthen their position by participating in the organisation of the war economy began to use internal regulations and arbitration as tools to strengthen their hold over their members, keep outsiders and new competition down, and force suppliers and customers to do business on

---

[23] Walther Pappenheim and Max Rheinstein, *Die Vollstreckung deutscher Schiedssprüche im Ausland* (Berlin, 1929); Mathies, 'Entwicklung', 5–8; Haffner, *Das ständige kaufmännische Schiedsgericht*, 56–61; Mittelstein, 'Recht und Praxis der Schiedsgerichte in Deutschland'.

rather one-sided terms. Initially many legal scholars and officials were pleased that private sector self-regulation was relieving state courts of a heavy burden. Yet by the late 1920s, some observers worried that this self-regulation had led to the development of a 'law created by business-men' enshrining anticompetitive practices and no longer controllable by weak and overburdened states.[24]

Second, merchants and exporters who did not belong to any of the large merchants' associations became interested in arbitration. Many small merchants and occasional exporters felt that, in an age of eco-nomic nationalism, law courts would treat foreigners unfairly, especially those from former enemy states, and that arbitration offered an altern-ative less susceptible to nationalist discrimination. In 1920, the Inter-national Chamber of Commerce (ICC) was established in Paris; it was dominated by business associations from France and the United States. The new organisation, which wanted to be seen as 'a businessmen's League of Nations', was active from the start in promoting and organ-ising arbitration.[25] It offered standard contracts and an arbitration system that any party could sign up for simply through a contractual provision. If a dispute arose over such a contract, the ICC would, for a small fee, select arbiters from lists provided by national business organisations and organise the proceedings. This kind of arbitration, available to every-one taking part in international business, made it increasingly important to have arbitral awards recognised by law courts, because in addition to strong and coherent merchant's associations that could mobilise peer pressure, enforcing such awards required a credible threat of state-court

---

[24] Hans Großmann-Doerth, *Selbstgeschaffenes Recht der Wirtschaft und staatliches Recht* 10 (Freiburg, 1933); Carl Leo, 'Welche Hauptgrundsätze sind für die Neuregel-ung des Schiedsgerichtswesens zu empfehlen?', *Verhandlungen des 34. Deutschen Juristentages*, 1926), 179–257; Arthur Nußbaum, *Die gesetzliche Neuordnung des Schiedsgerichtswesens. Denkschrift im Auftrag und unter Mitwirkung der Handelskam-mer zu Berlin* (Berlin, 1918); Nußbaum, 'Stand'; Schreiber, *Handelsbräuche*; Franz Böhm, 'Das Problem der privaten Macht. Ein Beitrag zur Monopolfrage', *Die Justiz*, 3 (1928), 324 ff. Knut Wolfgang Nörr, *Zwischen den Mühlsteinen: Eine Privatrechts-geschichte der Weimarer Republik* (Tübingen, 1988), 17 ff., 38 f., 53 f., 172 f., 231–34.

[25] See Frederick P. Keppel, 'The International Chamber of Commerce', *International Con-ciliation*, 174 (1922), 189–210 and Monika Rosengarten, *Die Internationale Handel-skammer. Wirtschaftspolitische Empfehlungen in der Zeit der Weltwirtschaftskrise, 1929–1939* (Berlin, 2000); the quotation is from George L. Ridgeway, *Merchants of Peace: Twenty Years of Business Diplomacy through the International Chamber of Commerce, 1919–1938* (New York, 1938), quoted in Rosengarten, *Internationale Han-delskammer*, 17.

enforcement. Departing from prewar practice, the ICC thus recommended that its arbiters always base their awards on national law. Dependence on the state's legal system ensured respect for national legislation.

It was, however, not at all certain that all states would actually recognise foreign arbitral awards. For this reason, the League of Nations brokered two conventions, one in 1923 and the other in 1927, on the recognition and execution of foreign awards. Germany signed up almost immediately, despite having been rather hostile to the League at the time the first convention was concluded. France signed up as well, thereby for the first time agreeing to recognise arbitration clauses in commercial contracts. The two conventions are interesting from the point of view of the actors and mechanisms of institution building: states concluded treaties determining how their national legal systems would recognise and deal with the private orders emerging on both a national and international level. Of course, when states signed up to an international agreement requiring their law courts to cooperate in the execution of foreign awards, they demanded that these awards respect national laws and public order. Arbitration thus seemed to develop into a private procedure of conflict resolution under partially public supervision.

In 1926, Arthur Nußbaum, one of the foremost specialists on arbitration and the founding editor of the *International Yearbook for Arbitration*, declared that in recent years 'hardly any legal problem has preoccupied specialists the world over as that of commercial arbitration has done'. Only a few years later, however, Nußbaum had to acknowledge that the 'era of the rapid ascension of arbitration has passed'.[26] Though there was consolidation rather than decline, it was clear that the project of organising the international economy on the basis of the rules made, interpreted and enforced by private business associations had failed. The ICC's arbitration procedure never won many adherents. Arbitration still worked only in a few enclaves that, because of their specific structure, permitted the establishment of 'self-enforcing institutions'. This was the case chiefly at the big raw materials exchanges, where tightly knit business communities had formed, with a small number of participants who regularly traded with each other and could not afford to be locked out by their peers. Elsewhere, such as in the highly competitive overseas export of European machinery, no stable institutions developed; there the business environment was, as described by merchants and

---

[26] Arthur Nußbaum, 'Vorwort', *Internationales Jahrbuch für Schiedsgerichtswesen* (1931), 3.

industrialists, an 'anarchy' where, basically, might was right.[27] This inter-war situation suggests that the creation of transnational private orders is more dependent than usually thought on the acceptance and support of states, which for their part thus have far more (though not necessarily benign) influence on the globalisation of economic institutions than usually acknowledged.

The revival of arbitration in the 1920s involved activity in the national and the international/transnational sphere by both private and public actors. It needs to be seen in the context of the ever-increasing density of economic regulation and legislation in the interwar years: states were now held responsible for social welfare, prosperity and fairness and for the distribution of the costs of the war among the various groups in society. States thus exercised much more control than before the war over the economy in general and over cross-border exchanges in particular. At the same time, many states perceived an increased need for coordinating institutions and wished to promote trade revival as a means of economic reconstruction, because it had come to be widely accepted that international cooperation was necessary to secure peace and prosperity. Hence in this context as well we may speak of continuity and change in the years around the Great War, with change mainly evident in the emergence of new actors and an increasing interpenetration of public and private, national and international rules. Again, the war did not put an end to attempts to institutionalise international economic relations, but it did change basic structures and conditions.

A similar narrative would fit many other aspects of economic governance in this period, in all these cases leading to a similarly unhappy ending: by 1931, small steps towards easier international economic exchange had lost much of their significance, with all the states involved pursuing unilateral policies to counter the effects of the Great Depression – requiring, for example, government approval for *all* cross-border payments.[28]

Conclusions

The changing nature and role of legal institutions in the years around the First World War need to be understood in a framework of larger transformations affecting the relationship of power, institutions and global

[27] See especially Großmann-Doerth, *Recht*; Schück, *Exportpraxis*.
[28] Harold James, *The End of Globalization: Lessons from the Great Depression* (Cambridge, MA, 2001).

markets. The types of risk involved in doing business changed profoundly during these years. Before 1914, risks of nature (accidents, natural disasters) and risks arising from the actions of trading partners (fraud, disputes over the meaning of a contract, bankruptcy) predominated. Many of these risks could be dealt with by nonlegal means such as insurance, credit information and making use of well-established standard contracts. The need for transnational legal institutions remained correspondingly limited; it is striking how little the parties to most prewar business transactions cared for legal detail. The 'avoidance of law', as Miloš Vec has put it,[29] was seen as a very simple way of increasing the efficiency of doing business. After 1918, a new source of risk appeared: economic policy and especially exchange rate policy. It was of course impossible to seek protection against the risks created by economic policy by legal means, because such protection would have to take the form of *evasion* of law.

This is but one instance of a larger transformation of statehood and state power around the First World War.[30] Before the war, many businessmen, especially in Germany, considered a progressive decoupling of the spheres of international business and international politics to be both possible and desirable. The war revealed this vision as illusionary because of the crucial importance of economic warfare and of national economies for the war effort. By the interwar years it was clear that new demands were being placed on the state, that new policy instruments – especially those of economic policy – had been placed in state hands, and that the objective function and ideological significance of borders had changed. The sphere of what was seen as the legitimate function and competence of the state had irrevocably expanded, encroaching on both private relations and the international order. The more the state was held responsible for economic outcomes, the more it sought to intervene in private transactions, becoming 'an invisible party to most legal proceedings between individuals or corporate entities'.[31]

Alongside the growth of the regulatory intervention of states, the activity of private bodies and public international organisations increased

---

[29] Miloš Vec, *Recht und Normierung in der industriellen Revolution. Neue Strukturen der Normsetzung in Völkerrecht, staatlicher Gesetzgebung und gesellschaftlicher Selbstnormierung* (Frankfurt a.M., 2006).

[30] Eckart Conze, 'Abschied von Staat und Politik? Überlegungen zur Geschichte der internationalen Politik', in *Geschichte der Internationalen Beziehungen: Erneuerung und Erweiterung einer historischen Disziplin*, eds. Eckart Conze et al. (Köln, 2004), 15–43; 26.

[31] Harold J. Berman, *Law and Revolution: The Formation of the Western Legal Tradition* (Cambridge, MA, 1983), 37.

as well. Although in this context it would be exaggerated to use the term 'organised capitalism',[32] there was a significant increase in efforts to create new institutions and rules for international business transactions by national business organisations, the International Chamber of Commerce, the League of Nations and so forth. This activity was a response to the need to coordinate regulatory activity and provide solutions to problems accentuated or created by the war – problems such as the increased importance of currency and trade controls, economic nationalism and discriminatory trade policies.

Institution building, conflicts and problem solving in global markets involve not only states but also complex configurations of private and public actors whose status is subject to negotiation and challenge. Private institutionalisation can occur only where state authority leaves sufficient scope for the process. Privately established institutions that develop on the basis of freedom of contract have been criticised for undermining the decisions and compromises worked out in democratic societies and enshrined in law. Yet the 'total' conception of national sovereignty maintained in the 1930s, demanding state control over all cross-border exchanges and over much of the social order at home, turned out to be incompatible with individual rights and 'global governance', economic or otherwise, leaving no room for international cooperation and replacing institutions with arbitrarily exercised power. In the end, both a 'mercantile internationalism' trying to isolate international business transactions from the sphere of international relations and the idea that public control over such transactions was somehow a necessary precondition for efficient and legitimate economic policies failed in the years under consideration. This suggests that economic openness cannot be secured unless it is based on an explicitly *political* decision favouring openness and interdependence. At the same time, the fact that, in the age of interdependent interventionist states, even private ordering depends on public permission and sanction creates a space for compromise. It also ensures that the influence of democratic institutions on the rules and institutions governing international economic transactions remains much larger than acknowledged in critical accounts of economic globalisation and 'private ordering'.[33]

---

[32] See the contributions in Heinrich August Winkler (ed.), *Organisierter Kapitalismus. Voraussetzungen und Anfänge* (Göttingen, 1973).

[33] See for example A. Claire Cutler, *Private Power and Global Authority: Transnational Merchant Law in the Global Political Economy* (Cambridge, 2003); Rodney Bruce Hall and Thomas Biersteker (eds.), *The Emergence of Private Authority in Global Governance* (Cambridge, 2002).

3

Against Globalisation

Sovereignty, Courts, and the Failure to Coordinate International Bankruptcies, 1870–1940

Jérôme Sgard

Even a cursory reading of the historical literature on international bank-ruptcies reveals a striking account: coordination in this field has tra-ditionally been limited, dysfunctional and difficult to improve. Whether one reads the landmark essay by Giuseppe Carle (1875), the brilliant con-ferences by F. Piggott (1884) and Leslie Burgin (1923), the mid-twentieth-century articles of Kurt Nadelmann or more recent academic literature, the story is the same, and time and again, the same conclusions come to the fore.

On the one hand, most authors agree that the economic logic of inter-national bankruptcies, or cross-border insolvencies,[1] clearly calls for the principles of *unity* and *universality* of proceedings. In other words, *all* creditors should be convened in a single forum where the *whole* stock of residual assets would be collected. If assets or creditors are located in dif-ferent countries, then any obstacle to smooth coordination between juris-dictions is certain to have adverse consequences. Consider, for example, the merchant whose assets are mostly in Bruges but whose debts are mostly in Florence (or Kansas and New York, if you prefer).

In stark contrast with this doctrinal consensus, what actually pre-vailed during the whole period under review in this chapter (1870–1940) was a fragmented and often chaotic international scene. Rather than universality, *territoriality* had the upper hand,[2] so that competition

---

[1] The second term is more common in the contemporary legal literature; here I use the two terms as synonyms.

[2] For a recent restatement of the debate between territoriality and universality, see the special issue of the *Michigan Law Review* 98 (2000), specifically Jay Westbrook, 'Global Solutions to Multinational Defaults', *Michigan Law Review* 98 (2000), 2276–328.

between parallel bankruptcy proceedings in different countries was most common – regardless of what diplomats, scholars and practitioners argued. The proximate reasons for this result are not difficult to see. When exploring the details of how a bankruptcy works, one immediately faces a host of practical problems and decisions that can easily derail international coordination. For example, should an opening judgment made in a given country have legal effect in another? And if such judgment impairs the professional capacity of the bankrupt merchant or allows for his or her imprisonment, should these rules have extraterritorial effect? May a sovereign state then allow a foreign trustee to seize, manage and possibly auction off assets located within its own territory? Think for instance of a German judge in 1875 Strasbourg who would adjudicate the bankruptcy of a (still French) trader just across the border between Alsace-Lorraine and France drawn in 1871. And what about the rights of senior or privileged creditors? Should they be governed by the law under which the creditors initially lent money (pursuant to agreed-upon collateral) or under the law of the country where the bankruptcy proceedings are initiated? Also important are the cases of debt discharge and of the continuation arrangements that are typically enforced against minority dissenters. Should English debt contracts be restructured by a Portuguese judge even when a clear majority of English creditors oppose the agreement?

In practice, very little progress was made on all these counts. As the 1930 Conference of the International Law Association concluded: '[T]he differences between the principal commercial countries of the world in matters of bankruptcy are fundamental, and it has been found both in Conferences of Governments and diplomats on the one hand, and in endless Conferences of international lawyers and International Law Associations on the other, to be impossible to reconcile the conflicting opinion and produce any measure of combined agreement'.[3]

In this chapter I try to account for the protracted resistance to cross-border coordination in matters of bankruptcy. I start with the actual practice of dealing with cross-border bankruptcies and then try to identify

---

[3] International Law Association, *Report of the Thirty-Sixth Conference* (London, 1930), 278. For comparable statements, see Friedrich Meili, *Moderne Staatsverträge über das internationale Konkursrecht* (Zürich, 1907) or Kurt H. Nadelmann, 'International Bankruptcy Law: Its Present Status', *University of Toronto Law Journal* 5 (1944), 324–51, especially p. 348: 'Indeed, the case of an international convention acceptable to all, or most of the countries of the world can be regarded as hopeless'.

the obstacles that proved so hard to overcome. However, soon the unique historical and political position of bankruptcy law will come to the fore, a position established in between the world of private contracts and property, on the one hand, and sovereign civil justice, on the other. In any liberal order the question of who has the right to seize the assets of a legally established firm or to intervene into the contracts of minority creditors is by no means a trivial one. Clearly, an arbiter or a private agent would have neither the authority nor the jurisdiction to do so. What about a foreign judge then?

This quasi-constitutional dimension of the problem is very much part of the discussion. At least since John Locke and Montesquieu – and clearly under the U.S. Constitution and the Napoleonic codes – the liberal compact was founded on a commitment to protect and guarantee individual rights in exchange for a transfer, or a recognition, of sovereign authority. Although the progress of individual rights has long remained uneven and uncertain, nineteenth-century Western states certainly did not take lightly any interference with regard to property and contracts or to their own sovereignty. This was a liberal and commercial age, although it was also an age when the interaction between nation-states was based more on realist and territorial principles than on contractual and universal ones. The dominant doctrine of international law was founded on a compact, self-standing notion of sovereignty that was reflected in poorly institution-alised interactions between states. Still, one way or another, global markets relied on some rules supported by some tangible authority, however fragile and dysfunctional both may have been. This is the viewpoint from which the experience of international bankruptcies should be observed: it brings to light the workings of early global markets, as well as the travails of their would-be regulators.

The second section presents the limited record in terms of actual bank-ruptcy treaties, including those within federations. The following section examines the successive attempts by diplomats, private-sector representatives and academic international lawyers to improve the overall international regime. In the fourth section I discuss how interest groups, especially those of senior creditors, could have successfully opposed improvements. The next section presents the arguments in favour of the 'judicial thesis' – the view that the legal nature of bankruptcy itself accounts for the difficulties encountered in international legal harmonisation. The sixth section makes explicit the link to the construction of sovereignty, and the final section concludes.

The Failure to Coordinate: Conventions, Empires and Federations

From the Napoleonic era to the 1930s, intergovernmental agreements on bankruptcy were comparatively rare but not entirely absent, though none were ever drawn up between the major players of the day. For instance, Germany and Austria held negotiations in 1878–79 on a treaty of judicial cooperation, but they failed to reach agreement on the issue of bankruptcy.[4] Although the two countries did reach agreement much later – in 1932 – the *Anschluss* prevented the agreement from actually being tested. Neither was there any treaty on the subject between France and Germany, between Great Britain and any nation on the Continent, or between any European nation and the United States. Although the United Kingdom signed two far-reaching treaties of judicial cooperation with France and Belgium in 1934, bankruptcies were once again excluded.[5]

Most actual agreements in fact emerged in 'post-imperial' networks. The first case occurred within the two decades following the abolition in 1804 of the German Holy Empire.[6] Quite rapidly, the legal and judicial order formerly regulated by the *Reichshofrat* crumbled as new independent states began to no longer recognise foreign judgments. Bavaria was the first to do so, as early as 1811. This led to a series of bilateral treaties among the states of Bavaria, Württemberg, Bade, and Saxony and then Prussia and Austria; some northern Swiss cantons were also part of the game.[7] One century later, a comparable movement was observed in the aftermath of the Treaty of Versailles and the destruction of the Austro-Hungarian Empire. Then, too, integration rapidly shifted to bilateral treaties signed between Austria and Bulgaria (1922), Czechoslovakia (1923) and Yugoslavia (1928); the latter two nations also signed a bilateral agreement in 1923, as did Czechoslovakia and Poland in 1934. In addition to these two Central European networks there were several accords negotiated between France and Switzerland (1804, 1828 and 1869), Belgium (1899), and Italy (1930) as well as one between Belgium

---

[4] See Meili, *Moderne Staatsverträge über das internationale Konkursrecht*.

[5] Hessel E. Yntema, 'The Enforcement of Foreign Judgments in Anglo-American Law', *Michigan Law Review* 33 (1935), 1129–68.

[6] The first known bilateral agreement on bankruptcy was signed by Holland and Utrecht in 1679; they were followed by France and the Kingdom of Sardinia in 1760 and then by France and some Swiss cantons in 1784.

[7] Jean Jacques Foelix, *Traité de droit international privé* (Paris, 1843); Kurt H. Nadelmann, 'Bankruptcy Treaties', *University of Pennsylvania Law Review and American Law Review* 93 (1944), 58–97.

and the Netherlands (1925). Last of all was a 1933 agreement between the Scandinavian countries – the first multilateral accord on bankruptcy ever signed.[8]

Federal countries offer a parallel set of examples in which political integration, rather than disintegration, was the issue. Here again, the adoption of a common bankruptcy law always proved difficult. In the United States, the 1787 Constitution expressly allowed the enactment of a federal bankruptcy law in addition to state laws. Three such statutes were enacted in 1800, 1841 and 1867, but rapidly shelved. Not until 1898 was an enduring federal framework adopted that required the Supreme Court to establish a specific judicial branch for bankruptcy with its own regulations and relation to appellate courts.[9] The second German Empire, founded in 1871, encountered less difficulty in establishing a federal law – possibly because of a less open and more centralised political system. Still, its 1877 bankruptcy statute was enacted only after the judiciary and the procedural law of the new empire had been fully redesigned on an integrated basis.[10] Switzerland is another example: coordination first took the road of 'concordats' between cantons (1804, 1810 and 1829) that belonged to their respective international law; that is, these matters were handled on a sovereign-to-sovereign basis. Discussions on a truly federal statute began only in 1868, but did not move forward until a federal constitution restructured the judiciary in 1874. Even so, a federal bankruptcy statute came into force only in 1889 – after some twenty years of protracted negotiations.[11]

A last case is the British Commonwealth, an empire that progressively developed some forms of judicial federalism. It is significant that the first step towards the mutual recognition of judgments among England, Scotland and Ireland did not occur until 1868 and concerned only their respective Supreme Courts; extension to the lower courts occurred in 1882. The same two steps were then taken with the Commonwealth countries in 1886 and in 1901, respectively, with a supplementary

[8] Nadelmann, 'Bankruptcy Treaties'.
[9] David A. Skeel Jr, *Debt's Dominion: A History of Bankruptcy Law in America* (Princeton, 2001).
[10] See Anke Maier, *Die Geschichte des deutschen Konkursrechts, insbesondere die Entstehung des Reichkonkursordnung von 1877* (Frankfurt a.M., 2003) and E. Thaller, *Des faillites en droit comparé, avec une étude sur le règlement des faillites en droit international* (2 vols., Paris, 1887); the reform of the courts and bankruptcy came into effect at the same time.
[11] See E. Roguin, *Conflits des lois suisses en matière internationale et intercantonale* (Lausanne, 1891) and the 1889 *Annuaire de Législation Etrangère*, pp. 606–17.

statute being adopted in 1912. Yet in these later cases, bankruptcy proved
again to be a stumbling block: although opening judgments and all attend-
ant acts by a court or trustee located in Great Britain were technically
enforceable in colonies or dominions, contemporary authors suggest that
the actual practice was not so smooth. Moreover, the reverse, 'upstream'
recognition – from periphery to centre – would certainly not exist, so
that parallel proceedings remained a possibility;[12] coordination between
colonial peripheries was apparently also deficient.[13]

These accounts highlight two main elements: (1) coming to agreement
on cross-border bankruptcies was demanding in terms of underlying political commitment and/or integration; and (2) the issue of jurisdiction and
the hierarchy of courts seemed to be part of the problem. Before exploring this line further, however, it is necessary to discard a straightforward
hypothesis: that the failure of coordination was not perceived as such.
Perhaps nobody cared, or perhaps private agents found their own way
around the problem.[14] In other words, to make sure that there was indeed
a coordination problem, one should first establish that agents did actually
care and also tried to solve it.

International Mobilisation

During the period under review, cross-border bankruptcies were discussed at length by three classes of agents: diplomats, representatives
of the private sector and international lawyers. Although their persistence attests to the presence of a real, practical problem, none of these
agents was able to achieve tangible results.

The Hague Conferences
There was actually one deliberate and consistent attempt through international diplomacy to establish a more satisfactory international bankruptcy regime. It unfolded within the Conferences on International Private
Law that were held at The Hague at the initiative of the Dutch government

---

[12] Yntema, 'The Enforcement of Foreign Judgments in Anglo-American Law'; G. C.
Cheshire, *Private International Law* (Oxford, 1938); Harrison Moore, 'Conflicts of
Laws within the Empire: Bankruptcy and Company Winding-Up', *Journal of the Society
of Comparative Legislation* 7 (1906), 384–91.

[13] Australasian Commercial Congress, *Centennial Year 1888: Report of Proceedings* (Melbourne, 1889).

[14] For examples of private businesspeople ignoring problems or bypassing the court system,
see the contribution by Niels P. Petersson in this volume.

from 1893 onwards.[15] Although their focus was primarily on noncommercial aspects of private law (marriage, succession, etc.), negotiations also extended to such concerns as bills of exchange and the mutual recognition of corporations. Cross-border bankruptcies were also brought to the table at the first Hague Conference, and a blueprint for an international convention was discussed at the second meeting in 1894. However, no vote or endorsement was obtained, and it seems the main conclusions of the debates amounted to a list of the many reasons why eventual convergence would be difficult. In 1902 the topic was discussed again – but it was added to the agenda at the last moment, so that most delegates did not have a mandate to discuss it. Deliberations were thus limited to the Netherlands, the Italian head of the commission and the Swiss rapporteur. In 1925 Great Britain finally joined the Hague Conference and promptly insisted that bankruptcy be brought back to the table. However, it withdrew from the conference altogether when confronted with insurmountable conflicts on this issue.[16] A draft convention for cooperation was eventually agreed upon, but it was not adopted by any sovereign government even as a working tool or blueprint.

The Private Sector

The thinking and action of private agents, across and within countries, are of course much more difficult to apprehend than that of diplomats and governments. Moreover, one may expect that reactions would depend upon the size and openness of each economy, its level of development or the microstructure of the enterprise and banking sector. Nevertheless, there were continuous debates on this issue in representative forums, national and international, and they should be indicative of contemporary views.

Take the Congrès International de Commerce et d'Industrie, organised in Paris during the 1878 International Fair. A full section was dedicated to international commercial law, including bankruptcies. The final declaration of this congress included the 'wish' (addressed to governments) that international conventions would ease and simplify the execution of bankruptcy judgments between countries, following the now classical principles of unity of jurisdiction and universality of effects. The Congrès met again in later years and evolved into a more French-centred affair,

[15] Kurt Lipstein, 'One Hundred Years of the Hague Conference on Private International Law', *International and Comparative Law Quarterly* 42 (1993), 553–653.
[16] See the respective editions of the *Actes* of the Hague Conferences.

explicitly controlled and managed by the Paris Chambre de Commerce. Its deliberations are a reliable approximation of what were the main 'policy wishes' of the French economic and financial establishment. Although such topics as labour regulations, external tariffs and monopolies definitely attracted most attention, cross-border bankruptcies regularly featured in these meetings. For instance, the 1889 Congrès discussed equality of treatment among creditors and voted against the adoption of a reciprocity clause, thus taking a rather liberal position in that regard. The 1890 meeting declared that the recognition of foreign judgments by the French courts (the *exequatur*) should be made easier, with limited discretion for the judge to review their substance.

In the United Kingdom, private lobbying in favour of better bankruptcy coordination seems to have been more focused on relations within the Commonwealth. The first intercolonial conference in Melbourne addressed the issue as early as 1863, and a Committee of the House of Commons in 1871 called for a unified status, though with no success; the 1887 imperial conference came back to the topic, as did the 1924 Congress of the Chambers of Commerce of the British Empire (both in London).

After the First World War, these private lobbies remained active in the field, along with a newcomer: the International Chamber of Commerce (ICC), a private multilateral organisation founded in 1920 in Paris. This organisation had a broader reach than its national equivalents, it held large international conferences every two years, and it had direct relations with such influential bodies as the Economic Committee of the League of Nations. The ICC indeed emerged as an active participant in the international economic debates of the interwar period, especially during the 1930s. As usual, the topic of international bankruptcies was not as 'hot' as those of international trade, foreign exchange and international cartels, but it rarely dropped off the agenda altogether. It was mentioned in the final declaration of the first ICC Congress in 1925, and it resurfaced during the 1930s: a standing commission was established[17] that again passed harsh judgment on the poor state of international cooperation and on the 'at times inextricable, or at any rate, costly and onerous difficulties' this caused.[18] The commission also drafted practical

---

[17] International Chamber of Commerce, *Bankruptcy: Berlin Congress, Document no. 8* (Paris, 1937).

[18] Fernand Levêque, *Bankruptcy and the Rights of Creditors: Tenth Congress of the ICC, Copenhagen, Document no. 13* (Paris, 1939).

recommendations that advocated, for example, equality of treatment between foreign and domestic creditors and the speedy recognition of confirmed arrangements.

An Emerging Epistemic Community

Having identified the private sector's interest in a better bankruptcy regime, one last link should be explored: the one that connects these interests to actual reform proposals – in other words, to those with the competence to formulate them. Indeed, there is no missing link here, because international lawyers repeatedly addressed bankruptcy matters and offered proposals.

After an early manifesto for an 'International Bankrupt Code' was published in London in the 1820s,[19] the 1870s saw a renewed interest in the topic. Giuseppe Carle (1875), André Weiss (1892), Josephus Jitta (1895) and Leslie Burgin (1923) put forward their own proposals. Appeals and blueprints were also adopted at international law conferences: the Association for the Reform and Codification of International Law called for such accord at its 1877 and 1880 meetings,[20] the Second Italian International Juridical Congress followed up in Torino in 1880,[21] and the Institut de Droit International addressed the issue several times.

This last institution is the most interesting one at this point not least because it rapidly established itself as the core player in an emerging epistemic community of international lawyers. Created in 1873 in Gent, the Institut consisted of a small number of self-selected members and associates who would meet (as today) every year or two and discuss reports prepared by ad hoc, multiyear commissions. Draft international conventions were then voted upon, article by article, and freely submitted to national governments.[22] In the words of Belgian lawyer Gustave Rolin-Jaecquemyns, who launched the Institut: '[B]eyond *diplomatic action* and

---

[19] Kurt H. Nadelmann, 'An International Bankruptcy Code: New Thoughts on an Old Idea', *International and Comparative Law Quarterly* 10 (1961), 70–82.

[20] See the corresponding *Proceedings*; in 1895 it renamed itself the *International Law Association*, and it still exists today under this denomination.

[21] Nadelmann, 'Bankruptcy Treaties'.

[22] See Martti Koskenniemi, *The Gentle Civilizer of Nations: The Rise and Fall of International Law, 1870–1960* (Cambridge, 2002), chapter 1 for an account of the political and intellectual context in which the Institut was created; see Guillaume Sacristie and Antoine Vauchez, 'Les 'bons offices' du droit international: La constitution d'une autorité non politique dans le concert diplomatique des années 1920', *Critique Internationale* 26 (2005), 101–17 for an analysis of the international community of lawyers before and after the First World War.

individual scientific action, a new and third factor of international law should be given body and life, namely *collective scientific action*'.[23] If the Nobel Prize awarded to the Institut in 1904 is any indication, then this endeavour was most successful.

The Institut repeatedly addressed cross-border bankruptcies: in 1891, 1894, 1902 and 1912. Although its universalist ideals were crushed by the First World War, it managed to resume its sessions in 1919, and in 1923 it created the Academy of International Law – where a large course on international bankruptcy law was taught in 1926, reflecting (among other factors) the new round of discussions on the subject during the 1925 session.[24] The International Law Association also returned to the issue in 1921, and in 1924 it created a special commission on the subject. It flinched at first when faced with the challenge and decided to work instead on the specific issue of trusteeship. But it took on the entire bankruptcy issue again in 1936 – though without result.

At the same time, a report on recent developments across countries was presented at the second congress of the International Association for Comparative Law, held at The Hague in 1935.[25] This was followed by a call for the creation of an 'International Bankruptcy Centre' to collect the highly diverse and increasingly complex national statutes.[26] This converged with a similar endeavour of the ICC that conducted its own twenty-two–country comparative survey of bankruptcy laws during 1937–39. It noted 'a very definite tendency to increase the number of privileged categories of creditors' – primarily the tax administrations and the workers. In other words, redistributive, discretionary policies pursued by national states were having a strong influence in bankruptcy law, making it more territorial and more differentiated. This national influence would drive a steady convergence at the academic level between international law and comparative law. In stark contrast with the debates of the 1870s and 1880s, the perception became very clear that progress at the interstate level would require a much better knowledge of how states regulated their domestic economies.

---

[23] Quoted by John Brown Scott, *L'Institut de Droit International, tableau général des travaux (1873–1913)* (New York, 1920), xiii [italics added].

[24] Albéric Rolin, 'Des conflits de lois en matière de faillite', in Académie de Droit International (ed.), *Recueil des Cours 1926* (Paris, 1927), 1–160.

[25] Louis-Frédéricq Baron, 'Transformation des procédures de faillite, rapport général', *Bulletin trimestriel de l'Institut Belge de Droit Comparé* (July–September 1937).

[26] Nadelmann, 'Bankruptcy Treaties'. During the entire period, the American Society of International Law, founded in 1907, remained much more focused on public international law and did not directly address issues of bankruptcy.

An Inconclusive Answer to the Puzzle: Special Interests

Both the policy relevance of bankruptcy coordination and the pervasive character of resistance against it were by the 1930s beyond any reasonable doubt. The diplomats, the private sector and the globe-trotting academics all had addressed the problem repeatedly, and all had failed to deliver. These failures played out during times that saw sustained levels of commercial and financial integration as well as large-scale efforts to reduce cross-border transaction costs via several international conventions or 'unions'. So what was so distinctive about bankruptcies? And what does this tell us, retrospectively, about how global markets may be regulated?

One straightforward strategy to answer these questions is to look first for private special interests that would have felt threatened by the prospect of an international accord and would have lobbied against it. Obvious candidates include bankruptcy professionals such as judges, lawyers, trustees and liquidators. Yet they fail the test, because there are only rare indications of these groups taking a position or mobilising on the issue. With hindsight, this lack of activity should not be so surprising: in a world where genuine multinational firms were a rarity, cross-border cases were doomed to remain a marginal part of the overall market for insolvency services; and it was far from clear that a rule-based division of judicial labour would have any tangible effect on the caseloads of the countries involved. The notion that private agents might go shopping for alternative forums was fully beyond the intellectual horizon of that time. The same account holds more generally: policy interests or 'substantive' preferences almost never made it to the floor. The usual hot issues of the domestic debates on bankruptcy reform were never heard about on the international scene; think, for example, of pro-creditor versus pro-debtor rules, the trade-off between liquidation and continuation, or the rights of such stakeholders as workers and local communities. In other words, the whole international debate was much less about the substantive law than about procedures and the interaction between national jurisdictions.

In fact, the sole obvious private interests that might have opposed coordination can be found among the parties of actual bankruptcy proceedings – specifically, among senior creditors. This would hold whether their senior claims on the distribution of proceeds derived from statutes (as in the case of churches, tax administrations and workers) or instead were contractual (as with mortgages and all other types of real securities). At first sight, the potential threat to coordination was indeed overwhelming. If, after the default of a transnational firm, some senior creditors were subject to a law different from the law under which they lent, then huge uncertainty would follow regarding the hierarchy of claims, the security of contracts and the ex ante perception of investment risks. The larger and the more internationalised the firm, the less predictable the outcome would be. Moreover, the accumulation of assets and debts located in different countries might, over the course of a firm's life, change (perhaps several times) its implied bankruptcy forum.

And for several reasons the problem's magnitude only increased over time. First, with economic development and increasing capital intensity, the relative volume of debts that could be protected by real securities also increased. Second, from the 1930s onwards, statutory privileges increased as the states began large-scale manipulation of creditor hierarchies. Bankruptcy then became the instrument of redistributive policies, which are local by definition. Yet these 'substantive' or political economic factors were *always* and *fully* set aside by all reform proposals. Whether in the 1820s, the 1920s or the early twenty-first century, all proposed and actual treaties left seniority rights untouched. They would be governed by 'the law of the site' and would not be compromised in an international negotiation. This undisputed principle explains the absence of private mobilisation around the issue.

Thus the original question of why politicians and diplomats failed to improve the overall bankruptcy regime, even at the margin, remains unresolved. Having rejected the standard political economy answer (i.e. private interests), an alternative argument should now be explored: namely, that the judicial character of bankruptcies was probably the main hindrance to progress. Because bankruptcy courts redistribute private property and rewrite contracts, they have always been strongly anchored in national judicial hierarchies that in turn operate with the delegated authority and the guarantees of the sovereign. This fact was already evident in the first medieval statutes adopted in Italy,[27] and the sovereignty dimension in bankruptcy only became larger in later centuries, as nation-states became much more active in integrating their polities and economies. This is the defining historical context in which lawyers conferred at the Hague Conferences or at the sessions of the Institut de Droit International.

[27] Umberto Santarelli, *Per la storia del fallimento nelle legislazioni italiene dell'età intermedia* (Padova, 1964).

Centrality of the Judicial Argument

Alternate Strategies for Global Governance

In broad terms, there are three generic strategies for limiting the consequences of jurisdictional fragmentation.[28] One is to agree on a single supranational rule that would apply to all countries. This method has been adopted by today's European Union with respect to a number of issues (e.g. currency and antitrust enforcement), though not bankruptcy.[29] During the nineteenth century, the possibility of negotiating a universal commercial code was discussed for such cases as bills of exchange and maritime law, but from the outset the approach was considered entirely impractical for the case of bankruptcy.[30]

The second strategy, then, is to negotiate international (multilateral or bilateral) treaties. For instance, states may agree that jurisdiction over bankruptcies will be governed by the nationality of the debtor or by its identified 'main centre of activity'. This route was illustrated by the aforementioned post-imperial networks, and it was the privileged option defended by the legal academy and by the Hague Conferences, though with limited outcomes.

The third strategy is simply what occurs in the absence of progress under the first two. Cross-border bankruptcies are then handled by default rules – that is, the part of national domestic laws addressing 'from the inside out' those civil and commercial cases in which a foreign agent or a foreign court is involved. Lawyers refer to this as 'international private law' or 'conflict of laws'. This body of law typically establishes, for different types of cross-border cases, whether or not domestic courts have jurisdiction, which law (domestic or foreign) should be followed, and how foreign judgments are recognised.[31] For instance, international private law stipulates what the courts of country A should do with a divorce judgment rendered in country B if the right of divorce is not even recognised in country A. The point is that, by construction, rules of this sort differ from country to country and do not warrant coordination.

[28] For a related discussion, see the contribution by Niels P. Petersson in this volume.
[29] However, see Jeffrey Golden, 'We Need a World Financial Court with Specialist Judges', *Financial Times* (9 September 2009) for a recent statement in favour of an international financial court.
[30] See, for instance, the *Annuaire, VI (1882–1883)* of the Institut de Droit International.
[31] See Foelix, *Traité de droit international privé* and Pasquale Fiore, *Droit international privé* (Paris, 1875) for early treaties; Cheshire, *Private International Law* for a classical textbook; and Adrian Briggs, *The Conflict of Laws* (Oxford, 2008) for a contemporary discussion.

For example, English law explicitly defended the principle of universality in the case of bankruptcy. In law, an English trustee could then collect assets abroad and would equally welcome all creditors under its umbrella, without differentiating among them by origin. Although foreign judgments would not be directly enforceable in England, their reception was comparatively easy; the action of foreign trustees in England was well accepted, at least as regards movable assets. In contrast, self-restriction of English courts in support of foreign proceedings was either discretionary (as regards, for example, immovable assets) or essentially closed. For instance, any debt discharge decided by a foreign court, and therefore most continuation arrangements, would not affect contracts written in England. In other words, whereas the overall law was relatively liberal, it did not include any built-in mechanism of coordination that would have guided constructive interaction with foreign courts. It worked rather on a 'take it or leave it' basis – especially outside the Commonwealth.[32]

French law followed similar rules: foreign debtors and creditors had the same rights as resident ones, the French *syndic* could legally act abroad, a foreign trustee could obtain access to assets located in France and so forth. The recognition (and hence the execution) of foreign judgments was essentially conditioned on the granting of an *exequatur* by a French judge. Though the principle was not controversial, its implementation gave the judge a right to review the whole case and consider whether it affected 'public order' – clearly a legal concept that allowed large room for interpretation. Hence, although French doctrine supported the principles of universality and unity of proceedings, implementation was cumbersome and clearly asymmetric (i.e. self-centric).[33] Italian law followed similar principles, and German law explicitly defended a territorial

---

[32] See F. T. Piggot, 'The International Recognition of Bankruptcy' *Law Magazine and Review* 254 (1884), 19–29; Yntema, 'The Enforcement of Foreign Judgments in Anglo-American Law'; Cheshire, *Private International Law*; and L. J. Blom-Cooper, 'Bankruptcy in English Private International Law', *International and Comparative Law Quarterly* 3–4 (1954–55).

[33] Charles Brocher, *Commentaire pratique et théorique du Traité Franco-Suisse du 15 juin 1869 sur la compétence judiciaire et l'exécution des jugements* (Geneva, 1879); Charles Lachau and Christian Daguin, *De l'exécution des jugements étrangers d'après la jurisprudence française* (Paris, 1889); J. Perroud, *Les jugements étrangers, étude théorique et pratique sur leur autorité et leur exécution. Extrait du Répertoire de Droit International* (Paris, 1929); J. Percerou, *Faillites, banqueroutes et liquidations judiciaires* (3 vols., Paris, 1935); Maurice Travers, *Le droit commercial international* (Paris, 1936).

approach to international bankruptcies.[34] Another remarkable case was
the Netherlands, which had no rule whatsoever providing for the domestic
recognition of foreign judgments.

What the Lawyers Argued

Shifting to how the lawyers actually tried to reform this regime, rich
information can be drawn from the extensive reports of the meetings
published by the Institut du Droit International and the Hague Conferences. Though a detailed analysis of these texts would go beyond the
limits of this discussion, the issues raised and fought over are illustrative
and significant.

The first generation of Institut associates strongly defended the notion
that individual civil rights should be defined by nationality and then be
mutually recognised so as to allow for exchange, communication and
progress.[35] Although this notion made sense when applied to marriage
or inheritance, it was less clear regarding commercial matters. Should a
Greek national, trading with Americans from London, be subject to Greek
law and courts? In other words, part of the problem was determining
whether international trade should be governed by an independent body
of law or by the same basic principles as the other chapters, such as
family law or citizenship. In the case of bankruptcy, the 'nationality'
option won the first round at the 1891 meeting, but a resolution adopted
in 1894 endorsed the alternate principle of domicile. Hence our Greek
merchant would have been required to appear in a London court.

Then came the question of unity of proceedings, a core point of the
dominant doctrine on cross-border bankruptcy. In the early modern
period the last remnants of which were rapidly disappearing, merchants
traded on their own credit or personal reputation rather than on hard
physical capital. Hence to a large extent, 'capital followed the person',
so both could be brought before the same court. This option came under
increasing pressure because of capital-intensive economic growth that
implied more immovable assets and more senior creditors, both of which
are bound to a particular place or jurisdiction. Therefore, the decisions
about who should have jurisdiction and how unity of proceedings should
be obtained became more conflictual by the day. Still, the existing doctrine was never radically contested. Most remarkably, there was an alternate option whereby a lead procedure would coordinate secondary ones,

---

34 Kurt Hess, *Konkurs und Vergleich in internationalen Privatrecht* (Giessen, 1934).
35 See the 1883 edition of the *Annuaire* of the Institut and the discussion of the 'Oxford
Rules'.

located in different countries: this promising, though heterodox option was occasionally brought forward but without success.[36] The Hague Conferences discarded it outright, and after recognising it (under strict conditions) in 1894, the Institut restated in 1902 the 'absolute unity of bankruptcy' principle.[37] This option would only reemerge decades later, during the 1980s, when the European Union took on the issue from scratch.

Third was the question of 'public order', or 'policy preferences' in today's language. The concept was already present in the French rules of *exequatur*, and its relevance only increased with the emergence of regulatory states. In 1894, for example, the Spanish representative at The Hague raised the case of failed railway companies that should continue to operate during bankruptcy proceedings because of their public service duty. In 1912, the Institut agreed as well that 'the interests of third parties' could be recognised when addressing the case of immovable assets. By the 1920s, all parties clearly perceived the underlying conflict between policy preferences and international coordination.[38] One result was the new interest in assembling and comparing national bankruptcy laws, as reflected in the later, parallel initiatives of the International Chamber of Commerce and the International Association for Comparative Law. In short, whereas the prerogatives of sovereignty had initially been embedded within the rights of nationality as held by individual citizens, these prerogatives were being increasingly invested in the state's capacity to implement a large array of public policies. As economic growth became more capital intensive and more closely regulated by policy-making states, cross-border cooperation actually became more difficult.

Sovereignty and the Regulation of Private Contracts

The debates on international bankruptcies offer a fine case study for analyzing how lawyers addressed these new problems and how they struggled

---

[36] At the 1925 Hague Conference, the English delegation defended the principle of multiple procedures, but presented it as a defensive measure rather than as a potential principle of international coordination; this apparently reflected the long-run (though as yet unsystematised) evolution observed within the Commonwealth.

[37] See, for example, Josephus Jitta, *La codification du droit international de la faillite* (The Hague, 1895).

[38] See, for instance, Ernest G. Lorenzen, 'Territoriality, Public Policy and the Conflict of Laws', *Yale Law Journal* 33 (1924), 736–51 and the classical textbook by J. Westlake, *Private International Law* (6th edn. London, 1922), 51: 'No attempt to define the limits of that reservation (public policy) has ever succeeded, even to the extent of making its nature clearer' (quoted by Lorenzen).

with their own legal concepts as well as with the existing international and domestic political orders. There is no doubt that most lawyers sincerely wanted to help solve a pressing, real-world problem, though at the same time they were constrained by the existing political construction of sovereignty, judicial integrity and international private law.[39] The unrelenting defence of the strict unity of proceedings should be understood in those terms: rather than being interpreted merely as the reflection of an abstract intellectual commitment or a conceptual fantasy, it should be traced to constraints exercised by the political and legal order of the day.[40]

To better understand this point, four features mentioned previously should be brought together: the record of post-imperial networks of bankruptcy treaties since the 1810s, the parallel experience of federal countries, the strong resistance to full judicial reciprocity (as previously described for England and France), and the clear rejection of a multilateral route to international coordination on bankruptcies (only bilateral treaties were considered). In fact, these factors all converge towards the same proposition: governments were not ready to compromise their domestic judicial order and procedural integrity for the sake of an international agreement. As was often remarked at The Hague, leaving one's national creditors in the hands of foreign courts presupposes not only a strong bilateral relationship but also a mutual recognition of the respective countries' constitutional and judicial orders. Signatories should have 'full confidence in their respective courts', as a Belgian representative stated.[41] This explains why multilateralism was out of the question: such an approach presupposes the recognition of a community of states, however limited its purpose, that would warrant a transitive interaction. But this was not possible in the present case; for example, Belgium had agreements with both France (1899) and the Netherlands (1925) but the latter two had no agreement between themselves.

---

39 David Kennedy, 'International Law and the Nineteenth Century: History of an Illusion', *Nordic Journal of International Law* 65 (1996), 385–420; Joel R. Paul, 'The Isolation of Private International Law', *Wisconsin International Law Journal* 7 (1988), 149–78; Alex Mills, 'The Private History of International Law', *International and Comparative Law Quarterly* 55 (2006), 1–49.

40 In his discussion of the disappearance of private international law as a separate field, Paul, 'The Isolation of Private International Law', mentions two possible reasons for this phenomenon: a purely intellectual one that would include a delayed response to Blackstone's *Commentaries* and 'the growing significance of international trade'. Kennedy, 'International Law and the Nineteenth Century: History of an Illusion', and Mills, 'The Private History of International Law', follow the same methodological line; for these authors, real-world (i.e. political and economic) factors are present as elements of the broader social context rather than as part of the actual history being related.

41 Third Conference (1900), p. 160 of the *Actes*.

In other words, a key element was the political compact that structured not only the interaction between sovereigns internationally but
also their respective domestic interactions with citizens, their property
and their debt titles. At stake was the liberal government of civil societies and domestic markets as a matter of both constitutional politics
and practical regulation. This may well account for the problematic yet
unyielding defence of the unity of proceedings, which de facto preserves
formal integrity under the rules and guarantees of a national constitutional compact. The alternate option – based on horizontal, decentralised
coordination between national courts – would require that national proceedings be 'opened up' to each other. Moreover, to be credible, any
such rule would also require that, when engaging in international transactions, courts would work in complete independence and establish their
own rules of international coordination. This would have run entirely
counter to the executive's monopoly on interstate relations, which was a
key feature of the realist, Westphalian regime in force at the time.

The possibility of articulating domestic constitutional rules and rules
of international cooperation in a viable manner was further weakened
by the fact that the latter were weakly institutionalised and often dominated by raw power politics. Interstate commitments did not carry much
weight, and international judicial regulation was of limited use for most
practical purposes. In addition to the widespread reliance on interstate
arbitration (i.e. on a rather weak form of rule), the mutual recognition
of civil judgments in general was cumbersome, international commercial
arbitration was limited to some highly specialised organisations, and no
international agency had developed an internal dispute settlement mechanism before 1914. In such an environment, the trade-off between cross-
border coordination and the protection of national judicial prerogatives
was usually unpalatable. This must have been especially true in the case of
bankruptcy proceedings, which dealt with the highly sensitive institution
of private property rights.

This point is strengthened when one briefly considers the remarkable
breakthrough recently achieved within the European Union, which at
last overcomes dilemmas of the nineteenth century. After four decades
of failed attempts, the European Union finally adopted a comprehensive
agreement on cross-border insolvencies that became effective in 2002.[42]
Remarkably, this agreement retained the principle of universality, but

---

[42] See Bob Wessels, Bruce A. Markell and Jason J. Kilborn, *International Cooperation
in Bankruptcy and Insolvency Matters* (Oxford, 2009) and Louise Ellen Teitz, 'The
Hague Choice of Court Convention: Validating Party Autonomy and Providing an

dropped the principle of unity. All parties to a failure now enter the same proceeding, although it may be administered by several, coordinated national courts. A lead procedure is designated to which secondary or ancillary ones report, and courts are then duty bound to coordinate on a decentralised basis. Judgments are immediately enforceable across borders, information flows freely, and lead trustees may appear before all national courts. Yet just as in the past, policy preferences and special interests have been left to local rules. Examples of such matters include real securities and the hierarchy of claims, the rights of workers and local communities, and preferences regarding continuation versus liquidation. These matters are all left to some ninety different national laws and regulations now in force across the European Union.[43] In other words, the coordination of procedures now goes far beyond anything envisaged in previous decades, although redistributive, more generally substantive issues remain very much territorial.

Conclusions

Since the 1870s, diplomats and lawyers as well as private lobbies have continually pushed for better coordination of international bankruptcies. Despite these efforts, progress has been rare. Furthermore, the puzzle of failed reform cannot be explained by a lack of reform proposals or by the opposition of private interests such as those of senior creditors. In this chapter I have argued that this situation arose from the interaction between two dimensions of sovereignty: first, the international political order between nation-states, which was very much shaped by raw power politics and allowed for only very limited institutionalisation; and second, the domestic dimension of sovereignty, whereby states progressively developed into the ultimate guarantor and regulator of private rights and national markets. These political dimensions are, indeed, two defining aspects of the evolution of capitalism during that period.

If this analysis is correct, then the present construction of global economic agents, or citizens, is likewise conditioned by two factors: the

---

Alternative to Arbitration', *American Journal of Comparative Law* 53 (2005), 543–58 for the parallel case of civil judgments.
43 See Anne-Marie Slaughter, 'Court to Court', *American Journal of International Law* 92 (1998), 708–12; Robert O. Keohane, Andrew Moravcsik and Anne-Marie Slaughter, 'Legalized Dispute Resolution: Interstate and Transnational', *International Organizations* 54 (2000), 457–88. Karen Alter, 'Delegating to International Courts: Self-Binding vs. Other-Binding Delegation', *Law and Contemporary Problems* 71 (2008), 37–76 reflects more directly on the issues discussed here.

endowment of rights, over which agents negotiate with their own sovereign, and the sovereign's willingness to let regulators (specifically, the courts) coordinate internationally on a decentralised, horizontal basis. These two factors explain why the security of private rights and contracts at the global level is arguably much stronger today than it was a century ago. Multiple jurisdictions, which once constituted a formidable problem (both politically and intellectually), have now become part of the solution. However, this change became possible only after the adjudication of private disputes was largely freed of the strictures of a past era, one marked by realist sovereign interaction and laissez-faire domestic politics.

4

Credit Information, Institutions, and International Trade

The United Kingdom, United States, and Germany, 1850–1930

Rowena Olegario

Beginning in the mid-nineteenth century, the search for new overseas customers prompted exporters in Europe and the United States to seek better ways to obtain credit information on potential buyers. International banks (banks with overseas branches) could supply some of the necessary information; so, too, could export agents and the informal networks that merchants had relied on for centuries. Yet the limitations of these sources drove exporters, especially smaller businesses hoping to develop overseas markets, to seek better solutions to the problem of information asymmetry.

The institutional remedies that emerged in Great Britain, the United States and Germany varied in form. Invariably, they involved the state, as when American exporters lobbied the federal government to improve the services provided by banks and consular offices, or when British exporters sought assistance from the Overseas Department of the Board of Trade.[1] Yet economic actors below the level of the nation-state also mobilised to solve the problem of information asymmetry. These institutions included for-profit credit reporting firms, not-for-profit credit bureaus or interchanges, and industry groups. Their solutions were diverse, controversial, sometimes expensive and all imperfect; nevertheless, they succeeded in creating a network of information exchange that allowed exporters to connect with a wider range of customers overseas.

---

[1] Thomas G. Patterson, 'American Businessmen and Consular Service Reform, 1890s to 1906', *Business History Review* 40 (Spring 1966), 77–97; Cuthbert Greig, 'Foreign Collections', *Credit Monthly* 31 (October 1929), 27.

The construction of transnational mechanisms for information sharing was part of the historical process of globalisation, a process that occurred haltingly over the course of many decades beginning in the middle of the nineteenth century. Until then, as Michael Geyer and Charles Bright have written, regional autonomy was very much the rule. And although it is tempting to invoke the notion of an overarching power, centred in the West, that oversaw the process of globalisation, in fact the linkages among regions were achieved not by formal transnational regimes but by 'specialized mediators and interlopers'. Collectively, they were responsible for creating many of the rules, practices and institutional structures that enabled commercial transactions to occur among previously autonomous regions. The systems they created, Geyer and Bright write, were for the most part 'not centrally administered, nor do they have more than limited accountability. They have hardly any publicity. Organised in information corridors and segmented webs of exchange, these systems are difficult to describe, let alone theorize'. Even today, they argue, '[i]t is not world governments but regimes of mostly private regulations and practices that maintain and service the process of globalization'. Thinking about globalisation in this way helps us to understand how the countries that became 'the West' managed to dominate other parts of the world, not through brute force backed by state power, but through the efforts of disparate agents who organised and linked the different regions using new communications technology and institutional procedures.[2]

In becoming transnational organisations, credit reporting firms, mutual protection societies and credit bureaus participated in this process. Yet they have been little studied; in the historical literature, banks have received the bulk of attention as the arbiters of creditworthiness in both domestic and international trade. Certainly, the willingness of banks (as well as note brokers) to discount a trader's notes was a critical indicator of how far he or she could be trusted. Even so, in a number of highly commercial countries, alternative institutions for determining creditworthiness emerged, indicating that banks did not perform this function sufficiently well. In the UK, by at least the 1770s, shopkeepers and merchants had formed mutual protection societies to share credit information on their customers. Such societies also developed in Germany. In both countries they consisted primarily of small businesses that did not have the

---

[2] Michael Geyer and Charles Bright, 'World History in a Global Age', *American Historical Review* 100 (October 1995): 1034–60, 1045, 1047–48, 1054–55.

resources to perform their own credit investigations. Entrepreneurs in the United States, a large country with a mobile population and fragmented banking system, invented a different organisational form, the for-profit credit reporting firm. In all of these cases, banks were either unwilling or unable to supply information on smaller or less established firms or on individual retail customers. Their inadequacies prompted the establishment of alternative institutions for obtaining the information that is so crucial to judging creditworthiness.

Scrutinising domestic customers was difficult enough; overseas customers presented even greater challenges. Merchants in all three countries expanded their information-sharing organisations to cope with the information asymmetries of overseas trade. From the 1850s to the 1920s, an extensive international network of private and semi-private actors worked to ease the exchange of credit information. The networks eventually spanned not only the United States, Canada, the UK and continental Europe (including Central and Eastern Europe), but also India, South Africa, Latin America, Australia and other parts of the world. A few entities, such as Dun & Bradstreet, Creditreform and the National Association of Credit Men (now the National Association of Credit Management), continue into the present. Yet many more have closed, and except for scattered allusions in obscure journals and books, few traces of them survive. The disappearance of these organisations makes it difficult to recover their routines and innovations.[3] Yet doing so is worthwhile, for without them, the rich story of the institutional responses to the problem of information asymmetry cannot fully be told.

This chapter offers a starting point for historical research. It synthesises archival work done in the United States with information from secondary sources in the UK and Germany to outline briefly the attempts of traders in each country to obtain credit information on their current and potential customers. It ends with a few reflections on the trajectory that future studies might take, drawing on neo-institutional theory to suggest potential questions that can guide the formation of larger conceptual frameworks.

---

[3] In the United States, for example, attempts were made to establish for-profit credit interchanges for both domestic and international commerce. At least one firm, Credit Clearing House, was founded on this model and lasted into the 1920s. I have not been able to locate any historical documents relating to this firm or others like it. Rowena Olegario, *A Culture of Credit: Embedding Trust and Transparency in American Business* (Cambridge, Mass., 2006), 187–88, 190, 198; Archibald J. Wolfe, *Theory and Practice of International Commerce* (New York, 1919), 366–67.

Credit Reporting: For-Profit Firms vs. Mutual Protection Societies

'Credit reporting' refers to the gathering and dissemination of financial and business information on individuals and firms. (It should not be confused with the credit rating of bonds and commercial paper performed by agencies such as Moody's and S&P. These organisations have a quasi-regulatory function that is absent from credit reporting firms and bureaus.[4]) Historically, credit information travelled through networks made up of family and close associates or through groups of merchants in the same line of business. These arrangements are so ancient that they appear scarcely to have a history at all, their origins seemingly as distant as those of trade itself. In the modern era, one of the first groups set up specifically to exchange credit information, and for which there is surviving documentation, was the Society of Guardians for the Protection of Trade against Swindlers and Sharpers. Established in London in 1776, its members exchanged both wholesale and retail credit information. This association was purely private; governmental authorities made no contribution to its formation or administration. Nearly a century later, in the 1860s, similar groups began to appear in Germany where they were formed with the active participation of the local chambers of commerce and boards of trade, bodies that in Germany perform a semipublic function.

The British and German groups shared several common features. First, they were nonprofit enterprises: members' dues paid for expenses, and no one made a profit from selling the information. Second, the exchange of information involved only those who had sold or were considering selling to a potential buyer. Access was restricted to members, and severe penalties were imposed on anyone who disclosed the information to outsiders. In both countries, the groups began as local endeavours but quickly established correspondence with one another to form large, cross-country networks of information exchange.

In the United States, a different solution to the problem of information asymmetry evolved in the form of credit reporting agencies (or, more accurately, firms). This institution first appeared in New York City in the 1830s and was formalised as the Mercantile Agency by the abolitionist

---

[4] For credit rating agencies, see Timothy J. Sinclair, *The New Masters of Capital: American Bond Rating Agencies and the Politics of Creditworthiness* (Ithaca, NY, 2005); and Richard Sylla, 'An Historical Primer on the Business of Credit Rating', in *Ratings, Rating Agencies, and the Global Financial System*, eds. Richard M. Levich, Giovanni Majnoni and Carmen Reinhart (New York, 2002), 19–40.

Lewis Tappan in 1841. The Mercantile Agency became the R.G. Dun Co. in 1849; in 1933 it merged with a competitor, the Bradstreet Co., to form Dun & Bradstreet (D&B).[5] Today D&B operates in 200 countries, and its 2008 revenues of more than $1.7 billion make it the world's largest business credit reporting firm.[6] Such firms differed from mutual protection societies by being third-party purveyors, gathering information on individuals and firms that they then sold at a profit to anyone willing to pay. Credit reporting firms spread to the UK, Germany and other parts of the world beginning in the late 1850s. Mutual protection societies, organised almost exclusively along industry lines, began appearing in the United States only towards the end of the nineteenth century – somewhat later than in Germany and much later than in the UK.

The following sections briefly outline the historical evolution of credit reporting firms and mutual protection societies in the UK, the United States and Germany, the three countries where the modern institution of credit reporting first developed.

British Institutions

Formal credit information sharing has a long history in Britain. In the late eighteenth century, attempts to stem fraud by improving the flow of credit information led English mercantile and retail creditors to band together into trade protection societies. Based loosely on the guilds, the societies were established in London and other commercial centres to protect members against fraudsters by formalising the transmittal of trade gossip. The earliest such group was the Society of Guardians for the Protection of Trade against Swindlers and Sharpers, established in London in 1776. A surviving list of members for the year 1812 indicates that the society at that time had approximately 550 members, nearly all in London. Members operated in a wide variety of trades, both wholesale and retail, and included druggists, stationers, flour factors, lead merchants and woollen drapers.[7] Members promised to alert one another about slow payers

5 On the history of mercantile credit reporting, see Olegario, *A Culture of Credit*; Roy A. Foulke, *The Sinews of American Commerce* (New York, 1941); James D. Norris, *R. G. Dun and Co., 1841–1900* (Westport, CT, 1978); and Scott A. Sandage, *Born Losers: A History of Failure in America* (Cambridge, MA, 2005).
6 Hoovers, http://www.hoovers.com/company/The_Dun_Bradstreet_Corporation, December 2009. Hoovers is part of Dun & Bradstreet Corp.
7 *A List of Members of the Society of Guardians for the Protection of Trade against Swindlers and Sharpers* (London, 1812).

or nonpayers and established a common fund to prosecute robbers and shoplifters.[8]

As the following two examples illustrate, the information could be highly impressionistic and idiosyncratic, with numerous assumptions about gender and class embedded in the descriptions:

April 23d, 1798. The Members are hereby cautioned against being imposed upon by a Young Woman, between 17 and 20 Years of Age, of rather a pale Countenance, having the Appearance of a Lady's Maid; and of a remarkably decent Address. – Such a Person having lately obtained Goods from Two Members, by representing herself as coming from Two Ladies of distinction, to whom she was, in consequence, supposed to be Servant; but on Enquiry of those Ladies the Transactions turn out to be Impositions.

October 26, 1798. The Members are hereby informed, that a person hath lately obtained, from a Member of this Society, the difference between the Price of Some Goods he ordered, and the Amount of a Draft or Cheque, he produced, upon 'Messrs. Robarts, Curtis, Were, Hornyold & Co', payable to 'Jno. [John] Smith', Esq. or Bearer' and signed 'Wm. Antrobus', but on presenting the same for Payment, it appeared that no such Person kept Cash at that House. He is a tall genteel young Man about 25 Years of Age, has dark Eyes and sometimes dresses in a Blue Coat and Pantaloons with his hair tied; and at others in Mourning with his Hair as a Crop.[9]

It is unclear how long the Society of Guardians remained in operation, but another group, the Society of Mutual Communication for the Protection of Trade (later the Mutual Communication Society), proved longer lasting. Modelled on the Master Tailors guild, the society was founded in 1801 at the British Coffee House in London's Charing Cross. Its constitution contained two principles that were to lie at the heart of all trade protection societies: 'Every Member is bound to communicate to the Society without delay, the Name and Description of any Person who may be unfit to trust, for the security and satisfaction of the other Members; and shall, on all occasions, impart, without reserve, any information that may be solicited by any of the Members'. The second principle decreed that the society was run not for profit, but solely as a service to its members; all expenses were to be paid from a common fund. Three further regulations governed the society: first, that the information would not be divulged outside of the membership; second, that members' decisions about whom to trust for credit would not be constrained in any way by the society;

---

[8] *A List of the Members of the Guardians; or Society for the Protection of Trade against Swindlers and Sharpers* (London?, no date but probably 1799), 35–36.

[9] Ibid., 29–31.

and finally, that no member would give false or malicious information or combine with others to deny credit to any individual. Tickets were issued so that only members had access to the society's records and a strict procedure was implemented.[10]

The mutual protection model soon migrated to other commercial centres in Great Britain. In 1823 John Smith, owner of the *Liverpool Mercury*, called a meeting of that city's businessmen at a local hotel, where they agreed to set up the Liverpool Society of Guardians. Three years later he convinced traders in Manchester to establish a society there. Similar groups were soon operating in Bath, the Yorkshire/Lincolnshire area (centred in Hull), Leeds and Leicester in England, and in Glasgow and Aberdeen in Scotland. In 1839 steps were taken to form the London Association for the Protection of Trade, and the society was officially established in that city's West End in 1842.[11] Membership requirements in all of the societies were strict to ensure that information was trustworthy. The Liverpool society bylaws, for example, specified that businesses wishing to join had to be recommended by two existing members. The entire membership voted on their acceptance during the quarterly general meetings. Withholding information, sharing information with nonmembers and bankruptcy were cause for expulsion, and the secretary kept a list of persons who were deemed inadmissible.[12]

National coverage appears to have been an early goal of these societies; from the beginning, the Liverpool society bylaws recommended that 'correspondence be established with similar Societies throughout the Kingdom'.[13] Some sharing of information appears to have occurred in the 1830s, when a number of the association heads (or 'secretaries') began meeting informally. The meetings became a more formal conference of secretaries in 1848, and in 1865 the National Association of Trade Protection Societies was established. Its constitution required all member societies 'to reciprocate with all and each of the other Societies, in procuring and giving information in answer to enquiries without undue delay', and to exchange circulars with one another. By 1868, according to its annual report, the confederation had 'solicitors, agents, or correspondents in 2,500 towns and places' throughout the United Kingdom.

---

[10] C. McNeil Greig, *The Growth of Credit Information: A History of UAPT-Infolink plc.* (Oxford, 1992), 12–14, 106.

[11] Ibid., 14–17, 21.

[12] Society of Guardians for the Protection of Trade against Swindlers and Sharpers. Established Feb. 26, 1823 (Liverpool, 1824).

[13] Ibid., 12.

By the end of the nineteenth century, the national association had seventy-six member organisations totalling some 40,000 individual members.[14]

Credit reporting firms took root in the UK in the 1850s with the establishment of a London branch of the U.S. firm, the Mercantile Agency (later R.G. Dun & Co.) Home-grown British firms like Seyd & Co. also appeared around this time.[15] The nineteenth century thus saw the creation in Britain of a dense network of credit information exchange. In the last decades of the century, the British mutual protection societies began corresponding with Germany's Creditreform associations (to be discussed later). After the First World War, the societies made increased efforts to improve their international credit reporting. The London Association for the Protection of Trade (LAPT) opened an office in Brussels in 1925–26 and one in Antwerp soon after, and it had ambitious plans to open many more. An LAPT report from that period referred to an agreement that had been reached with more than 700 local bureaus across continental Europe to share information on local firms and market conditions free of charge, an indication that credit bureaus had become widely established in Europe.

The LAPT's proposed offices on the Continent never materialised, and the Brussels office was closed in 1946, twenty years after it had opened. In 1927 the association changed its name to the International Association for the Promotion and Protection of Trade Limited, or IAPPT; in addition to its correspondence with European bureaus, it had working arrangements with trade groups in South Africa, India and Latvia.[16] In 1928, formal agreements were signed with 150 offices of the National Association of Credit Men, as well as with the National Retail Credit Association, a consumer credit bureau that had 900 offices in the United States. Agreements also were made with the Canadian Credit Men's Trust Association Limited and two agencies in New Zealand. By 1932, the IAPPT claimed to have more than 2,000 affiliated offices worldwide and had acquired

---

[14] Margot C. Finn, *The Character of Credit: Personal Debt in English Culture, 1740–1914* (Cambridge, 2003), 290, 299. By 1939, seventy societies were affiliated with the National Association of Trade Protection Societies (NATPS). The trade protection society movement declined dramatically after the Second World War. C. McNeil Greig argues that the societies' nonprofit orientation contributed to their demise. C. McNeil Greig, *The Growth of Credit Information*, 14–17, 19.

[15] I have not been able to determine when Seyd & Co. was established, but it was probably in the late 1850s. Allusions to its reports appear in American credit manuals as late as the 1920s.

[16] C. McNeil Greig, *The Growth of Credit Information*, 164–66, 184.

the Indian and Eastern Association, which had more than 80 members.[17]
Judging by these self-reported numbers, it appears that by 1930 British exporters had access to information from an international network of credit bureaus and credit reporting firms, in addition to traditional sources like international banks and export merchants.

American Institutions

Mutual protection societies had a slower start in the United States. A number of factors accounted for the lag, including the country's large geographical expanse, the high mobility rates of its population, and trade relationships that were less established than in Europe. The early establishment by entrepreneurs of credit reporting firms and the speed with which the two largest (R.G. Dun and the Bradstreet Co.) achieved national coverage may also have preempted the formation of mutual protection societies. Credit reporting firms were well entrenched in the United States by the 1890s, when American businesspeople and policy makers began to see foreign markets as a solution to domestic overproduction, cyclical depressions and unemployment. Robert G. Dun announced in 1896 that his organisation could provide reports on any business in the world. During the latter part of the 1890s, Dun produced at least two reports per week on foreign firms for which no information was currently available.[18] Much of the information came from Dun's foreign contacts or from American firms that had done business overseas. The data would have been impressionistic and patchy, because most foreign firms did not make financial statements available to credit reporters. Even so, foreign entrepreneurs such as harmonica maker Matthias Hohner, who was based in a village in Germany, availed themselves of the credit reporting firms' myriad services, not just to check the credit ratings of American importers but also to compile lists of potential customers and collect bad debts.[19]

Other sources of information on foreign businesses had been established by the First World War.[20] Of the trade groups, the most important

[17] Ibid., 168–69, 177, 268–74; Cuthbert Greig, 'Foreign Collections', 27; National Association of Credit Men, Meeting of the Board of Directors, October 9–11, 1928, Chicago, scrapbook ledger, 3, NACM Archives, Columbia, Maryland.
[18] Norris, *R. G. Dun & Co, 1841–1900*, 158.
[19] Hartmut Berghoff, 'Civilizing Capitalism? The Beginnings of Credit Rating in the United States and Germany', Inaugural Lecture at the German Historical Institute, Washington, DC, November 14, 2008, 22–23.
[20] Credit men could also rely on the Philadelphia Commercial Museum (founded in 1894 to promote American and foreign commerce), American consular offices, commercial

were the National Association of Manufacturers (NAM), formed in 1895 and still in existence today, and the American Manufacturers Export Association, founded around 1910. Their members were smaller firms that did not have the resources to establish their own overseas offices. By 1912, the National Association of Manufacturers reportedly had files on tens of thousands of foreign businesses, some gained by contacting the firms directly, others through special inquiries made to local banks, merchants and American export firms. NAM also maintained a collection bureau and lists of foreign attorneys. It had 1,400 correspondents – foreigners and Americans living abroad – who provided information on market opportunities in their localities.[21]

Yet many of the nation's credit men (as the practitioners, almost exclusively male, referred to themselves) complained that the reports obtained from these sources were inadequate. Crucially, the reports did not include specific information on past transactions, such as whether a buyer had paid with cash or credit, the terms of the sale and whether bills were paid promptly. (Such information was known as 'ledger experience' because it was recorded in merchants' books.[22]) Among the many business groups lobbying for a more robust foreign trade was the National Association of Credit Men (NACM), established in 1896. Members of the NACM argued that exchanging specific ledger experience on buyers rather than simply coming up with a consensus opinion based on hearsay was essential to providing American firms with the confidence to sell on credit to foreign customers. Past experiences taught them that building trust was the key to making such an arrangement work and that the task would not be easy. For years, activists within the NACM had pushed for the creation of both a foreign and a domestic credit information interchange (bureau). Although in theory credit information bureaus are beneficial, the credit men's attempts to establish them had run into several coordination problems. The most serious obstacle was the feeling among some credit men that the bureaus' benefits would not compensate for the time

attachés, trade commissioners, banks and the credit departments of export publications. L. John Bergman, 'Elementary Foreign Credits', *Credit Monthly* 22 (May 1920), 18–19, 18. Consuls, though, were forbidden by regulations to furnish credit reports. Ernst Filsinger, 'Credits in the Near East: Skilled Observer Says We Neglect Opportunities', *Credit Monthly* 28 (January 1926), 18, 26, 28–32, 30.

[21] William H. Becker, *The Dynamics of Business-Government Relations: Industry and Exports, 1893–1921* (Chicago, 1982), chapter 3.

[22] Address by Louis S. Goldstein, New Orleans, LA, June 23–26, 1914 (pamphlet), in Proceedings of the Nineteenth Annual Convention of the National Association of Credit Men, Rochester, NY, June 23–26, 1914, scrapbook ledger, NACM Archives.

and effort the system demanded. Small-town creditors felt that their counterparts in large commercial cities would gain far more from the scheme.
And because it relied so heavily on voluntary effort, including the timely
response to requests from fellow members, many credit men expressed
scepticism that a national bureau could be made to work at all.[23]

The goal of establishing national and international credit bureaus for
the exchange of ledger experience advanced fitfully in the United States.
The catalyst was the First World War; with the prospect of the war ending, more American credit men felt a heightened sense of urgency about
establishing an international credit bureau, both to rebuild international
trade and to take advantage of America's newly dominant position within
it. The war enhanced the United States' favourable balance of trade and
made it, for the first time, a net creditor nation: in 1919 American exports
outpaced imports by $4 billion.[24] Businesspeople and policy makers real-
ised that the country would have to import more from other nations even
as it depended on them to buy an ever-expanding amount of goods to
offset weaker domestic demand. Yet British and European customers had
been devastated by war and were suffering from the devaluation of their
currencies. U.S. government loans helped offset the problem somewhat,
but deteriorating demand at home made the opening of new international
markets more pressing. The anxiety that had first manifested itself during
the depression of the 1890s continued: American businesspeople feared
that a deflationary spiral of lower prices for goods, capital and labour
would recur unless they succeeded in cultivating new markets abroad.

They were well aware that American businesses lacked the trade infrastructure of British and German exporters.[25] U.S. foreign trade had
increased tenfold in the fifty years preceding the First World War, but
American finance capital had not kept pace. Because national banks in the
United States were legally prohibited from establishing branches in foreign countries, most of America's foreign trade was financed by European

---

[23] Olegario, *A Culture of Credit*, chapter 6.

[24] 'Keep the Foreign Trade Flag Flying!... An Interview with Philip B. Kennedy, Director
of the U.S. Bureau of Foreign and Domestic Commerce', *Credit Monthly* 22 (April
1920), 16, 34–35, 39, 16. See also Philip B. Kennedy, 'The Significance of the Edge Law
in Relation to Foreign Trade', *Annals of the American Academy of Political and Social
Science* 94 (March 1921), 133–41, 133.

[25] Siegfried Stern, 'The Role of Private Credit in Hemispheric Trade', *Law and Contemporary Problems* 8 (Autumn 1941), 737–51, 737; R. DeF. Boomer, 'Mexican Credit
Characteristics: Necessity of Imports for Mexico', *Credit Monthly* 23 (October 1921),
9–10, 10; Address by Louis S. Goldstein, 1914. See also Archibald J. Wolfe, *Theory and
Practice of International Commerce* (New York, 1919), 287 ff.

banks. One U.S. trade official spoke for the majority of exporters when he observed that 'there has been denied to the United States a factor which has been of inestimable value to Germany, England and France in the treatment of foreign credits'.[26] The Edge Act of 1919, which amended the Federal Reserve Act passed six years earlier, attempted to enhance the credit facilities available to American exporters by allowing the federally designated national banks to open subsidiaries abroad. Thus encouraged by the federal government and by the promise of new markets, a number of firms began exporting, mostly to Europe and South America. For many, the experience was short-lived. In 1920, a worldwide economic slowdown began, and although it did not last long (by 1923 economic growth was again on the upswing), numerous export businesses failed. Banks were forced to close their new foreign branches, and they long remained wary of reestablishing them.[27]

Formation of a Foreign Credit Interchange Bureau (FCIB) was finally approved by the National Association of Credit Men in 1917 (although it would take two more years to become operational).[28] FCIB survived the postwar vicissitudes; by 1926, it had 460 members. Two years later the organisation reported issuing well over 100,000 credit reports and had inaugurated surveys of credit and collection conditions in Latin America. FCIB published a weekly *Confidential Bulletin* containing information on the economic and credit conditions in foreign countries. It relied primarily on American sources such as American Chambers of Commerce around the world and the foreign branches of the U.S. Bureau of Foreign and Domestic Commerce.[29] The credit reporting firms, meanwhile, continued

[26] Address by Louis S. Goldstein, 1914. In 1914, the National City Bank of New York established a foreign branch, but generally U.S. banks did not do so until the country became a net creditor after the First World War. After a postwar retrenchment, the number of U.S. banks with foreign branches rose beginning in 1925. In 1930 they numbered 234, probably the highest in U.S. history, although 14 banks and trust companies accounted for nearly all the branches. The majority of U.S. banks, however, continued to rely on foreign banks as correspondents. Clyde W. Phelps, 'The Future of American Banking Abroad', *Credit Monthly* 32 (November 1930), 21–22, 43–45.

[27] William A. Prendergast and William H. Steiner, *Credit and Its Uses* (New York, [1906] 1931), 483–84.

[28] In 1918, the Foreign Credit Round Table, a related project involving a group of American exporters, began to meet monthly in cities like New York and Boston; by 1920, its membership had grown to eighty export managers.

[29] National Association of Credit Men, Convention Reports, Thirty-Third Annual Convention, June 1928, Seattle, Washington, 54, NACM Archives; P. M. Haight, 'Foreign Credit Work Gets Increased Attention from American Business', *Credit Monthly* 31 (July 1929), 39.

opening offices abroad. Credit man J. L. Thompson of Yale & Towne
Manufacturing Co. was able to state with confidence in 1924 that the
'honor' of a foreign merchant 'can be determined with remarkable accuracy' by using available sources of information.[30]

German Institutions

In Germany, mutual protection societies and credit reporting firms
appeared at roughly the same time, in the 1860s. The first credit reporting firms to appear were of German origin. In 1860 the Wolffsche Tele-
graphenagentur was founded by one S. Salomon in Stettin in the province
of Pomerania (now part of Poland). Salomon served only a regional client
base, but two years later, Lesser & Liman established a credit reporting
firm in Berlin – the Bureau for Inquiries regarding Business and Credit
Relationships – that covered a larger territory. A decade later, in 1872,
Wilhelm Schimmelpfeng opened a credit reporting firm in Frankfurt am
Main that later expanded outside Germany and became one of the largest
credit reporting firms in Europe (Dun & Bradstreet took over the firm in
1984).[31] It was not until 1876 that R. G. Dun opened a branch in Berlin, perhaps to take advantage of the greater levels of trade that German
unification in 1871 had made possible.[32]

   As already noted, the first mutual protection society in Germany also
was established in the 1860s. In 1863, a group calling itself Mutua Confid-
entia was founded for the purpose of debt collection, but it also circulated
blacklists of problem payers among its membership. The following year,
two tradesmen in the town of Dresden formed the Mutual Protection
Association for Trade and Small Business, aided by the local chamber
of commerce. Other localities soon copied the arrangement, and in 1867
the associations combined to form the Federation of Commercial Mutual
Protection Associations. By 1874, fifty-one of these associations were in
existence, with a total of 6874 members. Yet these large numbers are
deceptive: in reality, the associations did not work well, and the mutual
protection movement fared poorly.[33]

   The idea clearly had strong appeal, however, because in 1879 a group
of businesspeople in Mainz organised a Credit Reform Association that

---

[30] J. L. Thompson, 'Foreign Credit Practices: Adjusting Them to Present-Day Problems',
     Credit Monthly 26 (May 1924), 14, 47, 14.
[31] Berghoff, 'Civilizing Capitalism?', 26.
[32] Creditreform, *Annual Report*, 2003–04, 13, 15.
[33] *Ibid.*, 13.

covered a larger range of businesses and a wider geographic area than the earlier groups. Ironically, the original purpose of the association was to try to eliminate credit altogether by forcing buyers to pay in cash. Within a few months, the impossibility of the goal became clear, and the organisation modified its program, renaming itself 'Verein Creditreform zum Schutze gegen schädliches Creditgeben' or 'Creditreform Association to Protect against the Injurious Granting of Credit'. The new association encouraged businesses throughout Germany to form similar bodies, with the goal eventually of establishing correspondence among them. To explain Creditreform's aims, its agents called on local chambers of commerce, boards of trade and other business associations – groups that, along with banks, had traditionally acted as sources of credit information. The association pledged to help prevent the abuse of credit by lobbying for reforms.[34] Fifteen local associations were in existence by 1883, and they joined together into the Verband der Vereine Creditreform (VVC, or the Federation of Creditreform Associations). The federation held its first conference that year in Mannheim and a few years later began organising on a regional basis, moving its head office from Mainz to Leipzig. Small companies made up the bulk of the membership: about half had twenty-five or fewer employees, and a full one-quarter had five or fewer. On the eve of the Great War, there were twelve regional federations.[35] (Creditreform exists today in a number of European countries, including the newest members of the European Union. In 1995, nineteen associations formed Creditreform International, which continues to add new members.[36])

The individual associations within Creditreform remained self-governing, each with its own constitution and bylaws. They yielded their independence only in matters that affected the interests of the federation. The structure was hierarchical: each local association had subordinate offices or branches, which provided written and oral reports on businesses within their neighbourhoods. Above the locals were the District Unions, which united several locals with common interests – for example, those engaged primarily in manufacturing or mercantile activities. A newspaper, the *Union News*, kept members apprised of developments. From the

---

[34] Creditreform, *Annual Report*, 13–14; James G. Cannon, 'Plan and Scope of the Union of the Credit Reform Associations of Germany...read before the Philadelphia Credit Men's Association, March 22, 1898' (pamphlet), 4–6. Cannon reported that the group was formed in 1881, not 1879.

[35] Creditreform, *Annual Report*, 14–16.

[36] Creditreform International, http://www.creditreform.com, December 2009.

beginning, the federation was envisioned as international in scope. A 'Warning Bulletin' provided a list of fraudulent dealers throughout the world, and a 'search list' of debtors who had reneged on their obligations was issued as a supplement to the *Union News*. (The publication of such lists had recently been deemed legal by the Supreme Court in Germany.) As with all mutual protection societies, members were forbidden from sharing information with nonmembers. Bureaus that revealed information to a third party were fined heavily, and more serious transgressions were met with expulsion. Whether the ultimate penalty would be imposed was decided by the Executive Committee, and although expelled members could appeal its decisions, they could not take their grievances to the courts.[37]

By the mid-1890s, Creditreform reportedly had some 18,000 European correspondents, as well as a few in North America.[38] It claimed more than 50,000 members in 330 local associations, 326 branches, and 5 'Official Agencies'. In addition to Germany, these branches were located in Belgium, Bulgaria, Denmark, Great Britain, Italy, Holland, East Roumelia (now part of Bulgaria), Switzerland, Serbia, Turkey and Austria. (Great Britain, Holland, Switzerland and Austria were particularly well served.) The information provided appears to have consisted primarily of blacklists – businesses and individuals considered unfit for credit. Differences in legal and regulatory regimes among countries presented problems; for example, German courts had affirmed the right to publish blacklists, but other countries had not. Nor had the process of exerting pressure on debtors in the collection of bad debts been recognised in every country. A proposed solution was to decentralise into a federal structure, with each local office conducting business in conformity with the laws of its home country.[39]

The mobilisation of German business during the First World War seriously hampered the work of credit reporting organizations. The government was not overly concerned about the creditworthiness of businesses it dealt with; at any rate, hyperinflation made appraisals extremely difficult, and transactions increasingly were done in cash. The Treaty of Versailles in 1919 stripped Germany of territory, which reduced the number of associations. To better survive the postwar business climate, the country's largest business information providers – Creditreform, Schimmelpfeng,

---

[37] Cannon, 'Plan and Scope', 6–7, 11–13, 18, 20.

[38] Ibid., 15–16.

[39] Ibid., 21–22, 30–31; Creditreform *Annual Report*, 15.

Deutsche Auskunftei (previously R. G. Dun & Co.) and the Bürgel firms –
formed a cartel.[40] During the Weimar years, Creditreform resumed correspondence among its offices in Germany, the Netherlands, Austria and
Switzerland, and it established ties with Sweden and Czechoslovakia.
(Correspondence with American associations did not occur until after the
Second World War.) In 1927, Germany's leading business information
providers set up the Evidenzzentrale GmbH in Berlin as a clearinghouse.
Creditreform's reports became more detailed and included items such as
annual turnover, assets and number of employees.[41]

Conclusions and Directions for Further Research

To conclude: although the subject of information is well theorised in the
economic literature,[42] the actual practices of information-sharing organisations, particularly in the realm of credit, are not well studied relative
to their importance to the global economy.[43] This chapter has introduced
a historical dimension by tracing the evolution of institutional responses
to information asymmetry during the first era of globalisation. Much has
yet to be discovered about these organisations, especially the day-to-day
routines by which they created the networks that enabled global trade.
An additional complication exists in that credit reports, by their very
nature, are prescriptive; they do not tell us how merchants acted on the
information. For example, how willing were they to risk capital on individuals and businesses with imperfect credit ratings? Did their level of
willingness track the stages of the business cycle?

The following broad themes might also be kept in mind, for although it
is tempting to think of credit reporting as part of a general trend toward

---

[40] Creditreform, *Annual Report*, 15–17.
[41] Ibid., 18–19.
[42] Theoretical works on the economics of asymmetric information in credit markets include
George A. Akerloff, 'The Market for "Lemons,"' *Quarterly Journal of Economics* 84
(1970), 488–500; Dwight Jaffee and Thomas Russell, 'Imperfect Information, Uncertainty, and Credit Rationing', *Quarterly Journal of Economics* 90 (1976), 651–66;
Hayne E. Leland and David H. Pyle, 'Information Asymmetries, Financial Structure,
and Financial Intermediation', *Journal of Finance* 32 (1977), 371–87; Joseph Stiglitz
and Andrew Weiss, 'Credit Rationing in Markets with Imperfect Information', *American
Economic Review* 71 (1981), 393–410; and Tullio Jappelli and Marco Pagano, 'Information Sharing in Credit Markets', *Journal of Finance* 43 (December 1993), 1693–718.
[43] For recent surveys of the credit reporting industry worldwide, see Margaret J. Miller
(ed.), *Credit Reporting Systems and the International Economy* (Cambridge, MA, 2003),
which includes a helpful literature review; and Nicola Jentzsch, *Financial Privacy: An
International Comparison of Credit Reporting Systems* (Berlin, 2006).

more efficient markets, scholars also need to be sensitive to the power dynamics that ultimately helped to embed this institution into the global economic structure.

Convergence

Comparing our three cases suggests that the drive to create information-sharing institutions was affected by the structure of each country's international trade. In Britain and Germany, many large manufacturers did not sell directly to foreign customers, but instead went through export merchants and commission agents, who took on the task of assessing foreign customers and extending credit. Not surprisingly, smaller firms made up the bulk of mutual protection societies in these countries. Less able to access the services of the established export merchants, these smaller firms would have found membership in the societies beneficial. In the United States, large American manufacturers, especially those like Singer that dealt in relatively complex goods, came to prefer selling directly to foreign buyers in order to better control their distribution structures. The strategy employed by such firms may have inclined them to cooperate with other U.S. exporters to share information on their foreign customers.[44]

Whatever the impetus behind their founding, many similarities in form and practice developed among credit reporting organisations in these three countries. In 1957, American economist Hedwig Reinhardt remarked upon 'the tendency toward uniformity...in gathering credit information, evaluating credit risks, arriving at credit decisions, and other procedures' within credit departments and organizations in the United States.[45] Reinhardt did not expound on the phenomenon, but in the 1980s sociologists Paul DiMaggio and Walter Powell characterised this general tendency toward homogeneity among organizations as 'institutional isomorphism' – a process, they argued, that came about not because the favoured model is necessarily the most efficient, but because those who support it are able to win the confidence of outside stakeholders.[46] (In

---

[44] Wolfe, *Theory and Practice of International Commerce*, 350–51.

[45] Hedwig Reinhardt, 'Economics of Mercantile Credit: A Study in Methodology', *Review of Economics and Statistics* 39 (November 1957), 463–67, 463. Reinhardt cautioned that one should not interpret the growing homogeneity in practice to mean that creditors conformed to rigid rules. Instead, flexibility continued to be a hallmark of mercantile credit.

[46] Paul J. DiMaggio and Walter W. Powell, 'The Iron Cage Revisited: Institutional Isomorphism and Collective Rationality in Organizational Fields', *American Sociological*

the case of credit reporting, stakeholders would include trade creditors, legislators, investors and academics.) Their insights became one of the pillars of the 'new institutionalism', an approach that restored the study of power to institutional evolution.[47] This focus on power and on the tendency of organisations to copy one another during periods of uncertainty helped to displace the ahistorical and transcendent 'laws' of institutional evolution, in particular those founded on a narrow conception of adaptation and efficiency. Neo-institutionalism states that homogeneity among organizations occurs after the institutional fields become mature and well defined. Arguably, the field of credit reporting reached this stage by about the 1880s, when a general understanding prevailed among trade creditors in the UK, the United States and Germany that obtaining key pieces of information on borrowers was a beneficial practice.

Common experiences across the Atlantic world may explain the development of similar institutions, but they do not account for the timing of the different forms. Mutual protection societies and credit reporting firms appeared at varying times in the three countries (see Table 2). In the UK, mutual protection societies significantly predated the credit reporting firms, and a national network was in place by 1865. The United States, in contrast, developed credit reporting firms first, in the late 1830s, and did not establish a national network of mutual protection associations until 1896. (In the case of consumer, as opposed to trade, credit bureaus' national coverage was achieved even later, in 1960.[48]) In Germany, credit reporting firms and mutual protection associations took root simultaneously in the 1860s, and a national network of associations was achieved by the early 1880s.

Uncovering the tendency toward homogeneity (or conformity) among credit reporting institutions that span national borders and cultures

Review 48 (1983), 147–60; and 'Introduction' in Walter W. Powell and Paul J. DiMaggio (eds.), *The New Institutionalism in Organizational Analysis* (Chicago, 1991), 1–38. For an analysis of how DiMaggio and Powell's theories have been interpreted, see Mark S. Mizruchi and Lisa C. Fein, 'The Social Construction of Organizational Knowledge: A Study of the Uses of Coercive, Mimetic, and Normative Isomorphism', *Administrative Science Quarterly* 44 (Dec., 1999), 653–83.

[47] DiMaggio and Powell categorised power as 'coercive' or 'normative'. Mizruchi and Fein point out that, compared to Europeans, American organisational scholars have tended to slight the issue of power. In general, neo-institutionalism emphasises inertia and constraint rather than constant innovation and experimentation.

[48] Robert M. Hunt, 'The Development and Regulation of Consumer Credit Reporting in America', Working Paper no. 01–21, Federal Reserve Bank of Philadelphia, November 2002, 9.

TABLE 2. *Credit Reporting Institutions in the United Kingdom, United States and Germany*

Country	Institutional Form	Date of First Appearance	Date National Coverage Achieved
United Kingdom	Mutual protection societies	1776	1865
	Credit reporting firms	1850s	?
United States	Credit reporting firms	1830s	c.1870
	Mutual protection societies	Late 19th century	1919
	Consumer credit bureaus	1869	1960
Germany	Mutual protection societies	1860s	1880s
	Credit reporting firms	1860s	?

requires investigating not only the external pressures that gave rise to adaptations but also the extent to which exporters, credit practitioners and trade officials were aware of developments in other countries. Did such awareness influence their own conceptions of what it meant to be 'creditworthy' in an integrating world economy? For example, the wording of subscription terms of the British credit reporting firm Estell & Co. and the American firm R.G. Dun & Co. came to resemble one another.[49] Further, nearly all credit reporting organizations faced legal challenges that questioned the accuracy of their reports.[50] The lawsuits prompted them to implement similar safeguards, including explicit language that placed responsibility for the credit decision on the subscriber.

Documented instances of organizations actively learning from their counterparts in other countries are few, but they are suggestive. In the late 1890s, during an annual convention of the National Association of Credit Men in the United States, speakers drew attention to Germany's Creditreform association. Until then, very few American credit men appear to have been aware of the organization, even though it had existed for nearly two decades and reportedly had 650 local associations and branches scattered across Europe. The president of the NACM immediately wrote to the German organization and, 'after much difficulty', procured copies of its constitution and bylaws. The NACM paid for a translation and

---

[49] See *The Birmingham Commercial List, 1874–1875*, Estell & Co. (London, 1874), iii; and R. G. Dun & Co.'s reference volumes of the 1860s.

[50] Joseph W. Errant, *The Law Relating to Mercantile Agencies, being the Johnson Prize Essay of the Union College of Law for the Year 1886* (Philadelphia, 1889).

appointed James G. Cannon, vice president of the Fourth National Bank of New York, to prepare a report. In 1898, Cannon's 35-page 'Plan and Scope of the Union of the Credit Reform Associations of Germany' was printed for general distribution among NACM members. Interest in British and German foreign trade institutions intensified during and immediately after the First World War, as American businesses looked overseas for new markets. A number of American writers and academics studied the practices of the two countries in the hope of improving the infrastructure of American foreign trade. Their findings appeared in manuals and textbooks and in journals like the NACM's *Credit Monthly*.[51]

Another clear instance of cross-national learning occurred when Cuthbert Greig, secretary of the London Association for the Protection of Trade and the author of two textbooks on credit granting, travelled to the United States in the late 1920s to observe the workings of the National Association of Credit Men. Inspired by what he saw, Greig wrote that the UK ought to have a similar national information clearinghouse that would include all lines of business, as well as both manufacturers and distributors. At present, he wrote, the interchange of ledger information among UK manufacturers tended to be confined to firms in the same lines. Unless all trade creditors shared information with one another, he argued, swindlers in the UK could continue to defraud firms by switching from one line of business to another, secure in the knowledge that information did not cross trade and sector boundaries.[52] The Great War may have changed the old settled ways, Greig wrote, but the existing structures and methods remained largely intact. Signs of change were in the air, but much more needed to be accomplished before the UK caught up to America. He urged a transatlantic transfer of knowledge, in which '[t]he old country in the twentieth century goes to the new country to consider new applications of old principles'.[53]

The convergence of these institutional forms suggests that the norms upon which they were based may also have aligned. In the United States, the spread of credit reporters – most of whom worked for firms based

---

[51] See, for example, George W. Edwards, *International Trade Finance* (New York, 1924); George C. Vedder, *American Methods in Foreign Trade: A Guide to Export Selling Policy* (New York, 1919); Wolfe, *Theory and Practice of International Commerce.*

[52] Cuthbert Greig, 'All in the Same Boat: Here and Abroad Credit Problems are Similar', *Credit Monthly* 30 (November 1928), 5–6. Mutual protection societies in the UK appear increasingly to have specialized in consumer rather than trade or manufacturing credit.

[53] Cuthbert Greig, 'John Bull's Credit System', *Credit and Financial Management* 36 (November 1934), 18–19, 42, 19.

in New York City – to small towns and large cities across the continent facilitated the spread of ideas about which precise characteristics rendered a trader creditworthy.[54] Further study of the prevailing norms in the UK and Germany, and the means by which they spread, is needed to understand the embeddedness of credit reporting within those countries' customs and social structures.[55]

The Quest for Legitimacy

The evolution of credit reporting institutions was driven also by a quest for acceptance and legitimacy. As numerous lawsuits across countries attest, these organizations' appraisals of borrowers could sometimes be wildly inaccurate; both credit reporting firms and mutual protection societies had to contend with lawsuits that challenged the truth of their reports. For credit reporting firms, additional legal challenges revolved around the question of 'privilege'; that is, whether information bought and sold by a third party should be given the same legal status as information obtained strictly for creditors' own use. American courts decided for and against the credit reporting firms beginning in the 1840s, clearly struggling with the idea that the details of commercial transactions could be the concern of anyone other than the principals involved. By the 1880s, however, credit reporting firms had become deeply entrenched in American commerce, and the challenges to their right to exist diminished considerably.[56] Scholars need to ask how these organizations' ability to judge the creditworthiness of millions of individuals and firms became accepted by borrowers, creditors, government bodies, courts and academics in spite of continuing problems with their accuracy.[57]

Neo-institutionalism would posit that legitimacy grows out of mimicking high-status organisations. Yet the credit reporting institutions'

---

[54] Olegario, *A Culture of Credit*; W. C. Schluter, 'Factors Determining Terms of Sale', *University Journal of Business*, 1 (Feb. 1923), 138–49, 140. Nicola Jentzsch points out that path dependence and lock-in also play a role. Once an organization adopts particular technology and reporting standards, switching becomes costly. Jentzsch, *Financial Privacy*, 17–18.

[55] For the classic statement of how economic relationships are embedded in social networks, see Mark Granovetter, 'Economic Action and Social Structure: The Problem of Embeddedness', *American Journal of Sociology* 91 (November 1985), 481–510.

[56] Ironically, in the United States, credit reporting agencies achieved legal protection sooner than did trade associations that exchanged credit information. David L. Podell and Benjamin S. Kirsh, 'Credit Bureau Functions of Trade Associations: The Legal Aspects', *St. Johns Law Review* 1 (May 1927), 101–28.

[57] John Case, *From the Ground Up: The Resurgence of American Entrepreneurship* (New York: 1992), 25–6.

legitimacy was also driven by the desire of certain groups to solidify their social and professional status by enforcing normative practices. For many American credit men, the entire world became a potential field for their professional ambitions. From their perspective, unenlightened foreign merchants could be educated about the value of transparency, much like American businesspeople had been made to see the light in preceding decades.

In this regard the historical record can sometimes be contradictory. For example, a report in 1898 by the National Association of Credit Men states that although credit reporting firms had become de rigueur in England and the United States, 'in Germany, owing to the strictness of mercantile law and the inability of private concerns to secure access to the proper records, these [firms], if established, could not render effective service'.[58] Mutual protection societies like Creditreform were founded to fill the gap. A recent history produced by Creditreform itself, however, claims that credit reporting firms 'proved to be the more successful model, and from the 1870s on, the mutual protection associations were increasingly ousted by large business information agencies'. Only in 1894 did Creditreform win legitimacy in the eyes of the public, when it was awarded a silver medal at the Antwerp World Fair. A brochure published by the association that year claimed that until very recently, its business model had been misunderstood and distrusted even by businesspeople.[59] The contradictory evidence is a reminder that it can be difficult to establish precisely when an institutional form achieves acceptance from stakeholders.

The quest for legitimacy has been most fully documented for the United States, where credit men were motivated to a large degree by the desire to achieve professional status.[60] Ledger experience, with its aura of strict objectivity, fulfilled a growing wish to replace rules of thumb with more precise data as the basis for credit decisions. These impulses were part of a more general trend that swept the country in the last decades of the nineteenth century, when bankers, accountants and others sought to enhance their social prestige through the establishment of professional associations. Progressive ideals characterised these new bodies, as when the NACM presented itself as an organisation on the cutting edge of change. Members praised the cooperation that made their new association

[58] Cannon, 'Plan and Scope', 4.
[59] Creditreform, *Annual Report*, 13, 15.
[60] Olegario, *A Culture of Credit*, chapter 6.

possible and self-consciously contrasted it with the cutthroat competition among businesses that had characterised the past.[61]

The Foreign Credit Interchange Bureau was an important component of this mission and became something of an evangelical cause for some American credit men, who openly used terms such as 'missionary' to describe the spirit behind their crusade: 'Our foreign credit department is in effect a commercial missionary carrying to many lands the ideals, aims and aspirations of the National Association of Credit Men', declared credit man P. M. Haight of the International General Electric Company. He envisioned 'that day in the future when business in all the civilized countries of the world will be working for the same ideals, the same code of ethics' as the NACM.[62] Willingness to share information on one's business standing (what we today call 'transparency') was a reliable indication of a country's state of development: according to the writer of a 1919 textbook on foreign trade, '[n]o one in India or in Turkey or in many other countries can tell accurately what his neighbor is worth and the neighbor won't tell'. Foreigners were '[u]neducated to the fact that it is to [their] benefit to furnish an accurate statement'.[63] The writer's crusading attitude mirrored the one held by U.S. foreign policy makers, who adopted what diplomatic historian Emily Rosenberg terms a philosophy of 'liberal-developmentalism'. According to this philosophy, America's robust economic development was based on the tenets of nineteenth-century liberalism and could be applied universally – with the United States, of course, as the benign driving force. Free trade was not at the forefront of this ideology, because America itself was strongly protectionist. Instead, what Rosenberg describes as 'support for free flow of information and [American] culture' constituted one of its most important tenets.[64]

American credit men speaking to audiences abroad repeatedly stressed the desirability of open information sharing, and they almost always commented on the 'Americanness' of the practice. In 1925, Dr. John Whyte,

---

[61] On the professionalization movement generally, see Nathan O. Hatch (ed.), *The Professions in American History* (Notre Dame, IN, 1988).

[62] Proceedings of the Thirty-Second Annual Convention of the National Association of Credit Men, Louisville, Kentucky, June 6–10, 1927, 264, scrapbook ledger, NACM Archives, Columbia, Maryland.

[63] Wolfe, *Theory and Practice of International Commerce*, 361–63.

[64] Emily S. Rosenberg, *Spreading the American Dream: American Economic and Cultural Expansion, 1890–1945* (New York. 1982), 7.

head of the Education and Research Department of the National Association of Credit Men, and Assistant Professor of German in the College of the City of New York, gave a lecture at Leipzig Commercial University in which he described the credit interchange system as peculiarly American.[65] That same year, in a meeting of the International Chamber of Commerce in Brussels, another American credit man stated that 'the doctrine of cooperation' embodied by the interchange system was 'revolutionary in character' and did not exist anywhere but in the United States. 'Surprise has often been expressed by foreign firms', maintained yet another American exporter, 'at the generosity of the American business man in giving of his hard won experience [that is, information on his firm's customers] to other firms, even to competitors'.[66]

The credit men were correct in emphasizing the unique features of their Foreign Credit Interchange Bureau: the exchange of specific ledger information (both positive and negative) and the greater reliance on financial statements. In 1927, Bertram J. Perkins, European director of Fairchild Publications, confirmed that credit information in Europe tended to consist of 'glittering generalities.... What [a man] is rather than what he has'. In the United States, asking potential buyers for their financial statements had become more accepted (although by no means wholly so), but in the UK, to ask for a statement was still considered insulting because it inferred that an individual's word was not considered trustworthy.[67]

Yet from a comparative perspective we see that the Americans exaggerated the extent to which their association was 'revolutionary in character'. Creditors' mutual protection societies were neither new nor peculiarly American; they had existed for nearly 150 years in the UK and for many decades in Germany. American practitioners were aware of the German credit reform societies; in 1898, the NACM had issued a substantial report on the German model based on a translation of its constitution and bylaws. Even so, almost no American credit men seemed inclined to

---

[65] 'Germans Interested in Credit Interchange', *Credit Monthly* 27 (October 1925), 30. See also Wolfe, *Theory and Practice of International Commerce*, 356.

[66] Ernst B. Filsinger, 'No Counterpart in Europe: National Association of Credit Men Purely Indigenous', *Credit Monthly* 27 (July 1925), 23, 41, 23; Lewis S. Thomas, 'Credit Granting Abroad: A Delicate and Essential Feature of Export Trade', *Credit Monthly* 28 (March 1926), 10, 31–32, 36, 32.

[67] Bertram J. Perkins, 'What He Is, Not What He Has: Basis of Credit Reference in France and England', *Credit Monthly* 29 (November 1927), 18, 35.

acknowledge any foreign precedents to their own 'modern' endeavours –
an indication that the quest for legitimacy can sometimes lead historical
actors to overstate the uniqueness of their own institutions.

Social and Political Issues: Privacy

Perhaps no social and political issue connected to credit reporting has
attracted as much interest in recent years as the right to privacy. Because
information on small business owners is often hard to come by, American
creditors have relied more heavily on these owners' individual credit
reports, blurring the line between 'legitimate' business use and intrusion
into the private concerns of individuals. The creditors' tactic is perhaps
understandable. As Nicola Jentzsch reports,

[t]ests of small business scoring models in the U.S. found that one of the most
important indicators of loan performance were the characteristics of the business
owner rather than the ones of the business itself. . . . Small business lending is in
general more related to consumer lending than to commercial lending and the
main similarity is that the business owner's profile is closely linked to creditworthiness of the company.[68]

Jentzsch's global survey is the most complete one on the subject; it documents how regulations governing the ownership of personal data vary
among countries. In the United States, numerous laws protect the privacy
of individuals from government intrusion, yet credit reporting firms and
bureaus have managed to retain legal ownership of the data they collect.
Compared to Europeans, American credit reporting organizations have
wide discretion on how such data can be used. The leeway granted to
these associations and firms has led to the problem of 'purpose creep', or
the tendency to use information for objectives other than the one that was
originally intended. Legislation such as the Consumer Reporting Employment Clarification Act of 1998 states that consumer credit reports cannot
be used by employers to assess potential candidates.[69] Yet popular advice
books and television programmes continue to warn that employers and
landlords rely on credit reports to weed out undesirable prospects.[70] Precisely how these regulations will evolve as globalisation advances remains
to be seen. Will foreign companies be allowed unfettered access to the
credit information of individual consumers? Perhaps so, but if the past is

---

[68] Jentzsch, *Financial Privacy*, 177.
[69] *Ibid.*, 27, 39, 154–55.
[70] See, for example, the works of Suze Orman, a popular personal financial adviser, author
and television personality in the United States.

any indication, their right to this information will be fiercely contested. Unlike in the first era of globalisation, state power may well be invoked to protect individuals from the seemingly insatiable desire of business corporations around the world to obtain data that many ordinary people feel are private.

PART II

COLONIAL MARKETS AND NON-WESTERN ACTORS

5

The London Stock Exchange and the Colonial Market

The City, Internationalisation, and Power

Bernard Attard

> Victoria had a little loan,
> She fixed it up at par;
> And everywhere that loaney went
> The people called out 'b-a-a'.
> The brokers shouted loud and long
> 'Your loaney is a fiz;
> It leaves so little for us brokes (sic)
> We can't do any biz'.[1]

The rise of the City of London as a centre for global commerce and finance is one of the most striking examples of the internationalisation of markets before 1914.[2] Yet even within the City itself, the transformation of the securities market was a remarkable case. By the mid-nineteenth century the London Stock Exchange was already a well-established organisation, but it served primarily domestic needs. From the 1850s an influx of new foreign and colonial issues dramatically altered its orientation. Business increased enormously, but so too did risks. The Exchange's governing body quickly tightened the quotation rules for government loans and prescribed how they could be offered to investors; at the same time new

---

[1] *Melbourne Punch*, 18 January 1883, 29.

[2] For London in its international context, see Youssef Cassis, *Capitals of Capital: The Rise and Fall of International Financial Centres, 1780–2009* (Cambridge, 2010).

The research for this chapter was funded by ESRC Grant Number R000223775. I thank the Australian & New Zealand Banking Group Limited and Westpac Banking Corporation for access to, and permission to quote from, their archives. I am also grateful to the following for their advice and assistance: Philip Cottrell, Deborah Lasky-Davison, Julie Attard, Kerrianne George, Alan Hall, Peggy Kennedy, Peter Marinick and the editors of this volume. Any errors are my own.

submarkets appeared promoting further specialisation amongst brokers and dealers. Thus the Exchange responded to rapid changes in the securities market by both formal and informal means in order to exercise greater control over those wanting to employ British capital overseas.

Much is already known about the Stock Exchange's internationalisation before 1914. Research has focused on the organisation's comparative development, the impact of the communications revolution and the integration of national and overseas markets.[3] Considerably less is understood about how the sudden appearance and growing volume of a wide variety of new foreign and colonial securities affected the Exchange's regulatory and trading arrangements or the ways in which control over those arrangements conferred power in the new global economy. The significance of these developments becomes clear when they are placed in the context of a broader pattern of institutional and organisational innovation taking place in London during the mid-Victorian decades. These changes have been likened in importance to the 'Big Bang' of the 1980s, with attention focusing on the reforms of British company law and the associated rise of joint-stock organisation in banking and other financial services.[4] The contemporary developments in the securities market are noteworthy because they were part of this larger process of adjustment in London's service industries that simultaneously accommodated and provided greater scope for the enormous growth of international business after 1850.

This chapter explores these themes through the experience of one group of overseas borrowers – Britain's self-governing colonies of settlement (particularly the Australasian colonies) – which together constituted the 'colonial market' in London.[5] No special claims are made for their significance other than that they contributed to, and were affected by, the same processes of institutional and organisational change affecting all overseas borrowers from the mid-1850s; indeed, in some instances they were the catalysts for these changes. Unlike foreign governments, however, many stayed active in London long after other borrowers had started to look for capital elsewhere. The colonial market, therefore, offers a case study of the interaction between power and institutions

---

[3] See especially R. C. Michie, *The London and New York Stock Exchanges, 1850–1914* (London, 1987); idem, *The London Stock Exchange: A History* (Oxford, 1999).

[4] Philip Cottrell, 'London's First 'Big Bang'? Institutional Change in the City, 1855–83', in *The World of Private Banking*, eds. Youseff Cassis and Philip Cottrell (Farnham, 2009), 61–98.

[5] The Australasian group of colonies comprised New South Wales, Victoria, Queensland, South Australia, Western Australia, Tasmania and New Zealand.

spanning the entire long period from London's rise as a global securities market to its relative decline after 1914. Furthermore, the kinds of power the colonists encountered in the City operated independently of formal imperial authority. The case study thus provides insight into institutional mechanisms and modes of control that affected overseas borrowers more generally, most obviously the other developing societies of the non-European world.

The chapter is in four parts. The first briefly reviews the Stock Exchange's organisational and institutional development to 1914, focusing especially on the origins and nature of its internationalisation. It also considers the growing significance of colonial borrowers after 1850 and the forms of power to which they were subject. The next two sections distinguish between the Exchange's functions as a regulatory body – and hence as the source of formal institutions – and as a market with its customary usages and informal modes of organisation.[6] The first ('Institutions') assesses the impact of internationalisation on quotation rules from as early as the 1820s, but particularly in mid-century. The second ('Market') examines the process of mutual adaptation through which borrowers conformed to the requirements of the Exchange's membership and traders acquired specialist functions within the market for new debt. The final section shows how the oligopolistic underwriting arrangements that emerged at the turn of the century allowed Stock Exchange firms to continue to control the colonial market. Throughout, the relationship between institutions and power is a central theme.

The Stock Exchange, Internationalisation and Power

The London securities market originated in the city's coffee houses in the late seventeenth century and soon spread beyond, most notably to the Royal Exchange and the transfer offices of the Bank of England. Until the end of the Napoleonic wars, trade was almost exclusively in British government securities and related guaranteed obligations (the national debt or 'public funds').[7] For most of the period the market had been loosely organised and dispersed, and lacked a properly

---

[6] This follows North's distinction between 'institutions' and 'organisations' and also roughly corresponds to Michie's distinction between institution and market; D. C. North, *Institutions, Institutional Change and Economic Performance* (Cambridge, 1990), 3–5; Michie, *London Stock Exchange*, 1.

[7] The following three paragraphs are based on E. Victor Morgan and W. A. Thomas, *The Stock Exchange: Its History and Functions* (2nd edn. London, 1969) and Michie, *London Stock Exchange*.

constituted membership. Nevertheless, its characteristic modes of dealing, settling bargains and disseminating price information by means of an
'official list' were already well established. The 'separation of capacity'
between brokers and dealers was also recognised, although not rigidly
enforced: brokers acted as agents, executing buy and sell orders on behalf
of clients, whereas dealers, or 'jobbers', bought and sold on their own
account, thus providing a market for the brokers.

By the turn of the eighteenth century, both groups wanted to regulate trade more effectively by restricting access to the market's physical
space and membership. In 1801, they formally established the London
Stock Exchange with its membership comprising elected subscribers who
alone were permitted onto the trading floor. The new exchange 'not only
provided a market for securities but also incorporated regulations on how
business should be conducted'.[8] The proprietors were represented by a
Committee of Trustees and Managers, which had responsibility for the
Stock Exchange building – first opened in 1802 and rebuilt on the same
site several times – and fixed subscription fees. A Committee for General
Purposes (hereafter the Committee), chosen by the subscribers, regulated
the market itself. The Committee drew up and applied the organisation's
rules (publishing the first rule book in 1812), elected new members and
adjudicated disputes. The Exchange thus had a dual character. First it
was the regulatory organisation that controlled the formal institutional
framework for trading securities in London; at the same time, it was the
body of traders themselves – brokers and dealers – who comprised its
membership and whose interests the regulatory framework principally
served.[9]

Although after 1815, the national debt still dominated business, the
appearance of a handful of new borrowers enhanced the Exchange's
importance in the wider capital market. During the following decade, a
short-lived boom in foreign loans led to the opening of a Foreign Funds
market in a room adjacent to the main English market. This space also
soon accommodated dealings in the shares of several companies that
had been floated to exploit the new interest in overseas investments.
The boom soon collapsed in what would become a familiar combination
of sovereign defaults and corporate failures. Nevertheless 'the episode
of the Foreign Funds market... had been a watershed for the London

---

[8] Michie, *London Stock Exchange*, 35.
[9] This is an important theme in David Kynaston, 'The London Stock Exchange, 1870–1914:
An Institutional History' (PhD thesis, University of London, 1983).

Stock Exchange'.[10] In 1835, the foreign market disappeared as a separate organisation, but by then the capital demands of the new railway industry were stimulating a far greater boom. Indeed, the 'railway mania' of the 1830s and 1840s was the first major step in the diversification of the market away from its dependence on the national debt and transformed the Exchange into 'the biggest and most important of its kind in the world'.[11]

Yet the market was still only on the brink of internationalisation. After 1850, the remarkable surge of British capital exports and simultaneous expansion of British commercial enterprise turned the City into 'the undisputed financial centre of the world'.[12] A substantial share of securities trading was still accounted for by the national debt and domestic utilities, but issues by overseas governments and companies operating abroad – especially railway obligations – were also increasingly prominent. Besides the cosmopolitan nature of the financial instruments now circulating in London, internationalisation had many other dimensions. The market's size and liquidity attracted a growing volume of foreign orders and, with the contemporary communications revolution, created opportunities for specialist brokers to conduct a substantial arbitrage business with New York and the Continent. Links to the money and foreign exchange markets were consolidated by the dependence of the Exchange's members on short-term credits and the facilities they provided for buying and selling international securities such as French *rentes* and American railway stocks. In turn, all this activity was contingent on the conjunction of several favourable circumstances: the London Exchange's openness to new members from a variety of social and national backgrounds (between 1850 and 1905, membership rose from 864 to 5,567);[13] its flexibility in setting commissions; its willingness to list new issues (the number quoted increased from less than 500 in 1850 to more than 5,000 by 1913);[14] its responsiveness to new technology and the market's physical need to grow; and – in contrast with European bourses – the almost entire absence of government regulation. These factors were all the prerequisites for a

[10] Michie, *London Stock Exchange*, 60.
[11] Ibid., 70.
[12] Morgan and Thomas, *Stock Exchange*, 88; also P. L. Cottrell, *British Overseas Investment in the Nineteenth Century* (Basingstoke, 1975), and for service enterprise, P. J. Cain and A. G. Hopkins, *British Imperialism, 1688–2000* (2nd edn. Longman, 2001), chapters 3 and 5.
[13] Morgan and Thomas, *Stock Exchange*, 140.
[14] Michie, *London Stock Exchange*, 95.

spectacular expansion that inspired the New York agent of one English broking firm to declare in 1911, 'The London Stock Exchange is the only really international market of the world. Its interests branch over all parts of our globe'.[15]

Unheralded and not particularly fashionable, the British colonies came to London as borrowers at the beginning of the mid-Victorian boom and made their own contributions to many of the developments just described. With India occupying a separate category of its own, the rest of the Empire could be divided into two groups: the Crown colonies governed directly by Britain, and the self-governing migrant communities in North America, Australasia and southern Africa. In important respects, the British regions of recent settlement were no different from the new European societies of the Americas.[16] After their early colonisation, globalisation provided them with opportunities for long-term growth as suppliers of raw materials, minerals and food. However, the creation of export capacity required enormous investments in railways and other forms of social overhead capital. Much of this infrastructure was financed in London, with governments and other public bodies often taking the lead.[17] Although, on the eve of the First World War, the nominal value of all empire government securities quoted in London was just a quarter that of foreign government stocks, from the mid-1870s capital subscribed for the former generally far exceeded the amounts raised by foreigners (see Table 3 and Figure 2).[18] Over the entire period of 1865–1914, governments in British settler colonies and India accounted for just over half of investment in overseas government bonds and 15 per cent of all British capital raised by public issues in London. The Australasian colonies claimed two-fifths of this investment in empire. It was concentrated in the period 1874–92 and in the years immediately preceding the First World War.[19]

---

[15] Quoted in ibid., 70; Michie, *London and New York Stock Exchanges*, 90.

[16] For an excellent comparative study, see Donald Denoon, *Settler Capitalism: The Dynamics of Dependent Development in the Southern Hemisphere* (Oxford, 1983).

[17] For the Australian colonies, see A. R. Hall, *The London Capital Market and Australia 1870–1914* (Canberra, 1962); N. G. Butlin, *Investment in Australian Economic Development 1861–1900* (Cambridge, 1964); and L. E. Davis and R. E. Gallman, *Evolving Financial Markets and International Capital Flows: Britain, the Americas, and Australia, 1865–1914* (Cambridge, 2001), chapter 5.

[18] Michie, *London Stock Exchange*, tables 3.2 and 3.3, 88–89.

[19] All statistics calculated from I. Stone, *The Global Export of Capital from Great Britain, 1865–1914* (Basingstoke, 1999) and exclude borrowings by provincial and municipal bodies. 'Settler colonies' refer to Canada, Australia, South Africa and New Zealand.

TABLE 3. *Capital Subscribed to Issues by Overseas Governments in London, Public Sale (£1000)*

	1865–9	1870–4	1875–9	1880–4	1885–9	1890–4	1895–9	1900–4	1905–9	1910–14	Total
National	35,811	146,101	30,133	36,342	51,579	16,245	59,328	35,767	80,332	76,677	568,315
Colonial and provincial governments											
Canada	2,478	7,027	9,584	3,265	9,545	7,066	2,516	1,036	16,417	27,888	86,822
Australia	7,154	5,351	19,256	36,012	44,983	28,539	13,396	13,439	13,705	33,082	214,917
India	0	4,825	12,098	8,126	17,848	15,650	32,087	9,956	24,176	17,585	142,351
South Africa	598	113	8,563	12,946	2,620	6,358	5,101	51,940	14,527	10,840	113,606
New Zealand	2,461	4,627	9,010	5,260	7,112	138	2,310	2,767	750	12,508	46,943
Total of five colonial governments	12,691	21,943	58,511	65,609	82,108	57,751	55,410	79,138	69,575	101,903	604,639

Note: Municipal bodies excluded.

Source: I. Stone, *The Global Export of Capital from Great Britain, 1865–1914* (Basingstoke, 1999).

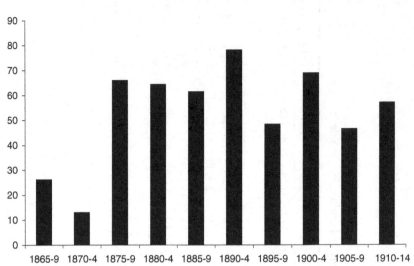

FIGURE 2. Capital subscribed to issues by major colonial governments as a proportion of total subscriptions to overseas government issues, 1865–1914 (per cent).

Australasian and other colonial governments thus participated in the London securities market as suppliers of debentures, bonds and inscribed stock. The Stock Exchange performed its dual function as a regulator and the body of intermediaries linking the colonists' supply of securities to the investors, who ultimately constituted demand. How did power enter these relationships? Most obviously, the colonists were subject to the Committee's power over whether their securities would be marketable, as well as to whatever power accrued to the Exchange's members from their willingness to trade. Both forms of power pertained to the normal requirements of any exchange: the institutional arrangements necessary for a market to function in an orderly manner and the prerogatives of traders both to deal voluntarily and to manage their risks. However, this power also created opportunities to influence, coerce or constrain significantly the choices of those wishing to borrow. Its potential uses, therefore, raise more fundamental questions about hierarchy and control in the global economy, to which we briefly turn.

The social theorist, journalist and economist, J. A. Hobson, famously described finance as 'the governor of the imperial engine, directing the energy and determining its work'.[20] In fact, Hobson distinguished

---

[20] J.A. Hobson, *Imperialism: A Study* (3rd edn. London, 1938 / 1988), 59.

between the 'new imperialism' in Africa and other tropical regions after 1870 – to which he was referring – and 'the colonization of sparsely peopled lands in temperate zones, where white colonists carry with them the modes of government, the industrial and other arts of the civilization of the mother country'.[21] Indeed, British colonists in North America and Australasia were amongst the main beneficiaries of a settler imperialism that also gave them considerable advantages in the City of London because of the relative ease with which information, money and people flowed within the Anglo world; the possibility of appeals by investors to metropolitan legal institutions; and the imperial government's willingness to grant occasional guarantees and enact legislation in the form of the colonial stock acts that made it safer to hold empire stocks.[22] Even had none of these advantages existed, the imperial government's strict adherence to laissez-faire policies precluded any direct attempts to interfere with the settlers' access to money.

Despite all this, ever since Gallagher and Robinson advanced their widely influential hypothesis about the 'imperialism of free trade', the self-governing colonies – no less than heavily indebted Latin American republics – could be viewed as being subject to an 'informal' British power that was no less effective because it fell short of direct rule.[23] Informal imperialism might take many forms, but its dynamics as far as the colonists were concerned were essentially the same: dependence on British investors and financial intermediaries narrowed their effective choices and compelled, or predisposed, them to conform to metropolitan expectations. In the argument's most recent formulation, Cain and Hopkins have characterised the British service sector, with its orientation towards the international economy, as a 'gentlemanly capitalism'; it exploited its connections with government and its capacity to determine the norms of economic behaviour (i.e. its structural power over 'the rules of the

---

[21] Ibid., 27.
[22] John Darwin, *After Tamerlane: The Global History of Empire* (London, 2007), 305; James Belich, *Replenishing the Earth: The Settler Revolution and the Rise of the Anglo-World, 1783–1939* (Oxford, 2009), 126, 132–3; David Jessop, 'The Colonial Stock Act of 1900: A Symptom of the New Imperialism?' *Journal of Imperial and Commonwealth History* 4 (1976), 154–63; and Gary B. Magee and Andrew S. Thompson, *Empire and Globalisation: Networks of People, Goods and Capital in the British World, c.1850–1914* (Cambridge, 2010).
[23] This is a large literature. For the classic statements see John Gallagher and Ronald Robinson, 'The Imperialism of Free Trade, 1815–1914', *Economic History Review* 6 (1953), 1–15; Ronald Robinson and John Gallagher with Alice Denny, *Africa and the Victorians: The Official Mind of Imperialism*, 2nd edn. (Basingstoke, 1981), ix–xxiii.

game') to create and maintain the most favourable conditions for British commerce and investment abroad.[24] In other words, in temperate regions no less than tropical ones, metropolitan finance could still be viewed as 'the governor of the imperial engine', with the only difference that it performed this function long after formal imperial rule had lapsed.

Whether or not one chooses to define imperialism as the exercise of power in these ways, the concept of informal imperialism offers a starting point for considering the wider significance of the powers of bodies like the Stock Exchange, particularly when their use was motivated by a desire to coerce or to ensure that borrowers observed metropolitan standards of creditworthiness. The extent to which the elaboration of the Exchange's rules up to the 1870s made both possible is the subject of the following section.

Institutions

As far as those wishing to raise capital in London were concerned, the Stock Exchange's most important institutional power was its determination whether or not to grant a special settlement to a new stock and include it in the Official List of securities and their prices.[25] The steady increase in the number of new issues, desirability of a quotation and recognition of the Committee's authority meant that, as its chairman observed in 1875, 'We have gradually grown up from a private body, that is to say a private tribunal for the regulation merely of our internal business, into a sort of public and *quasi* judicial position'.[26] Although exclusion from the Official List did not prevent a security from being traded, quotation brought it within 'a publicly recognised market' and provided the information needed by investors and creditors before they were willing to hold it or accept it as collateral.[27] For these reasons one broker complained to the

---

[24] Cain and Hopkins, *British Imperialism*, particularly chapters 1 and 21; A. G. Hopkins, 'Informal Empire in Argentina: An Alternative View', *Journal of Latin American Studies* 26 (1994), 469–84. This argument, although qualified, is now being incorporated into the canonical accounts of British imperialism; see for example John Darwin, *The Empire Project: The Rise and Fall of the British World System, 1830–1970* (Oxford, 2009).

[25] Morgan and Thomas, *Stock Exchange*, 151–52; Kynaston, 'London Stock Exchange', 158–68.

[26] House of Commons, 'Report from the Select Committee on Loans to Foreign States; together with the proceedings of the committee, minutes of evidence', *Sessional Papers 1875, Reports of Committees* (367), 29 July 1875, vol. 11, q. 467, 23; also see q. 468, 23.

[27] Michie, *London Stock Exchange*, 87.

Committee in February 1862, after some New South Wales debentures had failed to obtain a listing: 'Our Principals ... having received them as remittances, find themselves placed, by your decision, in the position of holders of unavailable assets'.[28]

From the outset the significance of a quotation, and even of a bond's prominence in the Official List, was clear to the financial agents responsible for marketing colonial debt. In 1857, the Crown Agent for Colonies applied to have the stocks of Canada, New South Wales, Victoria and South Australia marked under 'a distinct heading, say of "Colonial Government Securities".'[29] His motive was to make them 'more generally sought', and when the Committee granted his request the colonial market effectively came into existence.[30] Five years later, the secretary of the Union Bank of Australia (hereafter, the Union Bank) explained to the bank's Colonial Inspector in the colonies that the Stock Exchange

may assume to themselves undue powers ... but as the Committee carry general investors at home with them (for such parties may well seek to know what extent of obligations particular Governments may incur, their correctness, resources, &c., and they depend on the Stock Exchange Committee to ascertain at least sufficient of these particulars to justify the quotation of Debentures in their official list), they – the Committee – in making investigations and requirements, do not really prejudice, but probably support the interests of such Colonial Governments as look for, and may be entitled to, assistance from our money market.[31]

Arguably, by the 1860s the most important regulation affecting overseas borrowers had already existed for some time, being one consequence of the defaults that helped bring to an end the first foreign loan boom. In 1827 the foreign market's committee refused to recognise new issues by governments that had already stopped payment; the main Exchange

[28] Sewell Brothers to Committee of Stock Exchange, 25 February 1862, Applications for Listing, CLC/B/004/F/01/MS18000/022A/0976, London Metropolitan Archives.
[29] E. Barnard to Messrs, Mullens and Marshall, 27 February 1857, South Australia, Parliament, *Proceedings with copies of Documents ordered to be printed*, 1857–8, no. 126, 'Bonds, Correspondence with Agent-General, 12.
[30] Barnard to Colonial Secretary, South Australia, 11 March 1857, 'Bonds, Correspondence with Agent-General', 12; General Purposes Committee minutes, 20 March 1857, CLC/B/004/B/01/MS14600/024, fol. 164, London Metropolitan Archives.
[31] Secretary London to Colonial Inspector, no. 788, 24/27 October 1862, Union Bank of Australia, U/120/16, Australia & New Zealand Banking Group Limited (ANZ), Group Archive, Melbourne.

continued the ban after the merger of the foreign and domestic markets.[32]
By the early 1860s, its rule book stated,

> The Committee will not sanction, nor take any cognizance whatever of, bargains
> made in any new Bonds, Stock, or any other Securities issued by any Foreign
> Government, that has not duly paid the Dividends on former Loans raised in
> this country, unless such Government shall have effected and carried out some
> arrangement with the holders of such Stock, Bonds, or other Securities, on which
> the Dividends have been left in arrear (sic).[33]

Throughout our period, this rule was far more effective in bringing about
the settlement of outstanding debts than anything aggrieved investors
might hope to accomplish themselves by direct negotiation with delin-
quent governments. Yet borrowers of all descriptions also came to
recognise the potency of an appeal by disaffected parties to the Stock
Exchange's rule book even when they were most punctual in their payments. In 1859, the English shareholders of the Geelong and Melbourne
Railway Company threatened to sabotage the first important Australasian
issue in London – the initial instalment of a £7,000,000 railway loan for
the gold-rich colony of Victoria – when they protested to the Committee that they had not received dividend payments allegedly guaranteed
by the colonial government.[34] The shareholders were already negotiating
the railway's sale to the colony. When it appeared that the loan might
be denied a quotation, the London director of one of the banks involved
in the issue urged another of the financial agents: 'Pray write out [to
Australia]... that the Geelong & M[elbourne] Railway may be bought
up'.[35] In the event, the Committee soon decided to grant a quotation
after it was established that the colony's guarantee only extended to the
company's debentures.[36] Yet the colonial government was ignorant of all
this when it finally agreed to purchase the line, putting an end to what
the local correspondent of *The Times* described as 'the shabby attempts
to depreciate the credit of this colony'.[37]

---

[32] Morgan and Thomas, *Stock Exchange*, 93, 152; L. Jenks, *The Migration of British
Capital before 1875* (New York, 1927), 284.

[33] P. L. Simmonds, *Fenn's Compendium of the English and Foreign Funds*, 8th edn.
(London, 1863), 93.

[34] General Purposes Committee minutes, 17 January 1859, CLC/B/004/B/01/MS14600/
025, fols. 72–77.

[35] D. Larnach to Saunders, 17 January 1859, U/120/10.

[36] General Purposes Committee minutes, 31 January 1859, CLC/B/004/B/01/MS14600/
025, fols. 87–90.

[37] 'Victoria (From Our Own Correspondent)', *The Times*, 2 April 1859, 7.

Similar attempts (almost invariably by foreign-owned railway companies) to use the Stock Exchange's quotation rules to interfere with new colonial or foreign government issues were a familiar tactic in the Victorian and Edwardian capital markets, and they might be interpreted as one manifestation of imperialism – an imperialism of business – in its informal mode.[38] Yet even when there was no crude intention to coerce, the Exchange's refusal to grant a quotation might be an equally effective use of informal power (in this instance, structural) if it left borrowers with no choice but to adjust their institutional arrangements to make their credit more acceptable in London. This arguably was the case during the 1860s, when the Committee declined to recognise the issues of New Zealand's provincial governments because of uncertainties about the security of their fiscal resources and the means of legal redress should a province default.[39] Underlying the Exchange's decision was an implicit preference for large, marketable issues secured on the revenue-raising powers of a central government. Without the possibility of a quotation for provincial issues, the colony had little alternative but to abolish the provinces' borrowing powers and consolidate their issues into a single colonial stock.

Further research may uncover similar instances of institutional reforms undertaken to meet the Stock Exchange's standards of creditworthiness. Yet the Exchange's refusal to recognise an entire class of borrowers was probably exceptional. More typically, it responded to the enormous increase in the number of securities entering circulation from the mid-nineteenth century by adjusting its own institutional arrangements to prevent fraud, increase the information available to members and control the ways in which new stocks were sold.

[38] For examples affecting Argentine public borrowers, see Colin Lewis, 'British Railway Companies and the Argentine Government', in D. C. M. Platt (ed.), *Business Imperialism 1840–1930: An Inquiry Based on British Experience in Latin America* (Oxford, 1977), 412–13. Other Australasian examples involved Tasmania during the 1870s and 1880s, New Zealand in the 1890s and Western Australia in the 1900s. For 'business imperialism', see D. C. M. Platt, 'Economic Imperialism and the Businessmen: Britain and Latin America before 1914', in Roger Owen and Bob Sutcliffe (eds.), *Studies in the Theory of Imperialism* (Harlow, 1972), 297. Platt disputes the effectiveness of this form of business imperialism. The point here is that it was relatively commonplace.

[39] Bernard Attard, 'From Free-Imperialism to Structural Power: New Zealand and the Capital Market, 1856–68', *Journal of Imperial and Commonwealth History* 35 (2007), 505–27; Bernard Attard, 'Making the Colonial State: Development, Debt and Warfare in New Zealand, 1853–76', *Australian Economic History Review* 52 (2012), 101–27.

In early 1859 the Committee defined for the first time the conditions
on which a foreign or colonial loan would be granted a quotation. For
example, the contractor or agent was required to provide details of the
amount issued to the public and had to be represented by a broker when
the application was considered.[40] The immediate reasons for this new
regulation are not clear, but the rule was amended almost immediately
because of problems arising from the sale of Australasian securities. The
most common way in which these securities entered the market was by
private negotiation through the agency of a broker. Bonds were either
sold in London itself for the first time or, in the case of local issues,
resold after remittance by an original buyer in the colonies. Disputes
occurred between brokers and dealers because remitted bonds frequently
lacked information about where coupons were payable or the total issue
authorised.[41] After one disagreement over whether certain New South
Wales debentures were actually negotiable in London, the Committee
decided that in the future *all* remitted government bonds should be signed
by a financial agent in England, should specify the authority and amount
of the loan, and should list the numbers and denominations of the entire
issue.[42]

Three years later, after 'a long controversy' with the New South Wales
loan agent, the Committee agreed to ban the sale of new issues by private
negotiation altogether, resolving 'that all Colonial bonds issued in this
Country should be publicly negotiated (*sic*) by tender or otherwise'.[43]
Again, the Committee's minutes are not explicit, but the most likely
reason was the dealers' objections to the unpredictability of supply when
debentures were remitted or sold privately in small instalments. In October 1862, the Union Bank's secretary explained to the Brisbane manager
that the Exchange had been 'very anxious to induce Colonial Governments to desist from local sales of such Debentures as may be intended
for subsequent disposal here, and to prevent financial agents in London

---

[40] General Purposes Committee minutes, 7 March 1859, CLC/B/004/B/01/MS14600/025,
fols. 113–14.
[41] Bernard Attard, 'New Estimates of Australian Public Borrowing and Capital Raised in
London, 1849–1914', *Australian Economic History Review* 47 (2007), 155–77, 169–
71.
[42] General Purposes Committee minutes, 19 and 29 August 1859, fols. 233–34, 236–37;
26 September 1859, fols. 251–52, CLC/B/004/B/01/MS14600/025.
[43] Secretary to Manager, Brisbane, 23 October 1862, U/120/16; Steer Cuerton & Law-
ford to Committee for General Purposes, 15 October 1862, CLC/B/004/F/01/MS18000/
022A/976; General Purposes Committee minutes, 25 August, 6 October and 16 October
1862, CLC/B/004/B/01/MS14600/027, fols. 59, 78, 84.

from effecting private sales'.[44] In the event, the new rule was applied to foreign as well as colonial issues.[45]

This amendment effectively ended private negotiation through a broker as a means to sell new colonial debt in London, even when the sums involved were trivial.[46] Borrowers now converged on the practice of inviting competitive tenders for large loans and opening the tenders publicly on a nominated day. For the rest of the century there was only one further change to the way in which colonial loans were marketed, yet it also was initiated by the Stock Exchange. Until the early 1870s, loan agents kept the minimum or reserve price of new issues secret until tenders had been opened. Within a few years, the brokers' reluctance to bid unless the minimum was advertised virtually put an end to this practice. The Committee's role was now simply to reinforce an existing trend, accomplishing this without a rule change in February 1876 by the publication of a memorandum condemning the 'exceptional practice' and questioning whether 'it should not constitute a bar to Official Quotation'.[47] The mere threat to deny a listing was clearly considered sufficient.

By the mid-1870s, the Committee had established a set of rules and conventions that ensured that the colonists' market behaviour accorded with the preferences of the Exchange's members.[48] Subsequently, the most important formal institutional innovations, the Colonial Stock Acts of 1877 and 1900, were legislative and originated elsewhere. Until the end of the century, the arrangements for offering colonial loans within the Exchange's regulatory framework remained unchanged. However, these arrangements were also influenced by customary practice, preferences and organisational forms that originated within the market and to which the regulatory structure was itself an institutional response. It is to the consideration of these that we turn.

---

[44] Secretary London to Manager, Brisbane, 23 October 1862, U/120/16.

[45] General Purposes Committee minutes, 22 October 1862, CLC/B/004/B/01/MS 14600/027, fols. 89–90.

[46] In 1870, South Australia was forced into a pointless public offer of £30,000 debentures after the Committee refused to grant a quotation if they were placed privately; General Purposes Committee minutes, 17 June 1870, CLC/B/004/B/01/MS14600/034, fol. 170; *The Times*, 15 July 1870, 10.

[47] General Purposes Committee minutes, 31 January and 4 February 1876, CLC/B/004/B/01/MS14600/040, fols. 264, 275; memorandum, by order Francis Levien, Stock Exchange, 7 February 1876, enclosed with D. Larnach to S. Smith, 18 February 1876, Bank of New South Wales, GM204/12, Westpac Banking Corporation, Westpac Historical Services, Sydney.

[48] Coincidentally, Cottrell also marks the end of the mid-nineteenth century 'Big Bang' in the late 1870s; 'London's First "Big Bang"', 97.

Market

The extent to which the Stock Exchange's members participated in marketing new capital issues in London has typically been viewed as quite limited. Kynaston offers the best account, concentrating on the preparation of the prospectus, the arrangement of underwriting from the 1880s, applications for special settlement and quotation, and malpractices like pre-allotment dealing and stagging, all with particular respect to company issues.[49] Where the retailing of new stock was concerned, Davis and Gallman express a common view: 'The raising of capital by the sale of *new* securities was not done through the stock exchange, but through a loosely structured collage (*sic*) of new issue houses, company promoters and brokers, underwriters, and advertisements'.[50] It is certainly true that member firms themselves rarely acted as the agents or contractors for a loan. Yet as a mechanism for absorbing and distributing new stock, the Exchange was indispensable, particularly for colonial borrowers.

It is impossible here to give an adequate account of all roles played by the Stock Exchange firms in the new issue market for colonial loans, although some are already evident from the preceding section. It is sufficient simply to emphasise that Stock Exchange support was indispensable because its members more often than not were *themselves* the market in the first instance. An important reason for this was a customary practice scarcely mentioned by historians: the payment to Stock Exchange firms by issuers of a 0.25 per cent commission for any sales of new debt effected by them or for successful tenders obtained through their agency. By allowing this commission, financial agents gave the Stock Exchange a direct interest in handling the greatest proportion of any new loan.

The importance of the customary 0.25 per cent was acknowledged by everyone interested in an issue's success. One of the first decisions of the consortium selling Victoria's £7,000,000 loan was 'that all members of the Stock Exchange, whether dealers or brokers, be paid the usual brokerage'.[51] A decade later, when a new agent offered a New South Wales loan for the first time, its managing director in London was 'waited

[49] Kynaston, 'London Stock Exchange', 127–58.
[50] Davis and Gallman, *Evolving Financial Markets*, 155, emphasis in the original; see also, Michie, *London Stock Exchange*, 141.
[51] Minutes, London Committee, 30 December 1858, Victoria, Legislative Assembly, *Documents Ordered to be Printed*, 1859–60, C2, 'The Whole of the Correspondence between the late Government and the six Banks having reference to the Sale of our Debentures in London'.

on by some of the Brokers of the Stock Exchange', who told him that 'they would take no part in it unless we would pay them the full quarter per cent always allowed to Brokers'.[52]

Yet even had no commission been involved, the Stock Exchange's market-making functions meant that the dealers inevitably purchased the greater proportion of new colonial bonds and subsequently retailed them *via* the brokers in response to public demand. The customary 0.25 per cent was simply an added incentive to the firms involved in this chain of transactions. During the controversy over private sales in 1862, the brokers employed by the New South Wales loan agent explained to the Committee, '[T]he Bank only sell[s] the bonds on the demand of the dealers'.[53] Two years before that, the London secretary of one of the banks selling Victoria's £7,000,000 loan had informed the acting superintendent in Melbourne, 'A large number of the subscribers are jobbers, who are not permanent holders, but who sell again at a small profit to the public'. He added, '[I]t is well known that, unless any Foreign loan is favorably (*sic*) received on the Stock Exchange, it can never be placed successfully upon the market'.[54]

Its unpopularity with the jobbers was probably the main reason why the Committee disallowed private negotiation for the retailing of new debt. One banker warned as early as 1860 that 'the plan of selling in small portions is not a wise one; it tends to keep back the biddings from the Stock Exchange, and to make the operators in the money market unwilling to deal with the bonds'.[55] By contrast, the tender system on which all Australasian borrowers had converged by the middle of the decade best suited the Exchange's own preferences for how to handle the growing number of new issues in what had become a discrete colonial market.

Even during the operations to sell Victoria's £7,000,000 loan, brokerage firms bid for substantial amounts of stock by aggregating many separate tenders.[56] By the mid-1870s, the brokers themselves were organising

[52] Larnach to Smith, 30 October 1868, GM204/4.
[53] General Purposes Committee minutes, 16 October 1862, CLC/B/004/B/01/MS14600/027, fol.84.
[54] Secretary London to Acting Superintendent, no. 1145, 17 February 1860, A/51/13, ANZ Group Archive, Melbourne.
[55] J. Cummins to Colonial Inspector, no. 885, 26 November 1863, U/120/18.
[56] Between 1858 and 1862, Stock Exchange members submitted bids for between 86 to 98 per cent of the amounts sold; see the statements of account of each of these operations printed in Victoria, Legislative Assembly, *Documents Ordered to be Printed*, 1859–60, A45 and C2; 1860–1, no. 57, and 1862–3, no. 16.

these combinations of investors, which were now being described as 'syndicates' by analogy with the groups (sometimes including Stock Exchange firms and also known as syndicates) that were paid a commission by loan contractors and company promoters to guarantee the sale of all or the greater part of a new issue.[57] Syndicates of the latter kind were sometimes also known in the colonial market, but they were rare. Despite the confusion of some observers, the distinguishing characteristic of syndicates in the colonial market was that they were organised voluntarily by Stock Exchange firms, which acted independently of loan agents and did not receive any commission apart from the customary 0.25 per cent.[58] Profits arose solely from the difference between a debenture's original net purchase price and the amount for which it was eventually sold. In 1883, after a loan for Victoria failed because the syndicates did not believe it worth their while to bid (inspiring the rhyme quoted in the epigraph to this chapter), *The Financier* offered the best description of these 'useful intermediaries':

For many years past, Loans of this sort have been taken *in the first* instance not by the investing public but mainly by financial associations, 'syndicates', and so forth, who have sought to make their profit by 'nursing' the new Stock and – sometimes after the lapse of a considerable interval – parcelling it out amongst investors in proportion as the demand has made itself manifest through the market.[59]

During the 1870s these investor groups coalesced around a handful of Stock Exchange firms with particular expertise in colonial stocks, which served as one element in a much larger pattern of specialisation in the Victorian Stock Exchange.[60] In 1875, South Australia's Agent-General explained after his negotiations with one of the principal syndicate brokers,

You can count off on the fingers of one hand the names of all the brokers upon whose countenance and support the floating of every Colonial loan depends. The

---

57 'Syndicates', *Economist*, 16 August 1873, 994; also see Hall, *London Capital Market*, 77–80; Morgan and Thomas, *Stock Exchange*, 89–90. For a discussion and examples with reference to Japanese loans, T. Suzuki, *Japanese Government Loan Issues on the London Capital Market 1870–1913* (London, 1994), 25–27 and *passim*.

58 *The Economist*, which was unremittingly hostile to 'these cliques', persistently conflated the two types of syndicate, e.g. 'The Financing of the South Australian Loan', 7 February 1891, 168–69; for 'cliques', 'The Lesson of the Victorian Loan', 18 April 1891, 494. Hall also believed the two forms of syndicate were identical, *London Capital Market*, 101.

59 *Financier*, 10 January 1883; cutting in Public Record Office Victoria, Melbourne: VPRS 1225, box 1, file 83R/10115. Emphasis in original.

60 This is an important theme in Michie, *London and New York Stock Exchanges*.

Stock Exchange, *as a body*, don't go in for Colonial loans – there is little to be made out of them. They leave the tendering of the bulk to the four or five who get up the necessary information on Colonial subjects, and obtain such share for their own connexions from the tenderers, on the same terms, afterwards.[61]

Provided loans were attractively priced, the syndicates effectively underwrote new Australasian issues in London, as well as the issues of the other colonies and probably India as well. When Australian investments boomed during the 1880s, the successful applications by general investors sometimes exceeded allotments to the syndicates by a considerable margin, but the latter could always be relied upon to make up any shortfall. Their informal nature, however, meant that they were fundamentally unstable. If loans were priced too keenly (as in the case of Victoria's loan of 1883), credit dried up; if too much capital was already locked up in other speculative investments, the syndicates ceased to function. The weakening of Australian credit from 1889, combined the following year with the depressing effects of the Baring crisis on a wide range of stocks, had precisely this result. In the first half of 1891 no syndicates bid for new issues by South Australia, Victoria and Queensland, which all failed.[62] Soon after, the New Zealand Agent-General observed, 'The syndicates that a few years ago were always ready to make wholesale purchases of a large quantity of stock with the view of retailing it out to small investors now no longer exist'.[63]

The 1890s, in fact, marked the transition to a more formal system of underwriting in the London capital market that ultimately replaced these loose combinations. The payment of commissions to guarantee the success of a new issue slowly came within the pale of accepted practice, with the Companies Act of 1900 finally removing any lingering doubt.[64] For colonial loan agents, underwriting not only formalised the old system of stockbroker-led syndicates but also eliminated risk because underwriters were obliged to take up the unsubscribed portion of any loan. At the turn

[61] F. Dutton to Treasurer, 20 January 1875, South Australia, Parliament, *Proceedings with Copies of Documents Ordered to be Printed*, 1875, no. 98, 'Sale of Bonds and Consolidation of Bonded Debt'; emphasis in original.

[62] *The Economist*, 'The Financing of the South Australian Loan', 7 February 1891, 168–69; 'The Lesson of the Victorian Loan', 18 April 1891, 493–94; 'Colonial Finance and the Market for Colonial Loans,' 30 May 1891, 694–95; Hall, *London Capital Market*, 78, 101–2.

[63] W. Perceval to Premier, 9 June 1892, New Zealand, Parliament, *Appendices to the Journals of the House of Representatives*, B-21, 1893, 5.

[64] 'The Science of Underwriting', *The Economist*, 26 April 1890, 517–18; Hall, *London Capital Market*, 78–79; Kynaston, 'London Stock Exchange,' 134–36; Davis and Gallman, *Evolving Financial Markets*, 172–73.

of the century, when several Australasian borrowers wished to reenter an increasingly crowded market still wary of Australian credit, loan agents insisted that the new issues be underwritten, despite the additional costs involved.[65] The actual arrangements, however, were left to a tight circle of Stock Exchange firms, which required that loans be offered for subscription at a fixed price. One of these firms, J. & A. Scrimgeour, had been a key syndicate broker during the 1870s and 1880s. It now underwrote for New Zealand. A second, Mullens Marshall, had also been active in colonial securities since the mid-nineteenth century.[66] The most important, R. Nivison & Co., filled the gap created by the disappearance of many of the other syndicate brokers during the 1890s. Nivison eventually monopolised the underwriting of Australian, Canadian and South African loans and cooperated with Mullens over Indian issues.[67] In a study of the colonial market published in 1911, a German scholar commented on the prominence of these three firms, observing, '[W]ith the fixed-price issue, the role of the broker comes to the fore'.[68] After the First World War, the governor of the Bank of England described them as the 'issuing brokers'.[69]

Institutions and Market, 1900–1930

The three issuing brokers rose to prominence at the end of a process of specialisation by which Stock Exchange firms came to be the main links between colonial borrowers and the wider capital market. As a result, Nivison and the other brokers exercised considerable control over the terms and timing of new issues. After 1900, the price of all new colonial loans had to be agreed first with one or another of them. Moreover, just as during the 1870s and 1880s when the syndicate brokers acted as

[65] For further comments about the origins of underwriting in the Australasian market, see Hall, *London Capital Market*, 78–79, 101–2; Suzuki, *Japanese Government Loan Issues*, 29–30; Bernard Attard, 'Marketing Colonial Debt in London: Financial Intermediaries and Australasia, 1855–1914', conference paper, accessed at http://www.esrc.ac.uk/my-esrc/grants/R000223775/read/.

[66] Scrimgeour was the broker used by the Crown Agents of the Colonies; Mullens was employed by the Bank of England and the Treasury.

[67] R. S. Gilbert, 'London Financial Intermediaries and Australian Overseas Borrowing, 1900–29', *Australian Economic History Review* 10 (1971), 39–47, 41–45; R. T. Davenport-Hines, 'Lord Glendyne', in R. T. Appleyard and C. B. Schedvin (eds.), *Australian Financiers: Biographical Essays* (Melbourne, 1988), 190–205.

[68] T. Schilling, *London als Anleihemarkt der englischen Kolonien* (Stuttgart, 1911), 46.

[69] Montagu Norman Diary, 14 and 27 February 1928, ADM34/17, Bank of England Archive.

specialist intermediaries between borrowers and the rest of the Exchange, the issuing brokers now served similar functions in the Edwardian market. Their agreement to underwrite at a given price also served as an important signal. According to a former South Australian Agent-General in 1908, Stock Exchange firms were still the main sub-underwriters of Australian loans: 'Jobbers ask directly a loan is coming out: "Is Nivison in this?" If he is not they will not touch it'.[70]

With the connections between the issuing brokers and the financial institutions that supported them well established, and all the critical negotiations taking place between the loan agents and brokers beforehand, the floating of new Australasian and other colonial loans was increasingly a routine affair. Risk to borrowers and their agents had largely been eliminated, but at the cost of dependence on an effective oligopoly of the three underwriting firms. This dependence reflected the restrictive practices that were becoming more common in the London securities market immediately before the First World War. The most well-known of these were the strict enforcement of the separation of capacity between broker and jobber from 1909 and the introduction of minimum commissions in 1912.[71] Each undermined the Exchange's competitiveness and frustrated its more dynamic elements. Yet the war itself dealt the most powerful blows to London's international position. From 1915, private foreign lending was subject to an official embargo, and even when the embargo was abandoned in 1919 capital exports continued to be restricted in one form or another for most of the 1920s.[72]

Despite the more difficult conditions in London for all overseas borrowers after 1914, London's regulatory regime continued to favour the empire. Even during the war, British dominions were permitted to continue raising money for essential public works. After 1918, even though British capital exports failed to recover to their prewar levels, the empire increased its share of this diminished total: governments alone accounted for an annual average of 40 per cent of overseas issues during the

---

[70] *The Register* (Adelaide), 29 July 1908, quoted in R. S. Gilbert, 'London Financial Intermediaries', 42.

[71] Michie, *London Stock Exchange*, 113–16.

[72] Ibid., chapters 4 and 5; John Atkin, 'Official Regulation of British Overseas Investment, 1914–1931', *Economic History Review* 23 (1970), 324–35; D. E. Moggridge, *British Monetary Policy 1924–1931: The Norman Conquest of $4.86* (Cambridge, 1972), 199–227; Bernard Attard, 'Moral Suasion, Empire Borrowers and the New Issue Market during the 1920s', in R. C. Michie and Philip Williamson (eds.), *The British Government and the City of London in the Twentieth Century* (Cambridge, 2004), 195–214.

1920s. Australasian public bodies were particularly prominent.[73] The Stock Exchange Committee continued to exercise authority within its established sphere of responsibility. The concentrated arrangements for underwriting colonial loans, however, provided new ways to regulate empire borrowing. Even before 1914, the three brokers cooperated voluntarily to smooth the flow of new securities. After the war, the Bank of England sought to incorporate them into its own arrangements for regulating the capital market, at first through the operation of a loan queue and eventually by requiring them to seek its approval for any fresh issue.[74]

The Bank's inability to exercise anything stronger than moral suasion ultimately frustrated these efforts. However, the brokers' oligopoly did create a new vulnerability to those wishing to interfere in a colonial government's borrowing operations. This was particularly acute because of the participation of all of London's financial institutions that mattered in the underwriting arrangements orchestrated by Nivison and the others, as well as the readiness of those institutions to form a united front against any borrower that could be accused of breaking contracts with existing investors. During 1920–24, British pastoral companies with substantial holdings in Australia organised a boycott of Queensland government loans after the state Labour Ministry removed the statutory limit on how far Crown rents could be increased at each reappraisal.[75] The denial of a quotation was still an obvious weapon in London's armoury. At a meeting in June 1920, at which the state premier tried to explain his efforts 'to dissipate the idea that the Labour policy was destructive to capital', Committee members reminded him that they had the power to 'remove quoted stock from the List... prevent the publishing of the record of markings... and forbid dealing'.[76] Yet it was unlikely that the dispute would ever reach that stage: only a few days earlier, Nivison had made it clear to the premier that 'he would not be able to get it [a proposed loan] underwritten'.[77] The state was effectively locked out of the London market. Without the support of the banks and other financial organisations that backed Nivison, there was nowhere

[73] Attard, 'Moral Suasion', 196–7 and table 10.1.

[74] Ibid., 195–214.

[75] B. Schedvin, 'Theodore and the London Pastoral Lobby', *Politics* 6 (1971), 26–41, 33.

[76] Conference with Premier, 8 June 1920, General Purposes Committee, minutes of sub-committees of a non-permanent character, Stock Exchange, CLC/B/004/B/33/MS14609/007, London Metropolitan Archives.

[77] Cablegram to Acting Premier Fihelly, Brisbane, 6 June 1920, Queensland State Archives: item ID 862856.

else in London to turn. In the short term, the state withstood the boycott by finding money in New York, raising two small loans there in 1921–22. However, American capital was still too expensive for the majority of empire governments, including Queensland, to make Wall Street a genuine alternative. In 1924, with large maturities falling due in London, the premier had no choice but to come to terms with the pastoral companies.

Conclusion

This study of the market for colonial securities in London has explored two aspects of the Stock Exchange's internationalisation during the first great era of economic globalisation that ended during the Great Depression. The first aspect is the ways in which the Exchange adapted its institutional arrangements and informal organisation to cope with an influx of new borrowers and their securities during the mid-nineteenth century. The origins of the general expansion were domestic as well as foreign, but as I have argued here, internationalisation was one of the most powerful forces stimulating innovation in response to the new trading conditions.

The second issue considered in this chapter is the nature of power in the internationalised securities market that emerged after 1850. In the first instance, the Exchange's Committee exercised authority as the market's regulatory body. As we have seen, the Committee administered and modified the Exchange's formal rules to minimise risk, improve the quality of information, reduce uncertainty and ensure that loans were offered in a manner most acceptable to the Exchange's membership. As one might expect, self-regulatory power was liable to be used in self-interested ways, although after the First World War, the Bank of England attempted to exploit the issuing brokers' control of the colonial market to serve its own regulatory ends. Yet regulatory power always had a wider significance in a market partly constituted by dependent borrowers whose loan operations were vulnerable to disruption by third parties seeking redress for their particular grievances. In these circumstances, the Exchange's authority and market power might be used, or exploited, in ways that translated into a protean informal imperialism whose expressions ranged, as we have seen, from direct attempts to coerce to the subtler institutional pressures to conform to metropolitan standards of creditworthiness.

6

The London Gold Market, 1900–1931

Bernd-Stefan Grewe

In the early twentieth century, London still was a safe city. Day after day, a vehicle resembling a small furniture removal van arrived at N. M. Rothschild and Sons in St Swithin's Lane. The van's doors were opened, and a cargo of gold bars worth millions was unloaded by being passed hand to hand. The bullion van had no special protection and there was no armed guard – just one ex-policeman in a bowler hat and raincoat.[1] Since the 1840s, N. M. Rothschild had always been at the centre of the London gold market, by far the world's largest bullion market in the twentieth century. Before the First World War, more than a third of the world's annual gold production was brought to London and sold on this market.

Until 1914, the City of London indisputably had a hegemonic position in international finance, and it is not surprising that the biggest gold market was to be found there as well. Yet after the war, because of its huge debts Britain lost its leading position to the United States, which became the world's creditor, the dollar becoming a world currency and New York another important financial market. Surprisingly enough, London was able to defend its key position in gold trade for another half-century and continue to fix the gold price around the world. How was this possible, when London had lost its hegemonic position in world finance, and when Britain, after reestablishing its gold standard in 1925, had to abandon it again already in 1931?

Research on the history of gold in the early twentieth century is limited in two ways. First, most studies concentrate on the history of the functioning or abolition of the international gold standard within a frame of

---

[1] Michael Bonavia, *London before I Forget* (Worcester, 1990), 177–78.

monetary policy. Of course, under the gold standard, monetary policy had a major impact on the gold market. Yet demonstrably, other factors frequently omitted by macroeconomists also had an impact, thus indirectly affecting the international monetary system. Such factors include new discoveries of the precious metal and freight and insurance rates for its shipping. Second, the historically oriented economic research has a strong Eurocentric or U.S.-centric orientation.[2] Few studies take actors from the periphery into account and try to analyze their interests and agency. Hence the role of Indian, South African and Australian actors is rarely investigated in a similar way to that of Western reserve banks – that is, to a degree proportionate to their real influence on the international gold market.[3]

This chapter discusses the London gold market as an example of a global market in which contemporary players with quite divergent interests interacted: London bullion brokers who refined and traded gold by foreign order or on their own account; South African mining companies that produced the major part of the world's new gold; and reserve banks of industrialised nations like France and Germany as well as, from 1913, the Federal Reserve Bank of New York. Although each of these players exerted considerable influence on this market, the Bank of England held the key position. Until the outbreak of war in 1914, the London gold market was truly global, and although gold could be imported and exported without limitation, the rules were set by just one nation: Britain. How strong was the Bank of England's real impact on the world gold market? To what extent could the bank exert a form of de facto control over gold supply and prices?

The period studied in this discussion can be divided into four phases: (1) the prewar period when the classical gold standard held, (2) the period of the First World War, (3) the postwar years until 1925 when the British gold standard was reintroduced, and (4) the period from 1925–31 when Britain had to abandon the standard and devalue sterling.

The Prewar Gold Market

Before 1914 London was by far the world's most important gold market. Since the 1880s, the largest part of the gold for sale in London came

---

[2] Barry Eichengreen, *Golden Fetters: The Gold Standard and the Great Depression, 1919–1939* (New York, 1992).

[3] John McGuire, Patrick Bertola and Peter Reeves (eds.), *Evolution of the World Economy, Precious Metals and India* (Oxford, 2001), is a notable exception.

from the Witwatersrand in South Africa. In the four years before the war, more than 8.8 million ounces of gold – close to 274 metric tonnes – were shipped annually from Cape Town to London. Yet the London market had not always been unchallenged. At the turn of the century, German banking capital attempted to divert at least part of the flow of gold from the Rand to Berlin: the German East Africa Line offered very favourable shipping rates, and Deutsche Bank and Degussa contacted the mining groups of A. Goertz and Werner, Beit, promising them considerable cost savings on the overhead expenses involved in having raw gold assayed, refined and marketed in London. However, in the end only a comparatively small amount of gold found its way onto the German market. What made London so much more attractive?

There were four main reasons why the South African mining companies continued to ship their unassayed raw gold to London. First, the South Africans did not possess either a refinery or a mint and thus had to rely on England for this capacity. All South African coins were minted in London, and sterling was also the South Africa currency. Second, the large Witwatersrand mining houses raised most of their capital on the London money market. They were registered on the London Stock Exchange, had their head offices in the City and held their annual general meetings in London. Lloyds insured gold shipments, and the shipping facilities between Cape Town and London were better developed than on any other route to Europe or the United States. Shipping gold through the German East Africa Line from Lourenço Marques (Mozambique) via Suez to Hamburg took forty-seven days instead of the seventeen days from Cape Town to London, resulting in much higher insurance costs and loss of a month's interest. Third, the London bullion market was a free market, in the sense that it suffered from no restrictions such as gold premiums or central bank intervention. Finally, the Bank Charter Act of 1844 (Peel's Act) fixed the buying price for standard gold bar at 77s. 9d. per ounce and the selling price at 77s. 10 $\frac{1}{2}$d. – the Bank of England thus offering the mines a guaranteed market for all the gold they produced. Although the other markets saw to it that all transhipped gold could be sold immediately (e.g. the Banque de France sometimes offered higher prices than the Bank of England), they were not obliged to buy at a fixed price.[4]

The mining companies delivered their raw bullion to one of the two big local banks – the Standard Bank of South Africa or the National

---

4 Jean Jacques van Helten, 'Empire and High Finance: South Africa and the International Gold Standard 1890–1914', *Journal of African History* 23 (1982), 529–48, 538–42.

Bank of South Africa – responsible for organising the weekly shipments to England. These banks then contracted with the London refiners, which were also responsible for converting the gold into cash. About 60 per cent of all unrefined gold coming to England was refined by the Royal Mint Refinery, and the remaining 40 per cent by Johnson Matthey.[5] Rothschild had taken over the Royal Mint Refinery in the 1850s: this refinery had handled the flood of gold available from Australian discoveries and in the early twentieth century was the only one with sufficient financial power to advance the price of South African gold.

Bullion brokers or banks wishing to buy gold would contact one of the refiners and state their requirements. As a result of the Bank Charter Act, the refiners could satisfy any other demand on the market at 77s. 9¼d. before selling the remaining gold to the Bank of England.

'London good delivery' gold bars accepted by the Bank of England became a rigorous standard for gold on the world market. A good bar had to be at least 995 parts per thousand pure gold, with up to 999.9 being accepted; it had to contain between 350 and 430 troy ounces of fine gold and bear the stamp of one of the firms accepted as refiners and assayers. In the early nineteenth century, Mocatta & Goldschmid was the sole bullion broker authorised by the Bank of England. Then the bank's bullion office opened itself to the purchase or sale of gold bars belonging to any sworn broker; originally this involved a group of five brokers, who later became the members of London Gold Market Fixing Ltd. Alongside Mocatta and N. M. Rothschild were Sharps, Pixley & Co.; Johnson Matthey; and Samuel Montagu & Co. Ltd. The reason why 'London good delivery' became the global gold-bar standard is that having their bars accepted in London furnished refiners with a reputation and facilitated acceptance of the bars in gold markets from Hong Kong and Bombay to New York.

The Bank Charter Act had fixed the buying and selling price of gold in order to guarantee the value of the national currency, the pound sterling. In obliging the Bank of England to purchase and sell gold on demand, the act protected the stability of sterling and prevented any depreciation, which made sterling unrivalled as an international currency. From the 1870s onwards, other countries adopted the gold standard, so that the German mark, the French franc, the U.S. dollar and many other currencies had fixed exchange rates with the pound. In addition, the bulk of international transactions were still denominated in sterling; overseas banks held balances in the currency, and some reserve banks held part

---

[5] Rothschild Archives IX/35/64, Draft Memorandum on the Gold Market, 1937, 1–3.

TABLE 4. *Gold Reserves of the Central Reserve Banks Before the First World War (in Metric Tonnes)*

	1900	1905	1910	1913
Bank of England	198,47	199,21	223,37	248,09
Reichsbank (Germany)	211,00	267,00	240,00	438,60
Bank of France	544,23	835,92	952,46	1030,43
U.S. Treasury	602,59	1148,67	1660,52	2293,46
Bank of Italy	115,00	285,16	359,00	355,83
Bank of Russia	661,16	654,14	954,2	1233,00

or all of their main reserves in it as well. All this made sterling unrivalled as an international currency, 'on equal terms with gold'.[6] A. G. Ford thus suggested that the prewar gold standard can be seen as a sterling standard.[7] Consequently, the Bank of England simultaneously became the regulator of both that standard and the international payments system, the entire system being based on acceptance and convertibility of sterling (and other currencies) into gold. (In the nineteenth century, the expansion of the world economy and world trade had only been possible because of the discovery of big gold fields in California, Australia and South Africa. Only this new gold made it possible to extend the money supply and credit under a gold standard system.)

Surprisingly, British gold reserves were very low compared to those of other European countries (see Table 4). At the turn of the century, the French gold stock was twice as large as the British: it had doubled further by 1913, whereas the British reserves only grew by about 25 per cent.

The most convincing explanation of this disparity is that gold reserves did not bear interest. Although the Bank of England was responsible for managing sterling, it was also a private institution that had to make a profit for its investors, the City of London's bankers. This dual role could cause conflicts between its public duties and private interests. To hold higher gold reserves without any change in bankers' deposits would reduce the income of both the bank and its shareholders.[8] Gold stocks did not bear interest, and the bank's owners were not interested in holding

---

[6] W. M. Scammel, 'The Working of the Gold Standard', in Barry Eichengreen and Marc Flandreau (eds.), *The Gold Standard in Theory and History* (London, 2nd edition 1997), 104.

[7] A. G. Ford, 'Notes on the Working of the Gold Standard before 1914', in Eichengreen and Flandreau, *The Gold Standard in Theory and History*, 161.

[8] Richard S. Sayers, *The Bank of England, 1891–1944*, 3 vols. (Cambridge 1976), 61; Dieter Ziegler, *Das Korsett der 'Alten Dame'. Die Geschäftspolitik der Bank of England 1844–1913* (Frankfurt a. M., 1990).

dead capital. Even after the Baring crisis of 1890 – the threatened insolvency of London's Baring Bank had led to panic and a minor depression whose effects were mitigated by a governmental rescue – when George Goschen, the Chancellor of the Exchequer, stressed the urgent need to enlarge the country's gold reserves, London's bankers continued to reject this idea. Instead of increasing reserves, the Bank of England compensated by expanding its use of monetary policy techniques, becoming famous for an ability, when necessary, to 'attract gold from the moon' (the phrase is Walter Bagehot's).

Crucially, the bank's ability to protect the convertibility of sterling and attract gold depended on the London gold market. For that reason, it was of vital interest for the City of London bankers to keep the world's gold market in London, with the availability of gold there reinforcing the City's continued international financial leadership. To attract gold the Bank of England used several monetary instruments. For a start, it could raise the rate at which it offered credit to the other British banks. High interest rates restricted credit and attracted foreign investors, thus causing an inflow of gold. Next, it could use so-called gold devices: the option of operating on the open market and buying gold above the fixed statutory price, or increasing the selling price for foreign coins, or refusing to sell gold bars (in which case it still had to convert bank notes into sovereigns). Finally, the bank could offer credit to gold import businesses.[9] (Other central banks like the Banque de France and the Reichsbank bought gold at the borders and in ports to reduce the transaction costs for the sellers.) Because many other countries with considerable gold reserves such as Russia were highly indebted to Britain, there was a good prospect of London obtaining more gold if needed.[10]

In any event the hegemonic position of the City of London and the Bank of England in world finance had already begun to erode. With the growth of powerful joint-stock banks in Britain and of rival money markets in Germany and the United States, the bank rate's capacity to bring in gold had diminished.[11] For this reason, gold devices and thus London's gold market became even more important in protecting the preeminence

---

[9] Eichengreen, *Golden Fetters*, 39–40; Russell Ally, *Gold and Empire: The Bank of England and South Africa's Gold Producers, 1886–1926* (Johannesburg, 1994), 20–21; Scammell, *Working of the Gold Standard*, 104.

[10] The direct operations of the Bank of England on the gold market are best described in Sayers, *Bank of England*, I, 47–53.

[11] See the memorandum for the Chancellor of the Exchequer on the gold reserves (May 1914), in Marcelo de Cecco, *Money and Empire: The International Gold Standard, 1890–1914* (Oxford, 1974), Appendix A, 173–206; Ally, *Gold and Empire*, 20.

of sterling, and the City's position as 'banker of the world' depended all the more on maintaining its position as the world's gold market. As long as the weekly gold shipments from South Africa to London continued, this position was not in danger, because knowledge that new gold was always on the way inspired confidence in the Bank's ability to maintain specie payments. Although the City's interest in Transvaal gold cannot be considered the only reason for the Boer War,[12] that factor indisputably played a part in British decision making. During this war, which cut off gold deliveries from the Rand's mines, the Bank of England's gold devices still seemed able to attract enough gold to guarantee the convertibility of sterling. In fact, what was at work here was not the London market attracting gold from abroad but intervention by authorities in the India Office to prevent Australian gold from flowing to India. Such well-established patterns within the world's most important gold market changed profoundly after the outbreak of the First World War.

The First World War and the Gold Market

For some economic historians, the international gold standard was 'one of the first casualties of the outbreak of hostilities' inaugurating the Great War[13] – a war that, we recall, would kill six million people. However, the British gold standard was not immediately abolished when the fighting started on the Continent. Walter Cunliffe, the governor of the Bank of England, agreed with Keynes that practical steps should be taken 'to maintain specie payments, so as to meet foreign demands, while making it extremely difficult and inconvenient for the ordinary man to get gold'.[14] The Bank of England continued to change its notes into sovereigns, although some clearing banks had refused to do so since the end of July 1914. Soon after Cunliffe made this statement practically all gold coin circulation was stopped, with the Treasury issuing notes in its place. This call-in of sovereigns worked by moral suasion rather than by law and meant the effective abandonment of the gold standard, although it remained theoretically in force.

Yet even after the informal abolition of that standard, gold became much more important for government policy. All belligerents had to

---

[12] C. W. De Kiewiet, *A History of South Africa: Social and Economic* (Oxford, 1957), 140.
[13] Ally, *Gold and Empire*, 29.
[14] E. Johnson (ed.), *Collected Writings of John Maynard Keynes*, vol. XVI (London, 1971), 12; Sayers, *Bank of England*, I, 83–84.

borrow money to wage war, in particular to buy raw materials, munitions, weapons and food from either allies or formally neutral states like the United States or Sweden. Such states no longer accepted the currencies of the belligerents, instead insisting on being paid either in their own currency or gold. This was mainly because, to finance the war, most belligerents had suspended the convertibility of their currencies and issued unsecured paper money – an inflationary procedure that helped sustain the war's cost, but made it difficult to borrow money abroad. All the belligerents took extraordinary measures to protect their gold reserves and safeguard their credit. Significantly, gold holdings were considered a unique source of a country's wealth after hostilities had ended. In the short term, cutting off the enemy's access to the precious metal would undermine its capacity to raise money and buy goods abroad, and thus to wage war.[15]

There can be no doubt that the American refusal to accept sterling credits in payment for exports created a difficult situation for Britain. This refusal was the reason for several measures taken by the British government in respect to the gold market. First, British wartime legislation (the Realm Act) prohibited both the export of gold by private persons and the melting of gold coins; as a result the London gold market was practically closed. Second, Britain took measures to ensure that newly mined gold would not end up in the hands of the country's enemies. With gold shipped from Cape Town across the Atlantic now subject to sinking or seizure by German warships and submarines and, connected with this situation, with the nearly threefold increase in freight and insurance costs (from 4.34 pence per fine ounce to 12.72 pence) it had become almost impossible to continue the weekly gold shipments to London, something that in turn could endanger borrowing for the war. At the same time, the South African economy relied heavily on the export of gold.

To solve a problem that had become dire, an agreement was signed on 14 August 1914 between the Bank of England and the South African gold producers: the Bank agreed to continue to purchase all the gold mined in South Africa at the fixed rate of 77s. 9d. per standard ounce, and the producers agreed to sell all their gold to the bank, which would advance them 97 per cent of the value. The mining companies were to

---

[15] During the Second World War, German economists tried to learn the lessons from the First World War: Theodor Sonnemann, *Das Gold in der Kriegswirtschaft. Eine Untersuchung über die wehrwirtschaftliche Bedeutung des Goldes im modernen Kriege* (Berlin, 1944).

deposit the gold at the African Banking Corporation, the National Bank
or the Standard Bank of South Africa on behalf of the South African
Minister of Finance; when the Finance Minister acknowledged that the
gold was delivered to the banks, the advance would be paid to the mines.
This so-called August Agreement gave the British authorities exclusive
control over the disposal of South Africa's gold, a control they exercised
rigorously. In 1915, one of the mining companies tried to ship some of its
gold directly to the United States, rather than sending all of it to the Bank
of England, because gold prices in New York were higher due to the weak
sterling exchange. An ultimatum from the Bank of England led to quick
abandonment of this scheme. Had the company insisted on breaking the
agreement, the British government would clearly have commandeered
gold production, as it did in Australia. The Bank itself later confirmed
that 'South African gold producers would not have been permitted to
dispose of their output other than to the Bank of England acting as the
agents of the British Government'.[16] Like Britain, all its dominions soon
placed embargoes on exporting gold.

The growing British financial deficit with the United States pushed the
burden of the credit onto England's comparatively small gold reserves.
In October 1916, an interdepartmental British government committee
made the shocking discovery that, by March 1917, the reserves of gold
and other securities would be exhausted. The drain continued at a constantly accelerating rate as the deficit mounted. In the winter of 1916–17,
Britain was close to financial collapse – which was prevented by
Germany's initiation of a campaign of unrestricted submarine warfare
that led to the United States' entry into the war in April 1917.[17] Thus, the
financing of Britain's warfare was saved. In any case, because of the financial emergency London's gold market was closed for business between
1917 and 1919.

Another danger to Britain's war finances was the continuous need
for gold by India, prompting the British to restrict Indian access to the
metal. Yet India was another important source for vital war material and
faced serious problems maintaining the convertibility of rupee notes as
its currency reserves (sterling) diminished rapidly from 1917 onwards.
This could have caused the collapse of the Indian currency system and
endangered the procurement of war supplies for Britain. Because of the

---

[16] Ally, *Gold and Empire*, 34 f.
[17] John Milton Cooper Jr, 'The Command of Gold Reversed: American Loans to Britain,
1915–1917', *Pacific Historical Review* 45, 2 (1976), 209–30.

need to reserve gold stocks in London to finance the imports of war material from America, British financial authorities declined to send gold to India from London, but arranged a series of gold flows from both the empire (Australia and New Zealand) and one country outside it (Japan) to deal with the Indian currency crisis.[18] Finally, the United States helped manage the crisis by selling a considerable part of its unneeded silver reserves to India. This solved the problem of India's coin shortage, but because the Indian rupee was on a silver standard, it came under strong pressure when the price of silver rose during the war. (None of the leading economic powers were concerned about the stability of the world's silver price.) Another result of the crisis was the limitation of India's exports to necessities: unlike many other primary-producing countries, India would not experience a wartime export boom.[19]

During the war, discussions took place within the Bank of England about how to return to the gold standard and reestablish a free gold market in London after peace was restored. The huge public debt accumulated during the war would have to be repaid, and many bankers believed it would have to be paid in gold. The control over gold movements would thus become even more important for Britain than it had been in the prewar period.

A Free Gold Market in London (1919–1925)

In the spring of 1919, the economic situation was completely different from that of 1913. Britain was no longer the world's creditor; rather, it had itself become a debtor to the United States. The prewar exchange rate of $4.86 per pound sterling had depreciated to about $4.17. In London, the gold price remained fixed at 77s. 9d. per ounce, so that gold exports to New York were highly profitable. Hence to be able to offer a competitive price for gold, the gold standard had to be formally abandoned. Because an early restoration of the standard was unquestioned government policy, and because the existing embargo legislation would end with the ratification of the Treaty of Versailles, a new basis for the gold export embargo was required in 1920. The Act to Control the Exportation of

[18] Andrew Pope, 'Australian Gold and the Finance of India's Exports during World War I: A Case Study of Imperial Control and Coordination', *Indian Economic & Social History Review* 33, 2 (1996), 115–31.
[19] G. Balachandran, *John Bullion's Empire: Britain's Gold Problem and India between the Wars* (Richmond, 1996).

Gold and Silver Coin (7 February 1921) prohibited gold exports except
under licence. It would expire on 31 December 1925.[20]

South African gold producers raised strong objections with the British
authorities regarding the various restrictions on the sale of gold. During
the war, they had accepted the disadvantageous situation for the sake
of sustaining the British economy. However, production costs had risen
during the war while the price that could be obtained in London remained
unchanged. Sterling's depreciation further dented the mining companies'
profits. Many low-grade and deep-level mines, which already had to bear
high costs, were in danger of closing, with only a handful of mines able to
still operate profitably. It thus became very attractive for the South African
mining companies to sell their gold in New York instead of London.

In the City, there was a widespread belief that Britain had been the
centre of the world economy only because of international confidence
in sterling, which had been underpinned by the pound's free conversion
into gold. As a result it was felt that Britain should struggle to return
to the prewar gold system, which meant that London needed to again
emerge as the hegemonic bullion market. For the sake of controlling
South African gold production, amounting to more than a third of the
world's newly mined gold, the Bank of England concluded a new selling
agreement with the South African gold producers in July 1919. This was
a first step in reestablishing the gold market, given that an immediate
return to the prewar parity with gold was impossible because of the
postwar weakness of the pound. The agreement channelled the sale of
South African gold through the London market[21] – the gold producers
had to ship all refined and unrefined gold to England, and they were
offered a premium in London so they could obtain the same price there
as in New York. In addition, the producers were offered reexport licences
after refining so they could offer their gold wherever they wished. The
United States had already fully reinstated its free gold market in June
1919, so this agreement, allowing London to open such a market of its
own, prevented an immediate shift from London to New York as the
world's financial centre.[22]

As a second step, the Bank of England made further arrangements
with N. M. Rothschild to establish a free gold market in London. As the

[20] Sayers, *Bank of England*, III, 55–6.
[21] This agreement is in Ally, *Gold and Empire*, 152–3.
[22] Ibid., 47–133.

biggest bullion broker, refiner and owner of the Royal Mint, that firm was meant to preside over and manage the market. There was to be one official price for gold on any one day and no quotation for forward gold.[23] The proceedings for the London gold market were developed in September 1919 (and would remain much the same when the free gold market was reopened after the Second World War). The fixing of the gold price took place each weekday morning at 10:30 at the Rothschild Bank in St Swithin's Lane in the City. The brokers from N. M. Rothschild & Sons, Johnson Matthey, Samuel Montagu & Co., Mocatta & Goldsmid, Pixley & Abell and Sharp Wilkins arrived with their orders, and they settled on a gold price at which all supplies could be absorbed.[24]

A third measure to make London a more attractive gold market was arranged by Brien Cokayne, the Governor of the Bank of England. He had negotiated successfully with steamship companies for a reduction in freight costs from London to New York and with insurance companies for a reduction in insurance rates from Cape Town to London. These measures substantially reduced the economic advantage of shipping gold directly from South Africa to the United States.[25]

One reason why the South Africans signed the agreement and continued selling their gold in London was that the overall prospects for reestablishing a gold market in Europe seemed quite good. Most European countries wanted to stabilise their currencies on the basis of the prewar gold standard, which could mean increased demand for bullion and thus a higher price. However, after the start of gold fixing, demand from the Continent was quite limited compared to gold exports to the United States or India. Between 1920 and 1925, about 57 per cent of the gold sold on the London market went to the United States, and close to a quarter was shipped to India. On the supply side, about 82 per cent of the gold brought to the London market came from South Africa.[26] The data clearly indicate the economic impact exerted by the United States and India and, on the supply side, by the South African gold producers. This impact was also reflected in the development of the gold price.

[23] Draft Memorandum on Gold Market 1937, Rothschild Archives, XI/35/64.
[24] Timothy Green, *The New World of Gold* (Johannesburg, 1982), 107–14.
[25] Ally, *Gold and Empire*, 51.
[26] Calculation based on data from Annual Report of the bullion department at N. M. Rothschild. Rothschild Archive, XI/35/64.

TABLE 5. *Gold Prices in London*

	Highest Price	Lowest Price
1919	111s 3d	98s 6d
1920	127s 4d	102s 7d
1921	115s 11d	97s 7d
1922	98s 4d	88s 5d
1923	96s 11d	87s 5d
1924	98s	88s
1925	84s 11½d	77s 10½d
1926	77s 10½ d	77s 10½d

Source: Richard S. Sayers, *The Bank of England, 1891–1944* (Cambridge 1976), III, 84.

During these years, the price of gold closely followed the fluctuations of the New York exchange, even if for several months the keen competition from India was able to drive the quotation a few pence above the New York parity (see Table 5). Some years later, in a 1937 memorandum, Anthony de Rothschild described how the gold price was calculated before 1925[27]:

As soon as in September 1919 the export of gold under licence was permitted, the New York exchange became the real standard for the price of gold. The statutory price at which the U.S. Authorities would buy or sell gold was $ 20.67183 per ounce fine. The sterling price of gold was therefore ascertained by dividing the statutory dollar price by the New York exchange rate and deducting all costs of shipping gold from London to New York. For example:

the exchange rate being £1 = $ 4.17,
the sterling price of gold = 20.67813 / 4.17 = £ 4.9572 =   99s. 1¾d
less expenses (freight, insurance, interest, packing in London,
handling in New York and commissions)   ... 7¾d

     98s. 6d

Until Britain's return to the gold standard, the London gold market and the fixing at N. M. Rothschild thus no longer represented the world's hegemonic gold market, because both depended heavily on developments in New York. In this sense, the London gold market between 1919 and 1925 cannot be considered the world's leading gold market, because the price was set in New York and only differed by a premium offered to sellers to prevent them shipping their gold directly to the United States.

---

[27] Draft Memorandum on Gold Market 1937, Rothschild Archives, XI/35/64.

Because the market was also restricted by export licences, it is hard to disagree with Russell Ally's contention that it was at best the 'semblance of a free gold market'. The most striking argument to support this view is that, in practice, the London market worked more as a distribution centre for South African new gold than as a free gold market. An important element often overlooked by historians of monetary policy and the gold standard was the transport situation, which was favourable for London because of the well-established shipping connections with Cape Town, whereas the route between the Cape and New York was comparatively undeveloped.

The position of London as a gold market was clearly endangered after South Africa established a refinery in Germiston, at the Witwatersrand, in 1921 and a mint in Pretoria. The Transvaal Chamber of Mines founded the refinery as a shareholding company – Rand Refinery Ltd. – with shareholding being limited to the mining companies. The gold producers thus no longer depended on Britain for refining, while also excluding the South African government. Lower refining charges were the refinery's chief benefit.[28] At the same time, South African mining companies were able to export gold directly to countries offering the best prices. In 1922, they requested to end the selling agreement with the Bank of England, whose position had considerably weakened. The agreement was then watered down, the Bank being forced to agree to direct exports from South Africa, on the condition that it received complete information including dates of production and despatch, weight in ounces, destination and price per fine ounce obtained by the company. Governor Montagu Norman thus hoped to keep the Bank of England in a position to monitor international movements of gold.[29]

In any case London did not really have to fear that South Africa would export all its gold to other countries, because it still had a very close economic relationship with Britain. More than half of its imports came directly from the United Kingdom, and South Africa had a constant balance-of-payments deficit with Britain. Because the shipping facilities with Britain were much better than with any other country, it was still likely that the bulk of South African gold would be brought to London.

---

[28] Transvaal Chamber of Mines. Thirty-Fifth Annual Report. Year 1924, Johannesburg 1925, 64 (President's Address, M. Anderson). Sam Evans, the chairman of Crown Mines, the biggest mine at the Witwatersrand, calculated that for the period 1908–18, his company would have saved close to a half-million pounds if South Africa had possessed its own refinery and mint. Ally, *Gold and Empire*, 81.

[29] Ibid., 47–72.

It should be noted that the Bank of England's struggle was more about complete control over South Africa's gold production than about the danger of a supply shortage on the London gold market. A supply shortage would have little impact for British monetary policy, because all trade took place within the sterling area. London did need to cooperate with the South Africans, but it is more accurate to speak of reciprocal dependence than of British dependence on South African gold. One thing is certain, however: compared to the situation before the First World War, the Bank of England had lost control over South Africa's gold production. The mining companies had become less dependent on London and could now sell in other markets.

In its 1924 Annual Report, the Chamber of Mines announced that 39 per cent of its gold bars were now disposed of in New York, and another 35 per cent were shipped directly from Durban to Bombay. The advantage of this direct shipment was that the mining companies did not have to pay the freight. Only 1.420.415 ounces of standard gold (14.4 per cent) passed through the London gold market, to be resold to India. For the gold producers, the price differences were due to separate dealing methods, each marked by different charges borne by the company. The Gold Producers Committee in its report emphasized another argument against selling in London: local banks charged high rates on the transfer of funds from London to South Africa and absorbed a considerable portion of the so-called premium on gold.[30]

Under the gold standard and in the postwar years, the Bank of England had guaranteed the mining companies that it would buy all the gold they were not able to sell on the open market for the statutory price of 77s. 9d. It seldom had to do so before 1925, because the pound was depreciated and higher prices could be obtained elsewhere. Meanwhile, with the help and advice of the Bank of England, an independent South African Reserve Bank had been created in 1921. This new reserve bank began to increasingly take over the role formerly played by the Bank of England. From 1925 on, the South African Reserve Bank offered to buy all the gold the producers could not sell abroad for the fixed price of 77s. 9$\frac{1}{8}$d. This option became more important starting in 1926.

---

[30] Transvaal Chamber of Mines. Thirty-Fifth Annual Report. Year 1924, Johannesburg 1925, 125 and 126, 39. In any event the direct shipping of gold to Bombay soon declined again because of a decrease in demand for precious metals in India (see later discussion).

The South African government had supported the establishment of a mint, refinery and reserve bank to create a basis for taking charge of its own financial affairs. Global deflation had reduced the price of gold and threatened the survival of many mines. The gold mines had to reduce their workforce, pay lower wages or replace the comparatively expensive white miners with cheaper black workers. This was the main background for the strike and uprising of tens of thousands of white mineworkers in March 1922, later known as the 'Rand Rebellion', which the South African government suppressed with troops, tanks and aircraft. The mining companies were largely seen as driven by imperial interests, and the white workers became a main source of votes for the National Party, which stood for greater economic independence from Britain – something it saw as only possible once South Africa had its own monetary policy and could free its currency from the dominance of the imperial exchange system.[31] After the National Party's election victory in 1924, South Africa decided to return to the gold standard no later than 1 July 1925. For Britain this of course meant the risk of losing South Africa as part of the sterling system.

India, which as indicated played an important role in the so-called free gold market, presented another problem for the London bankers, who feared that strong Indian demand would absorb more gold and endanger the reestablishment of Britain's gold standard. To check this demand, the bankers successfully used their influence with the India Office in London; their influence was the main reason the rupee was the world's only currency to be revaluated after the war: in February 1920, it was 74 points above its 1913 parity.

To curtail gold imports into India, direct exports of gold to that country from South Africa remained prohibited even after the war. Yet the curtailment effort was not very efficient. Between 1920 and 1925 India imported about a quarter of all the gold passing through the London market, in total worth more than 83 million pounds.[32] In 1924, after the export ban for South African gold was lifted, gold worth close to 3.3 million pounds was imported directly from Durban, in addition to 11.5 million pounds from London and 'considerable amounts of bar gold from New York'.[33]

---

[31] Ally, *Gold And Empire*, 138–41.
[32] Rothschild Archive, XI/35/64.
[33] Transvaal Chamber of Mines. Thirty-Fifth Annual Report. Year 1924, Johannesburg 1925, 126; Rothschild Archive, XI/35/64.

For several reasons, the Indian share of the global gold market is much more difficult to assess than those of the United States, Britain and South Africa. For these countries, we have an institution or actor negotiating on their behalf – the Bank of England, the U.S. Federal Reserve and the gold producers' committees of the Transvaal Chamber of Mines – whose records can be examined. The most important gold market in India was formed by the bazaars of Bombay, which were decentralised and neither spoke with one voice nor produced written records. We can thus only roughly estimate the size and activities of the Indian market. Yet the available data do indicate the direction and order of magnitude of the trade. From 1921 to 1929, India imported a huge amount of gold, worth about 2.49 billion rupees; at the new 1926 rate of 18d. per rupee, this was the equivalent of 373.5 million pounds. In his annual report, the director of Rothschild's bullion department estimated the value of gold exports from London to India for the same period as about 92.4 million pounds. We still do not know where the rest of India's gold imports came from and how this trade developed in detail during the 1920s. A major part of the gold likely passed through the United States, and records indicate that some gold was sold by the French and Swiss and shipped from Marseilles.[34] Another source of India's gold may have been Australia, whose gold deliveries to the London market were remarkably low.

That the Indian demand for gold was clearly not satisfied on the London gold market, with little more than a quarter of the gold for India passing through London, again demonstrates that during the 1920s that market had lost its hegemonic position, with much of the gold trade now taking place independently of it.[35] Apparently, a gold market (re-)emerged in the Indian Ocean area, including India, Southeast Asia, and gold-producing countries such as Australia, New Zealand and South Africa. Yet buying and selling were not concentrated in one place such as in N. M. Rothschild in London. This may be the main reason why important functions of the London gold market such as the fixing of the international gold price were not taken over by another market. Whether lack of knowledge concerning this trade is due to Euro- and U.S.-centric historical perspectives, there is certainly a need for

---

[34] Ibid.
[35] If the whole of India's demand had been settled in London, the sum would have been much higher than exports to the United States (219.5 million pounds) and would have absorbed more than two-thirds of gold imports. In the absence of other gold imports, this would have caused a shortage of gold in London.

more research on the evolving network of gold trade around the Indian Ocean. Likewise very little is known about the same trade in the Pacific region.

The Restored Gold Standard (1925–1931)

On 28 April 1925, Winston Churchill, Chancellor of the Exchequer, announced in his budget speech that the 1920 Gold and Silver Export Control Act would lapse at the end of the year and that Britain would soon return to the gold standard. The Gold Standard Act obliged the Bank of England to again sell gold at 77s. 10½d. per ounce standard.[36]

Economic historians generally agree that restoring the gold standard at this price was a grave error because the pound was overvalued, thereby creating heavy difficulties for the British export industries and increasing unemployment. In his speech, Churchill characterised Britain's economic situation as buoyant because the war debts had been settled and the dollar exchange had been stable for some time. Both during and after the war, the policy of restoring the gold standard had been confirmed by all British government institutions (hence the driving force behind the restoration was clearly not South Africa's announcement of its return to gold). However, after the restoration took place, the expected financial stability did not occur. Because of its credit policy, the City of London had become extremely vulnerable to short-term capital outflows. This vulnerability, which was to prove catastrophic in 1931, substantially increased after 1927, because the Bank of England maintained the convertibility of the pound into gold at a fixed price through the manipulation of short-term rates.[37] The restoration of the gold standard was built on the hope that a global economic upturn would free Britain from the burden of its deflationary monetary policies.[38] There has been much debate on this question, but few studies have considered the effects of the restoration on the London gold market.

---

[36] Churchill's speech and the Gold Standard Act: Sayers, *Bank of England*, III, 80–84, 85–86. L. S. Pressnell, '1925: The Burden of Sterling', *Economic History Review* 31, 1 (1978), 67–88.

[37] The problem of the short-term policy became obvious when changes in the bank rate proved insufficient to prevent money outflow when London could not spare it. This was the case not only during the Wall Street crisis of 1929 but also from 1927 onwards when French money that had floated into London unnoticed in 1925–26 flowed back to Paris again. Sayers, *Bank of England*, III, 211–34.

[38] Balachandran, *John Bullion's Empire*, 220–28.

For N. M. Rothschild, this restoration marked the beginning of a 'dull period' for the free gold market. The gold fixing at the company had lost much of its importance because prices would only fluctuate within the limits set by the Bank of England's buying and selling prices. The brokers' meetings in St Swithin's Lane again became something like bullion distribution sessions. Likewise, the company was not happy with recent developments in the market for gold exported to England: first, gold from South Africa was no longer refined in England but by Rand Refinery Ltd.; second, the South African Reserve Bank shipped much of that gold directly to India; finally, supplies were small, with only a portion of the South African gold being shipped to London for the free market and then only when the price was higher than that offered by the Bank of England.[39]

Gold deliveries from South Africa were low in the first months of 1925, but increased considerably in 1926. This increase, however, did not mean that the fixed gold price had made London a more attractive place for selling gold. The opposite may have been true, because the price obtained by producers in 1922–24 was higher than the statutory price.[40] In fact, this surprising development was closely tied to the massive decline in Indian demand for precious metals from February 1925 onwards, with subsequent reduced gold shipments from South Africa and much gold diverted to the London market. The domestic and external reasons for India's diminished demand for gold are presently not well understood, with much research still needed.[41] Initially the development appears to have been connected with a partial failure of the monsoon, but Indian demand did not recover, remaining relatively low through the rest of the 1920s. Much of India's gold imports during these years came directly from Australia and South Africa.[42]

Because of the global economic crisis that began unfolding in 1929, Britain had to give up the convertibility of the pound into gold in 1931. A year later, South Africa abandoned the gold standard as well. The depreciation of sterling corresponded to an increase in the gold price to 131s. 11d. at the end of 1931. The South African mining companies made big profits, because the price they obtained for gold rose by

[39] Draft Memorandum on Gold Market 1937, Rothschild Archives, XI/35/64.
[40] Charles F. Feinstein, *An Economic History of South Africa: Conquest, Discrimination and Development* (Cambridge, 2005), 94 and 105.
[41] See also Balachandran, *John Bullion's Empire*, 228.
[42] Rothschild Archives, XI/35/64.

40 per cent while their costs, still in sterling, remained the same. On the other side of the Indian Ocean, most of the gold had been absorbed by India. Yet because of its own great depression, India became one of the main exporters of gold: the depression forced many peasants to sell their wives' gold jewellery, and the situation was aggravated by both the rupee's disadvantageous exchange rate and the worldwide decline of prices for agrarian products. Some bullion brokers in London even called this massive dishoarding 'the gold rush of 1932'.[43]

Conclusion

In the period after 1914, Britain experienced a considerable loss of economic power. The developments in the London gold market thus reflected a general trend in the postwar world economy. Britain's balance of trade had already shown a deficit much earlier, with India contributing substantially to the health of Britain's external accounts. Thus, the decline of British power was not a consequence of the outbreak of the First World War, but the war and the effective though not formal abandonment of the gold standard marked a watershed for Britain's hegemonic position in the world's gold trade.

During the war, this economic decline was not evident because India, Australia and South Africa helped sustain Britain in its fight against Germany. Once the war ended, however, the interests of the periphery could no longer be ignored. The weakness of the British position became obvious when South Africa started to seek independence from the control of the City of London. The bankers and bullion brokers in the City fought hard to keep the gold market in London and restore the gold standard, but eventually they lost the battle. The construction of Rand Refinery Ltd. and the South African mint, and the establishment of an independent South African reserve bank, allowed South African gold producers to sell their gold wherever they could obtain the best price, meaning that more and more gold was now traded independent of the London gold fixing.

In this context, the belief that reestablishing the gold market in London and restoring the gold standard would also restore the pre-eminent position of the City in the world financial system proved an illusion. The credit policy that backed the gold standard did not make

---

[43] Draft Memorandum on Gold Market 1937, Rothschild Archives, XI/35/64.

the financial system stronger, but increased its vulnerability to short-term outflows of money. Other factors, such as the importance of a British export industry that could hardly compete with its European and American counterparts when the currency was substantially overvalued, had been underestimated as well. In the end, the London gold market lost its primacy – although it still managed to retain a central position in the world's gold trade.[44]

[44] Churchill was thus not wrong in observing, in his budget speech in the House of Commons, 28 April 1925, that England 'is the centre of the Empire, and...in spite of all its burdens, has still retained, if not the primacy, at any rate the central position, in the financial systems of the world'. Sayers, *Bank of England*, III, 84.

7

The Boundaries of Western Power

The Colonial Cotton Economy in India and the Problem of Quality

Christof Dejung

Between December 1911 and January 1912, Arno Schmidt Pearse, the secretary of the International Federation of Master Cotton Spinners and Manufacturers, visited India to gather firsthand information on cotton cultivation and trade on the subcontinent. In his report, he revealed shock at certain practices he had encountered. 'In India, many fraudulent customs are common in the handling of cotton, probably more than in any other country', he wrote. He had found evidence that seeds of different cotton types were mixed before sowing, rendering more difficult the growth of high-quality long-stapled cotton varieties. Furthermore, he had observed that Indian cotton was regularly watered in certain regions to raise its weight and that cotton bales were often tampered with by enclosing dirt, stones, cotton waste or lower quality cotton in them. It was evident 'that every spinner who receives such cotton sustains a heavy loss'.[1]

How could it be that Indian cotton was still being offered in such a deplorable state on the world market at the beginning of the twentieth century, more than five decades after the onset of direct British rule on the subcontinent? Why were the British not able to counter practices so obviously damaging for Western industry? What role did quality play in the cotton industry, and how did attributes of a certain kind of cotton – for instance, the length of the staple – influence the geographical reach of

[1] Arno Schmidt Pearse, *Baumwollkultur in Indien. Bericht über Reise nach Indien, Dezember 1911–Januar 1912*, hg. vom Internationalen Verband der Baumwoll-Spinner- und-Weber-Vereinigungen (no place or year), 34 and 84 f.

I would like to thank Sven Beckert, Harold James, Claude Markovits and Niels P. Petersson for their comments on earlier versions of this chapter.

markets on which it could be traded? This chapter addresses these questions, which lead to related questions of imperial rule and indigenous agency; of the differing agendas maintained by colonial bureaucrats, European merchant houses and Indian traders and peasants; and of the development of non-European industries in colonial times. I argue that, although the nineteenth- and twentieth-century global economy was unquestionably dominated by expanding European political and economic power, global economic relations were nonetheless shaped even then by local conditions and power structures.

Thus this chapter focuses on processes of 'glocalization', as Roland Robertson has termed such entanglements of local and global structures, and it investigates Arjun Appadurai's claim that with globalisation the global often 'did not eliminate the local, but that the local and the global "cannibalized" each other'.[2] Such effects can be witnessed in the efforts by European powers to promote the growth of cotton in their colonial possessions in the second part of the nineteenth century. European industrialists and governments were particularly motivated to increase their cotton production by the cotton famine that broke out during the American Civil War. As Sven Beckert has indicated, the decades after Appomattox saw a new round of state intervention and an unprecedented commitment of states to secure raw materials and markets for their domestic cotton industries. However, integration into the global cotton economy of such countries as Egypt, India, Togo and Turkmenistan required new ways of incorporating indigenous agricultural labour into world capitalism; because after the end of the Civil War cotton production on plantations by slave labour became unsustainable, it also called for new ways of managing the relation between peasants and the land they were cultivating.[3] Such management was far from easy, partly because ignorance and misjudgment of local economic structures often handicapped colonial endeavours. In Africa for instance, colonial buying agencies sometimes aimed to purchase cotton at fixed prices that were below local market prices, so that peasants preferred selling their harvest

[2] Roland Robertson, 'Glocalization: Time-space and Homogeneity-Heterogeneity', in Mike Featherstone, Scott Lash and Roland Robertson (eds.), *Global Modernities* (London, 1995), 25–44; Arjun Appadurai, *Modernity at Large: Cultural Dimensions of Globalization* (Minneapolis, 2000).

[3] Sven Beckert, 'Emancipation and Empire. Reconstructing the Worldwide Web of Cotton Production in the Age of the American Civil War', *American Historical Review* 109 (2004), 1405–38; Sven Beckert, 'From Tuskegee to Togo: The Problem of Freedom in the Empire of Cotton', *Journal of American History* 92 (2005), 498–526.

to local traders rather than to Europeans. In other cases, African peasants were denied credit, the argument being that African cultivators were in no need of capital to cultivate their crop, whereas European settlers were provided ample advances for their farms. Furthermore, the Europeans antagonised local populations by forbidding cultivation of foodstuffs and by urging the peasantry to concentrate on cultivating cotton for export. It is no surprise, then, that many colonial cotton projects in sub-Saharan Africa were less successful than German, French or British officials had expected.[4]

Yet even where colonial powers were successful in raising the volume of raw cotton exports, as in British India, in part by employing the services of Indian merchant networks and Indian capital, they still had to worry about achieving the cotton quality demanded by textile industrialists at home. Industrial textile production required not only ever-growing quantities of cotton fibres but also distinct characteristics, varying widely depending on the country of origin, length of staple, colour and firmness. Whereas Indian and Chinese cotton traditionally had a short staple, American, Brazilian and Egyptian cotton had longer fibres, thus being suited for finer textiles of the sort produced in Lancashire. This was the reason the British were so eager to introduce long-stapled cotton varieties to India in the second part of the nineteenth century.[5] However, as indicated by the earlier cited complaints of Arno Schmidt Pearse and those that many British officials made in the course of the whole colonial period, the cultivation of high-quality cotton varieties was much more difficult than had been imagined in the mid-nineteenth century for two reasons: rural agriculture's social and economic complexity on the subcontinent and the consistent aversion of Indian merchants and peasants to the intrusion of the colonial bureaucracy.

It is clear that establishing an export-oriented colonial cotton economy had dramatic effects for India. In a seminal study, Laxman Satya has described how Indian peasants were urged to give up their subsistence-oriented and village-centred production methods and concentrate instead on cotton cultivation for the world market. As a result, they became

[4] Allen F. Isaacman, *Cotton Is the Mother of Poverty: Peasants, Work, and Rural Struggle in Colonial Mozambique, 1938–1961* (Portsmouth, 1996); Beckert, 'From Tuskegee to Togo'; Jonathan Robins, '"The Black Man's Crop"': Cotton, Imperialism and Public-Private Development in Britain's African Colonies, 1900–1918', *Commodities of Empire Working Paper* 11 (2009).

[5] Peter Harnetty, *Imperialism and Free Trade: Lancashire and India in the Mid-Nineteenth Century* (Manchester, 1972).

dependent on global market prices and could easily face starvation if the market and their revenues declined.[6] Despite this dependence and European export firms' market power after the 1860s, European control of the Indian cotton trade was much more restricted and much more inconsistent than Satya's analysis reveals. For a start, it was always influenced by the agency of indigenous merchants and peasants. As Chris Bayly, David Washbrooke and Rajat Kanta Ray have pointed out, throughout the colonial period Western merchants had to rely on Indian middlemen to do the spadework for them, because they were dependent on both the close social network of these middlemen and the peasantry and the financial capacity of Indian capitalists to raise agricultural credits.[7] Furthermore, European merchants and the colonial bureaucracy often disagreed about the extent to which the state should interfere with business. For this reason, establishment of the colonial cotton economy was a rather complex and ambiguous process, with European traders, colonial bureaucrats, Indian capitalists and Indian peasants interacting in various ways, sometimes leading to results unforeseen by the colonial government. To a considerable degree this reality explains why Indian peasants never produced the long-stapled cotton types required by the mills in Lancashire, Indian cotton thus being mostly consumed in mills on the European continent and, after the 1890s, in India and East Asia. Thus, when studying India's economic history in the colonial period, we had best not limit our view to the relationship between India and Britain, but should also consider that between the subcontinent and other parts of the world such as continental Europe, China and Japan.[8]

This chapter is organised into four sections. The first section shows that the colonial government's attempts to control the Indian cotton quality by legal means were hindered by the constant British fear of antagonising Indian merchants and peasants on the one hand and a lack of cooperation from European merchants on the other hand. The second section describes the changes in the cotton trade after the construction of the Indian railways and the establishment of telegraphic communication,

[6] Laxman D. Satya, *Cotton and Famine in Berar* (New Delhi, 1997).
[7] David A. Washbrook, 'Law, State and Society in Colonial India', *Modern Asian Studies* 15 (1981), 649–721; C. A. Bayly, *Rulers, Townsmen and Bazaars: North Indian Society in the Age of British Expansion, 1770–1870* (Cambridge, 1983); Rajat Kanta Ray, 'Asian Capital in the Age of European Domination: The Rise of the Bazaar, 1800–1914', *Modern Asian Studies* 29 (1995), 449–554.
[8] This argument is also made by Sven Beckert, 'Emancipation and Empire', 1421.

developments that allowed European merchants a backward integration of inland purchase and pushed Indian traders out of the export trade to Europe after the 1860s. In the third section, I argue that, although the Europeans gained control over the export trade, they were unable to interfere with the social and economic microcosm in the Indian hinterland. The fourth section discusses the improvement in cotton quality made by Indian industrialists after the First World War – something the colonial government had not been able to achieve throughout the nineteenth century. In light of the significant loss of European influence in the global cotton trade after 1918, I also argue that the interwar years were less a period of economic deglobalisation than of a de-Europeanization of the global.

Attempts to Control Cotton Quality on the Subcontinent Through Colonial Law

In the mid-nineteenth century, Great Britain was considered the 'workhouse of the world', producing about 20 per cent of global manufacturing output.[9] With the textile industry being of paramount importance, 'the one hundred millions of our capital, and the livelihood of near four millions of our countrymen' depended on the supply of raw cotton, as the British official James A. Mann remarked in 1860. It was, he continued, 'a matter so serious and of such magnitude, as to make the question one of the state'.[10] Yet at that time, about 80 per cent of all cotton consumed in the United Kingdom was imported from the United States. Because of tensions in that country between the North and the cotton-growing southern states, British industrialists became convinced that Lancashire should secure other sources for cotton.[11] Yet where was such a source to be found? In Mann's eyes, 'the only manner in which the certainty can be assured is in the liberal encouragement of the cultivation in our colonies, and in brief to have as many sources of supply, to guard against a local failure'.[12]

---

[9] Paul Bairoch, 'International Industrialization Levels from 1750 to 1980', *Journal of European Economic History* 11, 2 (1982), 296.

[10] James A. Mann, *The Cotton Trade of India: A Paper before the Royal Asiatic Society* (London, 1860), 3.

[11] Daniel R. Headrick, *The Tools of Empire: Technology and European Imperialism in the Nineteenth Century* (New York, 1981), 181.

[12] Mann, *The Cotton Trade of India*, 3 f.

India was the world's second largest supplier of cotton after the United States,[13] a fact that stimulated the imagination of British officials and industrialists alike. The annexation of the cotton-producing provinces of Berar and Nagpur in 1853 and the founding of the Cotton Supply Association in Manchester in 1857 were both driven by the wish to make India a reliable supplier for Lancashire.[14] Yet realisation of that plan proved much more difficult than anticipated, with the quality of the fibre, in particular, turning out to be a permanent nuisance for British officials. The botanist John Forbes Royle thus lamented that 'the gathering of the crop is everywhere careless' and that the 'cultivator, who, in many ways, seems to combine the independence of the freeman with the indifference of the slave, is . . . little interested in the quality, and seldom in the extension of his crop'. A further problem came from indigenous middlemen who 'with perverse ingenuity, seek . . . to change the nature of [their] purchase, and think . . . to add to its value by making additions to its weight'.[15] The resulting impurity of Indian cotton and its short staple were the reasons British spinners preferred the American plant for producing the fine cloth that was a speciality of Lancashire.[16] Hence if India was to replace the United States as a cotton supplier, cotton quality had to improve significantly.

Legislation was one way to achieve this goal: colonial governments generally used the introduction of European law to alter the economic conditions of their overseas possessions according to their own interests.[17] The British had tried to implement British commercial law on the sub-continent since the mid-eighteenth century. The first charters of the East India Company in the Presidency Towns had stipulated that if Hindus or Muslims were involved in a dispute, their respective laws had to be considered; British mercantile law could only be applied if all parties

---

[13] Clara Ratzka-Ernst, 'Welthandelsartikel und ihre Preise. Eine Studie zur Preisbewegung und Preisbildung' (n.p., ca. 1910), 236; Alonzo B. Cox, *Department Bulletin No. 1444: Cotton Prices and Markets* (Washington, 1926), 12.

[14] Harnetty, *Imperialism and Free Trade*, 4 and 36–40.

[15] J. Forbes Royle, *Culture and Commerce of Cotton in India and Elsewhere* (London, 1851), 60.

[16] Thomas Ellison, *A Hand-Book of the Cotton Trade: Or a Glance at the Past History, Present Condition, and Future Prospects of the Cotton Commerce of the World* (Liverpool, 1858), 37–9.

[17] Wolfgang J. Mommsen and Jaap A. de Moor (eds.), *European Expansion and Law: The Encounter of European and Indigenous Law in 19th and 20th Century Africa and Asia* (Oxford, 1992).

agreed.[18] What could have been a source of confusion worked rather well in practice. Right from the start, Indian merchants were willing to use British courts because they were considered efficient and fair, while at the same time continuing to rely on traditional indigenous business rules.[19] All in all, it seems that British mercantile law was not that different from indigenous trading customs. In 1845, Sir Lawrence Peel, Chief Justice of Bengal, could thus observe 'that the English law as to contracts . . . is so much in harmony with the Mahomedan and Hindoo laws as to Contracts that it very rarely happens in our courts . . . that any question arises on the law peculiar to those people in actions on contracts'. This is why the British decided to abandon the exclusion of certain ethnic groups from contract law in 1855.[20]

Yet mercantile law could act as a formal structure only for transactions between European and wealthy Indian merchants, who were both well educated and geared to a similar merchant's culture.[21] It did not succeed in regulating business with cultivators or petty traders upcountry and thus failed to improve the quality of cotton offered for sale in local Indian markets. Whereas commodities such as tea, coffee and indigo were produced on large plantations whose European owners were in direct contact with exporters and thus were unable to risk selling adulterated merchandise, the cotton trade was much more fragmented.[22] Indian cotton was cultivated by *ryots*, petty farmers who planted cotton in addition to other crops and were never able to gather more than one or two bales on their land. Because they lacked capital, they had to sell their crops in advance to local moneylenders who resold them later. The moneylenders, however, were not wealthy enough to do business without obtaining credit from traders in large inland towns; these inland traders in turn often acted as agents for wealthy Indian merchants from Bombay and other coastal cities. Hence until the construction of India's railway system, the country's cotton crop was transferred from owner to owner after harvest

---

[18] C. O. Remfry, *Commercial Law in British India* (Calcutta, 1912), 3 f.

[19] Sheila Smith, 'Fortune and Failure: The Survival of Family Firms in Eighteenth-Century India', *Business History* 35 (1993), 44–65; Ritu Birla, *Stages of Capital: Law, Culture, and Market Governance in Late Colonial India* (Durham, 2009).

[20] Quoted in George Claus Rankin, *Background to Indian Law* (Cambridge, 1946), 90.

[21] Bayly, *Rulers, Townsmen and Bazaars*, 3–6, 31, 239–42; Christof Dejung, 'Bridges to the East: European Merchants and Business Practices in India and China', in Robert Lee (ed.), *Commerce and Culture: Nineteenth-Century Business Elites* (Aldershot, 2011).

[22] J. Forbes Watson, *Report on Cotton Gins and on the Cleaning and Quality of Indian Cotton. Part I: Summary and Conclusion* (London, 1879), 162.

until finally arriving at the coast, from where it was shipped to Europe
or China. The *ryot* who sold his cotton in advance received no reward
for high quality and suffered no penalty for poor quality. He was simply
obliged to provide a certain quantity of cotton to the moneylender from
whom he had received an advance. The same was true for the other
dealers in the inland trade. And because cotton generally was sold by
weight, each owner was tempted to water it down or mix in dirt, seed
or lower quality cotton. Finally, because all cotton was equally adulterated before reaching the coast, the European or Indian merchants who
exported it to Europe and China had no choice but to accept it.[23]

In 1829, the British had unsuccessfully tried for the first time to eliminate these practices by legal means; with the manipulations meanwhile
intensifying, they made a new effort after India came under direct colonial
rule. In the 1860s, the British introduced the Cotton Fraud Act in Bombay, India's first export harbour for cotton. Yet this law never became
operative, because against the backdrop of the shock of the Mutiny of
1857, the colonial government was anxious not to provoke conflict with
Indian merchants and peasants. In any case the law not only encountered
resistance from Indians but also provoked opposition from the European
mercantile community. The Bombay and Manchester Chambers of Commerce were against it because the Indian government raised a duty on
every bale of cotton the officials examined, thus jeopardising the competitiveness of Indian cotton on the world market. Furthermore, merchants
argued that as long as East Asian and continental European spinners were
willing to purchase the cotton, government interference was not desirable.
For instance, Gaddum & Co., one of the most important cotton exporters
in the country, resisted the governmental order to clean several bales of
cotton in 1874 by claiming that the material's unclean condition posed
no problem because the firm took it into account by paying a lower price.
Paying a higher price for cleaned cotton had, the firm argued, already
been tested, with the result being 'that although the dirty cotton readily
found a market, we were quite unable to sell the cleaned cotton at a fair
price and had eventually to sell it at a very heavy loss'.[24] In a general

[23] Samuel Smith, *The Cotton Trade of India. Being a Series of Letters Written from Bombay in the Spring of 1863* (Liverpool, 1863), 12, 21 f., 28; Harnetty, *Imperialism and Free Trade*, 101 f.; Dietmar Rothermund, *Government, Landlord, and Peasant in India: Agrarian Relations under British Rule, 1865–1935* (Wiesbaden, 1978).
[24] Maharashtra State Archives, Mumbai (MSA), Revenue Department, 1874, vol. 26, no. 658: Cotton – Complaint made by Messers. Gaddum & Co. against the Cotton Inspector at Dhollera for seizing eight bales of cotton of low quality purchased by them: Letter

manner the merchants complained that the government was penalising the wrong party: the *ryots* and village middlemen responsible for the adulterations hardly ever were prosecuted, whereas the exporters who had done nothing wrong were held accountable.[25] For the government, this opposition from the European mercantile community was quite frustrating. In 1869, an inspector from the Bombay Cotton Department thus complained about 'the extreme sensitiveness generally exhibited by the European and Native cotton exporters to our interference with their cotton, which is permitted only on sufferance, not as a matter of right'.[26] As a result of the persistent opposition, the Cotton Fraud Act was withdrawn in 1882.[27]

Because governmental regulations had not worked out, both British officials and European merchants placed their hopes on Bombay business circles being able to organise a system of quality control on their own. Such a system had been established in the American cotton trade in the mid-1870s, after European merchants had complained about adulteration and contamination of cotton deliveries similar to that occurring in India. The pressure of European merchants – who had threatened to boycott deliveries from ports that did not attend to the problem – had been strong enough for controls to be implemented on every bale of cotton shipped from ports in the American South. The American system differed from the one implemented in India by dispensing with any legislative sanction or government agency; the bylaws and constitutions of the various American cotton exchanges had to be consistent solely with the laws of the United States and the federal state in question.[28] At the same time, measures were introduced on the authority of the cotton exchanges alone, and the exchanges also appointed supervisors and levied fees.[29]

from Messrs. Gaddum & Co., Bombay, to the Chief Secretary to Government, Revenue Department, Bombay, 25th February 1874.

[25] MSA, Revenue Department, 1875, vol. 27, no. 501: Cotton – Report of the Commission appointed to enquire into the working of the Cotton Frauds Act, Part I: Report of the Commissioners to enquire into the working of the Cotton Frauds Act (of 1863); with minutes of evidence and other appendices, Bombay 1875: Government Central Press – Appendix A: Minutes of Evidence.

[26] MSA, Revenue Department, 1869, vol. 8, no. 90: Cotton – Report on the working of the Cotton Fraud Department for 1868–69, Appendix H: J. H. Merritt, Inspector of Cotton, Bombay, to G.F. Forbes, Esq., Officiating Inspector-in-Chief, Cotton Department, Bombay, May 28, 1869.

[27] Harnetty, *Imperialism and Free Trade*; Charles W. MacAra, *Trade Stability and How to Obtain It* (Manchester, 1925), 204–6.

[28] Cox, Department Bulletin No. 1444, 25.

[29] Watson, *Report on Cotton Gins*, 163.

There were several reasons why a control system like that in the United
States did not take root on the subcontinent, despite the similarities
between the structure of the cotton trade in the American South and
in India. As in India, many American tenants – former slaves freed at the
end of the Civil War and poor white farmers who had migrated from
the East Coast – were in debt to merchants from the country's interior
or local shop owners and thus had to fear dispossession.[30] Also as in
India, until the late nineteenth century, trading in the American interior
was characterised by a chain of commission agents who delivered the raw
cotton to Europe and to factories in the industrialised North. It was only
in the 1880s that merchant houses such as Alexander Sprunt and Son
initiated commercial relations between the cotton fields and factories by
opening up buying agencies, gins, presses and warehouses in the cotton
districts.[31]

Despite these parallels, the establishment of an agrarian capitalism
had been successful in the United States, whereas it failed in India, not
least because capitalist entrepreneurs did not have to deal with the same
local mercantile structures in America as on the subcontinent. From the
beginning, American cotton was cultivated for consumption on the global
market. The country's plantations were generally bigger than those in
India, which increased the uniformity of the crop and made control easier.
Whereas some Indian cultivators could gather only a half-bale of cotton
on their land annually, the average American farm had an annual harvest
of ten bales, with no farm producing less than three.[32] Furthermore, the
regulations of the American cotton exchanges were much easier to enforce
than those of India's colonial government or the Bombay Chamber of
Commerce. On the subcontinent, cultivators were extremely suspicious
of governmental interference. In addition, language barriers complicated
communication, corruption was widespread, and officials always had to
consider the political situation – as indicated, they could not afford to

[30] Joseph P. Reidy, *From Slavery to Agrarian Capitalism in the Cotton Plantation South:
Central Georgia, 1800–1880* (Chapel Hill, 1992), 222–47; Jürgen Osterhammel, *Die
Verwandlung der Welt. Eine Geschichte des 19. Jahrhunderts* (Munich, 2009), 997.
[31] John R. Killick, 'The Transformation of Cotton Marketing in the Late Nineteenth Cen-
tury. Alexander Sprunt and Son of Wilmington, N.C., 1884–1956', *Business History
Review* 55 (1981), 146–53.
[32] Alston Hill Garside, *Cotton Goes to Market: A Graphic Description of a Great Industry*
(New York, 1935), 35; Watson, Report on Cotton Gins, 159–65; Arno S. Pearse, *The
Cotton Industry of India being the Report of the Journey to India* (Manchester, 1930),
31.

antagonise the indigenous mercantile community. Whereas the cotton economy on the subcontinent suffered from the lack of a basic social consensus within the colonial framework,[33] in the second part of the nineteenth century the needs of American cotton merchants and spinners were sustained by a general transformation of the United States into a capitalist economy.

The Realignment of the Indian Cotton Trade after the 1860s

Although colonial legislation did not have the desired effect on the Indian cotton trade, the acceleration of transport and communications fundamentally altered both the inland and export trade after the 1860s. With the outbreak of the American Civil War and the disruption of cotton deliveries from the southern states, the British government, working together with British capitalists, moved to import cotton gins and presses and build roads and railway lines to make India a steady supplier of cotton to Lancashire.[34] Stimulated by high cotton prices during the Civil War, cotton production on the subcontinent had begun to boom. Although prices went back to their regular level at the war's end, cotton production continued to expand after 1865. Overall, production increased on the subcontinent from 226 million pounds annually in the 1850s to 920 million pounds in the decade after 1910.[35]

The economic integration at work between various countries from the 1850s onward has been often described as the first wave of globalisation, and hence a precursor of a development that would characterise the late twentieth century. Approached from this perspective, the efforts of the British colonial government in India seem double-edged: on the one hand, they were clearly aimed at reducing American cotton imports and securing cotton production within the empire, a process that would have interfered with the Atlantic cotton trade, one of the most important sectors of international trade at that time. They can thus be regarded as an act of imperial mercantilism standing in stark contrast to the ideology of free trade then prevailing in Britain. On the other hand, the British efforts

---

[33] Jürgen Osterhammel, 'Symbolpolitik und imperiale Integration. Das britische Empire im 19. und 20. Jahrhundert', in Bernhard Giesen, Jürgen Osterhammel and Rudolf Schlögl (eds.), *Die Wirklichkeit der Symbole* (Konstanz, 2004), 401.

[34] Smith, *The Cotton Trade of India*; Harnetty, *Imperialism and Free Trade*; Beckert, 'Emancipation and Empire'.

[35] Beckert, 'Emancipation and Empire', 1423.

integrated ever more producing areas on the subcontinent into the world
market and were thus indeed a significant aspect of the unfolding of global
capitalism.

In any case, the establishment of a colonial cotton economy fundamentally altered the structure of the Indian cotton trade. Until the late
1860s, the major part of that business was controlled by indigenous merchants, who not only organised the inland trade from the cotton-growing
areas to the coast but were also responsible for half of the cotton transports to Liverpool, which before the opening of the Suez Canal was the
only significant European inlet for Indian raw cotton. The vast majority
of these exports were organised on consignment. Because most European
merchant houses established in India were not wealthy enough to export
on their own account, they had to rely on advances from European spinners or from wealthy Indian merchants acting as guarantee brokers.[36]

The construction of the Indian railway network allowed European
exporters to bypass the indigenous merchants who until then had transported the merchandise to the coast. After the opening of the first line
between Bombay and Thana in 1853, the network grew rapidly. In the
1880s, it already covered 10,000 miles and connected not only all major
towns on the subcontinent but also the upcountry cotton districts with the
harbour cities on the coast.[37] From that point on, European merchants
were able to come into direct contact with dealers in those districts, something they had tried to do since the early 1800s but had failed at because
of poor transport conditions and the difficulty of providing inland agents
with adequate sums of ready cash.[38] In addition to benefitting from an
increasing number of buying agencies in that region, in the second half of
the 1860s European trading firms began to build up ginning and pressing
factories for preparing the raw cotton for transport to Europe.

By the late 1800s, large European merchant houses had gained overall
control of the greatest part of the commodity chain, involving purchase
of the raw material, ginning and pressing, and export.[39] The opening

[36] Marika Vicziany, 'Bombay Merchants and Structural Changes in the Export Community
1850 to 1880', in Kirti N. Chaudhuri and Clive J. Dewey (eds.), *Economy and Society: Essays in Indian Economy and Social History* (Delhi, 1979), 170–75; August F.
Ammann, *Reminiscences of an Old V.B. Partner* (Winterthur, 1921), 8–10.
[37] Headrick, *The Tentacles of Progress*, 62; Rothermund, *Government, Landlord, and
Peasant*, 17; Brian Roger Tomlinson, *The Economy of Modern India, 1860–1970*
(Cambridge, 1993), 55 f.
[38] Bayly, *Rulers, Townsmen and Bazaars*, 249–45.
[39] Kagotani Naoto, 'Up-Country Purchase Activities of Indian Raw Cotton by Toyo
Menka's Bombay Branch, 1896–1935', in Shinya Sugiyama and Linda Grove (eds.),

of upcountry buying agencies in India gave them more direct access to producers. The establishment of certain standardised types of cotton in the 1870s – classified according to colour, length of staple and firmness – transformed the business, bringing Indian cotton standards into line with one of the most important set of standards in the global trade, that used on the Liverpool cotton exchange. Negotiations between merchants and spinners could now be based on some common understanding about the quality of the goods on sale.[40]

The establishment of telegraph communication between Europe and India in 1865 further promoted a commercial realignment, leading to the introduction of firm offers in place of consignments. This communication advance enabled European spinners to know which cotton qualities were on the market and at what price they were being offered by the various trading companies. Offers for consignment were increasingly difficult to obtain, because, as a former employee of the Swiss trading company Volkart Bros. put it in his memoirs, 'why, indeed, should intending buyers bind their hands by giving orders of which they could not foresee whether they would prove workable or not, when they could make sure of having the goods they were in need of by accepting the most tempting of the firm offers laid before them'?[41] Both the introduction of such price lists and the drawing up of contracts by telegraph also had an impact on how the cotton trade was financed. Purchasers no longer had to grant advances, as they had done in on-consignment trade until the 1860s; rather, they paid when their merchandise arrived in Europe. However, after the early 1870s, because of the ever-rising volume of raw cotton shipped from Indian ports, credit from Indian guarantee brokers was no longer adequate for financing cotton exports. To counter the strain on liquidity, European exporters from then on had to rely on credit from European commercial and merchant banks, which were much better prepared to finance shipments of such quantities on a global scale.[42]

The decades after 1850 saw a drastic rise in cotton exports, with the technological innovations of the 1860s reducing price differences between

---

Commercial Networks in Modern Asia (Richmond, 2001), 205–08; Rajat Kanta Ray, 'The Bazaar: Changing Structural Characteristics of the Indigenous Section of the Indian Economy before and after the Great Depression', *Indian Economic and Social History Review* 25 (1988), 286.

[40] *Calculationstabellen Gebrüder Volkart Winterthur* (Winterthur, 1873), 14.
[41] Ammann, *Reminiscences of an Old V.B. Partner*, 10.
[42] Vicziany, 'Bombay Merchants and Structural Changes', 167–81.

India and Europe. Economies of scale thus became increasingly important in the cotton trade. Consequently, a rapid consolidation process took
place in the 1870s. Small and medium-sized exporters were pushed aside,
while the more successful traders emerged as multinational firms with
huge turnover and with agencies in both the producing areas and spinning districts of the industrialised nations. By the late nineteenth century,
the leading export houses such as Volkart and the Anglo-Greek Ralli
Bros. shipped between 50,000 and 100,000 bales of cotton annually,
representing about 10 per cent of all cotton exports from the subcontinent to Europe.[43] To counter the ever-present danger of price fluctuations that could easily bankrupt the firms because of their huge turnover,
European merchants began to hedge their transactions at the Liverpool
cotton exchanges. Standardised cotton types were indispensable for such
operations on the futures markets, which remain only possible when the
goods traded are fungible – that is, when a merchant requires goods
of a certain specified quality regardless of origin, rather than specific
goods.[44]

The realignment of the Indian cotton trade shifted the balance between
Indian and European merchants. Whereas Indian merchants had accounted for a substantial share of cotton exports to China and Europe and had
extended credit to both European and Indian exporters, they were unable
to follow the changes in export trade after the 1860s. Unlike Western –
and, after the turn of the century, Japanese – trading firms, they lacked the
resources to invest in the establishment of buying agencies, ginning and
pressing factories, and warehouses in the country's interior. They found
it much more difficult than the Europeans to hedge their transactions at
the European cotton exchanges and obtain credit from European banks.
European merchants could raise metropolitan capital at a cheaper rate
than Indian traders, offering an advantage in financing exports. Using
such resources to establish greater control over the commodity chain and
exploiting the institutional innovations of modern finance, European and
Japanese traders took a dominant position in the Indian cotton trade
starting in the early twentieth century. Indian merchants had to look

---

[43] *Reports of the Bombay Chamber of Commerce for the Year 1898*; *The V.B. News, Pub-
    lished by Volkart Brothers, Winterthur, and Devoted to the Interests of their Employees*,
    no. 9, December 1923, 14–16.
[44] For the emergence of the cotton futures market see Nigel Hall, 'The Liverpool Cotton
    Market: Britain's First Futures Market', *Transactions of the Historic Society of Lan-
    cashire and Cheshire* 149 (1999), 99–117. For an overview of the role of hedging in the
    global cotton trade see Garside, *Cotton Goes to Market*, 208–75 and 307–14.

for different opportunities to invest their capital, which they found, for example, in industrial production or in granting credit for domestic trade and agricultural production.[45]

The Failure of Colonial Hopes

As indicated, making India a steady supplier of cotton for the Lancashire mills was one of the main reasons why the British government and British capitalists built railways, telegraph lines and roads on the subcontinent. In the eyes of many Westerners, this infrastructure development was not an act of economic exploitation but a step to modernise the country and a prerequisite for its industrial development.[46] However, the colonial situation in India and the scarcity there of capital rendered the establishment of what Europeans would have considered a suitable cotton market very difficult. Whereas they were able to control the many thousands of miles linking various gathering places – *mandis* – in the Indian interior and the spinning factories in Europe, they were completely incapable of controlling the first ten to twenty miles of the commodity chain between the cotton fields and the *mandis*, something they had not expected when setting out to open South Asia for business. The extent of their illusions is illustrated in an 1848 observation by John Chapman, promoter of the Great Indian Peninsular Railway, to the effect that many British merchants considered the railways of India 'nothing more than an extension of their own line from Manchester to Liverpool'.[47]

When it came to the cotton trade, the British were convinced that installation of a modern infrastructure would lead to the elimination of the middlemen who had made business so troublesome and hence to the emergence of an efficient market. Initially, this seemed to happen: for example, the British trading firm of W. Nichol & Co. informed C. F. Forbes, the colonial cotton commissioner, in 1868 that due to the construction of a railway line to Bombay, the quality of cotton from Berar had improved significantly. The company was convinced that the same development would take place in Dharwar, 'were they blessed with Railway communication with the Coast. . . . The Ryots would be brought

---

[45] Vicziany, 'Bombay Merchants and Structural Changes', 163–96; Rajnarayan Chandav-arkar, *The Origins of Industrial Capitalism in India: Business Strategies and the Working Classes in Bombay, 1900–1940* (Cambridge, 1994), 45–52 and 61.

[46] Headrick, *The Tools of Empire*, 181–88.

[47] Cited after David Thorner, *Investment in Empire: British Railway and Steam Shipping Enterprise in India, 1825–1849* (Philadelphia, 1950), 96.

into direct communication with the agent of the Bombay purchasers, and would speedily see that it was to his advantage to bring his Cotton to market well cleaned and of good quality'.[48] Several years later, J. K. Bythell, chairman of the Bombay Chamber of Commerce, was pleased to note that in the cotton markets of Kangaum and Oomrawutnee, 'every morning during the season . . . a very large number of the ryots bargain directly with the European buyer and discuss as keenly and acutely as any one the latest news from Liverpool as given by Reuters daily in these markets'.[49]

However, it was not long before these high hopes proved to be wishful thinking. Throughout the colonial period, European trading firms had rarely purchased directly from cultivators in the cotton districts but continued to rely on local intermediaries.[50] Many of these were petty traders or moderately wealthy peasants who borrowed money from Indian merchants to act as *sowkars* (rural moneylenders) and give loans to the *ryots*. Initially, European exporters tried to circumvent the moneylenders and purchase directly from the peasants. However, from their strong position in the villages, the *sowkars* could counter these efforts with a strategy of noncooperation,[51] a strategy that eventually forced the Europeans to cooperate with them. The Europeans gained from using moneylenders in several ways: first the *sowkars* were better placed than they were to assess the solvency of the *ryots*, and they were in a much better position to collect debts.[52] Second, no European merchant had the capital necessary for offering advances to thousands of cotton planters. The notion, suggested by several historians, that Western exporters provided the credit for agricultural production in India is thus inaccurate.[53] Merchant houses established in India, such as Volkart, Ralli and – after the turn of the century – the Japanese trading firm Toyo Menkwa, only paid for inland

---

[48] MSA, Revenue Department, 1868, Vol. 4, No. 844: Cotton – Cotton cultivation and trade in the Southern Maratha Country: Letter of W. Nichol and Co. to C.F. Forbes, Cotton Commissioner, Bombay, 29th July 1868.

[49] MSA, Revenue Department, 1874, Vol. 27, No. 351: Cotton – Opinion of Officer of Cotton Dept. in reference of the statement made by the Bombay Chamber of Commerce on the present state of the Mofussil cotton trade: Letter from J. K. Bythell, chairman of the Bombay Chamber of Commerce, Bombay, to the Chief Secretary to Government, Revenue Department, Bombay, 11th March 1874.

[50] See M. L. Dantwala, *Marketing of Raw Cotton in India* (Calcutta, 1937), 31.

[51] Satya, *Cotton and Famine in Berar*, 242.

[52] Chandavarkar, *The Origins of Industrial Capitalism*, 50; Dantwala, *Marketing of Raw Cotton in India*, 114–16.

[53] Tomlinson, *The Economy of Modern India*, 68; Satya, *Cotton and Famine in Berar*, 126 f.; Beckert, 'Emancipation and Empire', 1425.

cotton deliveries at the moment of arrival in the ginning factories; long-term advances to the peasants came solely from *sowkars*.[54] In this way the colonial cotton economy depended to a considerable extent on cooperation between merchants from Europe and India, enabling the European trading firms to purchase the crop within the country. European merchants avoided giving risky advances to the peasants and instead relied on the intermediary role of the Indian mercantile community to connect the rural Indian economy with the world market controlled by European trading firms.[55]

However, the strong position of the *sowkars* did pose fundamental problems for the colonial cotton economy as a whole. After the mid-nineteenth century, Indian agriculture began to lose its self-sustaining character. Both moneylenders and colonial bureaucrats urged cultivators, who traditionally worked to meet the needs of the local rural economy, to grow cotton for the world market. Moneylenders were eager to provide agricultural credit to peasants, to be repaid with excessive interest; colonial bureaucrats were interested in augmenting cotton production on the subcontinent and receiving real estate taxes, which the peasants had to pay after the introduction of colonial land reforms. The establishment of an export-oriented agricultural system altered the relation between peasants and rural moneylenders in a basic way. The *sowkars* had provided agricultural credits for many centuries. However, in the precolonial period – and also in the princely states during colonial times – the authorities had introduced checks to prevent their profiteering, oblige them to sustain peasant families when they ran out of food, and provide seed-grain for the next harvest. As David Hardiman has indicated, the colonial cotton economy, based on free-market ideology, severed such social ties, which had stabilised the relation between creditors and agricultural labour in the rural areas, thereby destroying the 'moral economy' of the villages. As a consequence, during periods of scarcity grain riots became a far more likely possibility in areas under direct British rule

[54] *Minutes of Evidence taken before the Indian Cotton Committee: Volume IV: Commercial. Part I: Minutes of evidence from United Provinces, Central Provinces, Burma, Sind and Bombay; Volume V: Commercial. Part II: Minutes of Evidence from Madras, Bengal, Imperial Officers, Central India, Baroda and Hyderabad* (Calcutta, 1920).

[55] Ray, 'The Bazaar'. In the early nineteenth century a similar interdependency had existed between indigenous moneylenders and shroffs on the one hand and the British East India Company on the other hand: Asiya Siddiqi, 'Some Aspects of Indian Business under the East India Company', in Dwijendra Tripathi (ed.), *State and Business in India: A Historical Perspective* (New Delhi, 1987), 79.

than they had been in the past and were more frequent than in the princely states.[56]

Throughout the colonial period, British officials lamented the indebtedness of the peasants, who were, according to a British observer from 1861, 'little better then slaves to the money lending class'.[57] Yet in condemning the *sowkars* for their purported extortion, the British failed to grasp the deeper causes of the problem, especially the fact that the colonial state was unable to provide any alternative system of agricultural credit and had to rely on the funds of indigenous merchants to finance cotton cultivation. The idea of India as a paradise for indigenous middlemen, whose chokehold on the peasants was responsible for the poor state of Indian cotton, thus represents a Western projection, as Neil Charlesworth has argued. That idea fails to take account of the considerable risks the *sowkars* had to take on, such as the permanent risk of a bad harvest due to the failure of the monsoon or the risk of price fluctuations on the world market.[58] Consequently, it is unlikely that the rural moneylenders could make substantial profits – in contrast to those taken in by European merchant firms and a thin layer of upper-class Indian merchants.[59] The colonial state also contributed to the situation by introducing colonial courts that could be used by the *sowkars* to keep the illiterate peasants in check. Although the moneylenders hardly ever brought an insolvent cultivator to court because they aimed for control of agricultural production and not for possession of their property, the threat of a trial was certainly an intimidating factor.[60]

Another example of how the British altered the rural microcosm in ways they had not foreseen involves the introduction of land rights; that is, the provision of land-title deeds to the peasants. Even when given these deeds, however, the peasants were not considered outright owners, but rather tenants of the state who could be ousted from their holdings if they failed to pay their land tax. This was a radical departure from the previous system, in which the state was not considered to have any general right to dispossess peasant proprietors.[61] The new system brought about

---

[56] David Hardiman, 'Usury, Dearth and Famine in Western India', *Past and Present* 152 (1996), 113–56.

[57] Smith, *The Cotton Trade of India*, 20.

[58] Neil Charlesworth, *Peasants and Imperial Rule: Agriculture and Agrarian Society in the Bombay Presidency, 1850–1935* (Cambridge, 1985), 83 f. and 89.

[59] Satya, *Cotton and Famine in Berar*, 197.

[60] Ibid., 208 f.; Rothermund, *Government, Landlord, and Peasant*, 17.

[61] Hardiman, 'Usury, Dearth and Famine in Western India', 125.

an additional change in the relation between peasants and *sowkars*. The peasants had to take out credit to pay their land taxes, in addition to loans for seed and agricultural equipment. They obtained the needed credit by selling their crop to the *sowkars* in advance at a fixed price, often even before it was sown. For their loans, the moneylenders demanded interest rates starting at more than 30 per cent a year. If the cultivators failed to deliver the stipulated amount of cotton after harvest – which was not unlikely because of the perpetual menace of drought – they had to take out another loan, which of course reinforced their dependency on the *sowkars*. As a result the vast majority of cultivators were deeply in debt, with moneylenders controlling up to 80 per cent of the cotton crop in the villages.[62]

The permanent indebtedness of the cultivators was the main reason the quality of Indian cotton remained low despite the colonial government's efforts. The cultivators had no reason to reap cotton carefully, because the crop was already in the possession of the moneylenders. Often it was left on the ground for several days before being gathered. In contrast, the grain still in possession of the peasants was always harvested with care.[63]

The British were unsuccessful in other respects as well. They failed in their introduction of new cotton varieties into India that were particularly suited for the requirements of Lancashire. After the 1860s, for instance, the colonial government aimed to promote the growth of Dharwar American, a long-stapled type of cotton; however, it neglected the fact that in the Indian climate, traditional cotton types had the advantages of growing faster and being easier to gather, thus producing higher yields, so that the new variety could not generate higher profits, despite its higher value. In addition, the seeds of American Dharwar were constantly being mixed with the Indian cotton variety called *kumpta*. In part this mixing occurred by neglect; in part it was a deliberate process because the mixed seeds could be sold as American Dharwar and thereby obtain a higher price than the Indian varieties. Finally, none of the economic actors involved in the Indian cotton trade – neither European merchants nor Indian traders and peasants – understood why they should bother to adopt new cotton varieties when the traditional short-stapled types were finding an ever-growing demand outside the country.

[62] Satya, *Cotton and Famine in Berar*, 208–28; Rothermund, *Government, Landlord, and Peasant*, 17.
[63] Satya, *Cotton and Famine in Berar*, 241.

The End of European Dominance after the Turn of the Century

Because the British were not able to control the social and commercial realities in the Indian hinterland, India never became the source of raw material for Lancashire mills that the colonial bureaucrats had envisioned. Soon after the end of the American Civil War, British spinners were again using American cotton in their factories.[64] All told, only 3 per cent of cotton exports from India went to Great Britain at the end of the nineteenth century.[65] Although British administrators still lamented the poor quality of Indian cotton,[66] this became less and less an urgent issue for the government. By the century's turn, the textile industry was no longer a leading sector in the British economy because of the development of businesses tied to the 'Second Industrial Revolution' such as machine production and the manufacture of chemicals. India was still important as an outlet for British manufactured goods, but no longer as a cotton-producing area. For its part, Indian cotton was increasingly aligned with industrial powers outside the British Empire. Since the 1850s, it had found a good market on the European continent, but after the 1890s it was increasingly consumed in Japan. In addition, China had represented an important market for Indian cotton since precolonial times, and in the late nineteenth century that market was augmented by the newly established Chinese textile industry. The fabric was attractive to both China and Japan because it was significantly cheaper than its American equivalent; furthermore, continental and East Asian mills had installed machinery particularly well suited for the use of Indian cotton.[67]

The onset of Asian industrialisation and the development of a proper textile industry at the end of the nineteenth century had a huge impact on the Indian cotton trade. The number of spindles in Japanese cotton mills, for instance, increased from 76,000 in 1887 to more than 970,000 in 1897.[68] Because Indian cotton had, as indicated, become very popular in Japan, most of the raw fabric went to that country rather than Europe after 1897.[69] For European merchants, exporting to Japan was extremely troublesome, in part because of protectionist measures imposed at the

---

[64] Ellison, *A Hand-Book of the Cotton Trade*, 39.

[65] *Reports of the Bombay Chamber of Commerce for the Year 1908*, 135.

[66] See F. I. Macara, *Trade Stability and How to Obtain It*, 204–06.

[67] Harnetty, *Imperialism and Free Trade*, 83–100.

[68] Gary Saxonhouse and Yukihiko Kiyokawa, 'Supply and Demand for Quality Workers in Cotton Spinning in Japan and India', in Michael Smitka (ed.), *The Textile Industry and the Rise of the Japanese Economy* (New York, 1998), 183 f.

[69] Volkart Archives, Winterthur, Dossier 3: Bombay I, 4. Table of Events 1851–1961/2.

end of the nineteenth century, which for instance encouraged Japanese spinners to use only Japanese vessels for cotton shipments. Furthermore, Japanese cotton trading firms were part of huge industrial conglomerates, the so-called *zaibatsu*, which owned industrial facilities, banks and trading houses. Because cotton trading firms and mills belonged to the same corporate group, Japanese traders could offer conditions to the country's mills with which the Europeans could not compete. As a result, the three largest Japanese trading houses – Toyo Menkwa, Nippon Menkwa and Gosho, which had established their own buying organisations in India at the turn of the century – were responsible for 80 per cent of all imports of raw cotton into Japan.[70] In China as well, the Europeans had to leave the majority of cotton imports to Japanese firms, not least of all because the Chinese textile industry was largely in Japanese hands.[71] The Japanese put European cotton merchants under pressure not only in East Asia but also on their home turf by opening branches in India, Africa, the Americas and Europe.[72] As a consequence, Japanese traders controlled about 15 per cent of Indian cotton exports to Europe at the end of the 1920s. In 1930, a British observer thus warned in the *Journal of the Royal Statistical Society*, 'If Lancashire does not look out she will soon have to buy her Indian cotton from Japanese firms'.[73]

The first three decades of the twentieth century also saw a growth of textile production within India. As a result, consumption of Indian cotton increased from 1.8 million bales in 1923–24 to 2.7 million bales in 1935–36.[74] All these developments naturally affected the direction of the Indian cotton trade. Whereas in 1908 more than 30 per cent of cotton delivered

[70] Barnard Ellinger and Hugh Ellinger, 'Japanese Competition in the Cotton Trade', *Journal of the Royal Statistical Society* 18 (1930), 195–201; Naoto, 'Up-Country Purchase Activities of Indian Raw Cotton', 199 f.; David J. Jeremy, 'Organization and Management in the Global Cotton Industry, 1800s–1990s', in Douglas A. Farnie and David J. Jeremy (eds.), *The Fibre that Changed the World: The Cotton Industry in International Perspective, 1600–1990s* (Oxford, 2004), 204–16.

[71] Jürgen Osterhammel, *China und die Weltgesellschaft. Vom 18. Jahrhundert bis in unsere Zeit* (Munich, 1989), 264.

[72] Ellinger and Ellinger, 'Japanese Competition in the Cotton Trade', 198; John R. Killick, 'Specialized and General Trading Firms in the Atlantic Cotton Trade, 1820–1980', in Shin'ichi Yonekawa and Hideki Yoshihara (eds.), *Business History of General Trading Companies* (Tokyo, 1987), 263.

[73] Ellinger and Ellinger, 'Japanese Competition in the Cotton Trade', 201. For the market shares of different trading companies in the cotton export from Bombay to Japan, China and Europe in the season of 1925–26, see Dorabjee B. Contractor, *A Handbook of Indian Cotton for Merchants, Shippers, Mills, Factory-Owners and Others Interested in the Cotton Trade* (Bombay, 1928), 38 f.

[74] East India Cotton Association, *Bombay Cotton Annual No. 17*, (Bombay, 1935/36), 95.

from the Indian interior to Bombay was exported to continental Europe, the figure had dwindled to 15 per cent by 1926. In contrast, 50 per cent of all cotton from Bombay then went to Japan and 10 per cent to China, with roughly 25 per cent being consumed in Indian mills. Exports to Great Britain hardly ever surpassed 5 per cent.[75] In addition, the mills in India, China and Japan began to produce increasingly fine-quality cloth for which the traditionally short-stapled Indian cotton was not suited. Asian spinners thus purchased ever greater quantities of long-stapled cotton from Egypt and the United States.[76] Most of these imports were under the auspices of non-European merchants, with American cotton traders such as Anderson Clayton and McFadden opening selling agencies not only in Europe but also in China and Japan after the end of the First World War.[77] In turn, Japanese trading houses such as Toyo Menkwa and Nippon Menkwa opened agencies in the United States to export American cotton to East Asia during the interwar years.[78]

At the same time, European trading firms such as Volkart and Ralli that until then had confined their operations to the trade between Europe and the subcontinent were beginning to expand their activities globally. Volkart, for example, opened up new subsidiaries in China, Japan and the United States in the 1920s, becoming one of the main importers of American cotton to Asia after 1930.[79] Many of these trading firms had to trim back their organisation after the fall of raw material prices on the global markets after 1924 and particularly after the beginning of the Great Depression. The price for raw cotton dwindled to one quarter of its value between 1924 and 1932.[80] After huge losses in 1931, Ralli, for many

[75] *Reports of the Bombay Chamber of Commerce*, 1898 to 1931.
[76] Rajat Kanta Ray, *Industrialization in India: Growth and Conflict in the Private Corporate Sector, 1919–47* (Delhi, 1979), 61; Stephan Steinmann, *Seldwyla im Wunderland. Schweizer im alten Shanghai (1842–1941)* (Dissertation, University of Zurich 1998), 146.
[77] Ellen Clayton Garwood, *Will Clayton: A Short Biography* (Austin, 1958), 78–95; Killick, 'The Transformation of Cotton Marketing', 154–68; Killick, 'Specialized and General Trading Firms', 256–63.
[78] Ellinger and Ellinger, 'Japanese Competition in the Cotton Trade', 198; Killick, 'Specialized and General Trading Firms', 263.
[79] Christof Dejung and Andreas Zangger, 'British Wartime Protectionism and Swiss Trading Companies in Asia during the First World War', *Past and Present* 207 (2010), 181–213.
[80] League of Nations, *Economic Instability in the Postwar World* (Geneva, 1945), 85; Charles Kindleberger, *The World in Depression, 1929–1939* (London, 1973), 88; Harold James, *The End of Globalization: Lessons from the Great Depression* (Cambridge, MA, 2001), 27 and 102 ff.

decades one of the most important cotton exporters from the subcontinent, had to abandon its Indian cotton-purchasing agencies.[81] Nevertheless the fact that many trading firms were extending their operations onto a global scale only after 1918 and that non-European merchant houses were successfully competing with European merchant houses in world trade can be taken as an indicator that, at least for the international cotton trade, the interwar years were not a period of simple de-globalization, as often argued in the scholarly literature, but rather one of something like de-Europeanization of global trade.

The dwindling influence of the Europeans in Asia and the advance of the Indian textile industry not only altered the structure of the Indian cotton trade but also led to an improvement in the quality of Indian cotton, something the colonial government had fruitlessly worked towards for many decades. An expression of the increasing demand for Indian self-rule after the First World War, the Government of India Act of 1919 transferred several administrative realms to indigenous control; these included the realm of agriculture. In 1921, the Indian Central Cotton Committee was founded in Bombay to improve cotton production and better control trade on the subcontinent.[82] The committee was not a colonial government institution but part of the mercantile community, with Indian merchants and industrialists playing an important role in its operation. In the 1920s, it introduced new laws prohibiting cotton transports from one Indian state to another (these usually served the sole purpose of mixing fibres of different qualities), and it obliged gins and presses to mark all bales, rendering them traceable to the factory if adulterations were found.[83] Further attempts to improve cotton quality were made by agricultural cooperatives – meant to give peasants better control over their crops and especially to make them less dependent on credit from moneylenders – supported by interest-free government loans.[84] Finally, irrigation was improved in Panjab and Sind, which allowed the

[81] http://www.rallis.co.in/aboutus/hist1854.htm (15 May 2009).
[82] H. L. Dholakia, *Futures Trading and Futures Markets in Cotton with Special Reference to India* (Bombay, 1949), 15 f.
[83] Contractor, *A Handbook of Indian Cotton*, 33; Dantwala, *Marketing of Raw Cotton in India*, 47 f.
[84] Nehru Memorial Library, New Delhi, Manuscript Section, Purshotamdas Thakurdas Papers, File No. 6: Surat Factory, Kapas, 13.1.1913 to 18.6.1923: Gulabbhai Nagarji Desai, Divisional Superintendent of Agriculture, Northern Division, Surat, to the Deputy Director of Agriculture, Poona, 11th December 1918; R. B. Ewbank, Registrar Cooperative Societies, Bombay Presidency, Poona, to Purshotamdas Thakordas, Bombay, 3rd May 1919.

production of long-stapled American cotton in these regions. Whereas until the 1920s, the British had tended to research measures for improving cotton quality isolated from the subcontinent's social and economic reality, the Central Cotton Committee examined the cotton question in India as a whole. It not only aimed to legally prevent practices such as damping, mixing and adulteration but also tackled commercial questions, because the problem of securing the cultivator a proper price for cotton was closely connected to the enhancement of quality.[85]

The combination of the committee's measures resulted in significant quality improvement after 1930. In 1926, only 6 per cent of Indian cotton had a staple allowing production of fine-quality cloth; in 1932 the share of long-stapled cotton had increased to 18 per cent.[86] A crucial factor in this success lay in the advance of the Indian textile industry, as purchasers of Indian cotton no longer came from Europe or East Asia alone but were also based in the subcontinent itself. Indian spinners had a vital interest in the purchase of good quality cotton for finer cloth and could exert their authority in the local mercantile community.[87] During the interwar years they became very successful in producing such cloth by using long-staple India-grown Cambodia cotton, thus even beginning to supersede their Manchester competitors in the Indian market.[88] It is an ironic twist that it was precisely Indian merchants displaced from the export trade by European firms who at the end of the nineteenth century began to invest in industrial production, in this way becoming the founders of Indian industrialisation.[89]

Conclusion

Although the global economy of the nineteenth and early twentieth centuries was dominated by European states and economic bodies such as

---

[85] B.L. Sethi, 'History of Cotton', in Indian Central Cotton Committee (ed.), *Cotton in India: A Monograph* (Bombay, 1960), 16.

[86] Thomas Peters, *Modern Bombay and Indian States* (Bombay, 1942), 50; Ray, *Industrialization in India*, 61 f.

[87] Nehru Memorial Library, New Delhi (NML), Manuscript Section, Purshotamdas Thakurdas Papers, File No. 142: Lancashire Meeting, 2.6.1933 to 20.11.1935: Summarised Report of First Indian Tour by Mr. H.C. Short, Commissioner of the Lancashire Indian Cotton Committee, 30th July 1935; Purshotamdas Thakurdas Papers, File No. 323: Indian Central Cotton Committee, 28.4.1944 to 12.8.1958: Inaugural speech of Purshotamdas Thakurtas at the Sixth Conference on Cotton Growing Problems in India on 5-2-55.

[88] Ray, *Industrialization in India*, 33.

[89] Rajnarayan Chandavarkar, *Imperial Power and Popular Politics: Class, Resistance and the State in India, c. 1850–1950* (Cambridge, 1998), 55–68.

merchant banks, commodity exchanges and multinational trading firms, in order to understand the complex social relations shaping economic transactions, it is crucial to examine the limits of Western power. The colonial cotton economy on the Indian subcontinent was shaped by many actors, each having a distinct agenda and operating within a different geographical range. The colonial bureaucracy's plan to organise the Indian cotton through legal regulation and introduce new varieties of cotton suitable for use in Lancashire was doomed not only by the resistance of Indian peasants and merchants and the lack of a social consensus in the colonial situation but also by the objections of European merchants to governmental intrusion. Although they relied to a large extent on formal institutions and on the political stability realised by the colonial state, their business interests were not entirely congruent with it. Whereas the state aimed at making India a supplier for the British textile industry, the merchants had no problem with shipping Indian cotton to Germany, France, Belgium, China and Japan, as the local spinning mills in these countries were eager to purchase cotton from the subcontinent. After the First World War, the Asian textile industry not only began to compete with textile imports from Manchester but Indian businessmen were also able to establish formal institutions and an economic infrastructure allowing an improvement in Indian cotton quality – something the colonial government had itself not been able to achieve. Furthermore, Japanese and American merchant houses began to compete with European trading firms, which is why European business suffered a remarkable diminution of importance in the global cotton trade after 1918. Hence when considering the economic relations of a colonial possession such as British India, restricting the analysis to colony and metropole would be too narrow. Not only were these relations always shaped by local structures and the agency of those who were colonised but they were also influenced by developments outside the borders of imperial power; consequently, they always had global scope.

8

The Colonised as Global Traders

Indian Trading Networks in the World Economy, 1850–1939

Claude Markovits

In the prevalent historiography of the world economy during the 1850–1939 period – a period that saw Western political and economic domination spread over the globe – the focus is understandably on Western governments and Western firms as the two main agencies for the remarkable advances in world economic integration that took place. Although it is not my intention to deny their central role, I would like to qualify it by calling attention to a different set of economic actors: non-Western traders, more particularly traders from the Indian subcontinent. On the rare occasions when these Indian traders do figure in narratives of the world economy of the era of Western imperial domination,[1] they are generally relegated to footnotes – a fate shared with many other groups of non-Western traders. For example, Philip Curtin, author of a widely acclaimed book on the role of trade diasporas in world history,[2] views their role as ended in the nineteenth century by global Westernisation; yet as the editors of a recent collection of essays on 'diaspora entrepreneurial networks' point out, 'the only reason why trade diasporas seem to have disappeared is that they long remained invisible to scholarship'.[3] Regional accounts of economic development, in particular those focusing on Africa and Southeast Asia, can ill afford to ignore such diasporas, given the

---

[1] There is no mention of Indian traders in standard histories of the world economy such as James Foreman-Peck, *A History of the World Economy: International Economic Relations since 1850* (Hemel Hempstead, 1995).

[2] Philip D. Curtin, *Cross-Cultural Trade in World History* (Cambridge, 1994).

[3] Ina Baghdiantz McCabe, Gelina Harlaftis and Ioanna Pepelasis Minoglou, 'Introduction', in I. Baghdiantz McCabe, G. Harlaftis and I. Pepelasis Minoglou (eds.), *Diaspora Entrepreneurial Networks: Four Centuries of History* (Oxford, 2005), xx.

prominent role that non-Western expatriate traders, particularly Indian traders, played in the development of commercialised economies in these two regions. My contention is that the importance of the Indians was not purely regional, but that they had an impact on a more global level. To establish this claim, I mostly rely on previously published research on two international trading networks from the Sindh province in present-day Pakistan; I complement this research with evidence collected from various primary and secondary sources.

I begin by considering an often poorly understood issue – that of the economic agency of the colonised – to show that, although Western economic domination placed obstacles in the path of 'indigenous' economic actors, it could not shut them out completely, even unwittingly creating a set of opportunities that some could exploit. Yet focusing on these successful actors does not mean a globally positive appraisal of the effect of Western economic domination, and I take care to distance my arguments from those of apologists of imperial globalisation such as Niall Ferguson.[4] Having thus sketched the broad contours of the context in which Indian trading networks operated and analyzed the structure of opportunities available to them, I turn in the second section to a discussion of the institutional framework. In a third section, I examine the impact of the First World War on Indian international trading networks, with the aim of showing a degree of operational continuity between the prewar and postwar periods.

The Global Economic Agency of Colonial Subjects: The Case of Indian Traders

Tying the notion of 'agency' to colonial subjects might seem paradoxical, but even a cursory look at the case of colonial India reveals that native traders were always able to maintain areas of economic activity relatively independent of British capitalists. The Indian historian Rajat Ray has suggested naming this realm of autonomous indigenous economic activity the 'bazaar',[5] and although the term arguably has an 'Orientalist' flavour, it does reflect an extensive reality. In any event, the important point in this context is that, alongside their activities in India's internal economy, Indian traders retained and in some ways even

---

[4] Niall Ferguson, *Empire: How Britain Made the Modern World* (London, 2003).
[5] R. K. Ray, 'Asian Capital in the Age of European Domination: The Rise of the Bazaar, 1800–1914', *Modern Asian Studies*, 29, 3 (1995), 449–554.

increased their international trading role in an era of Western economic domination. There are two main explanations for this persistence. The first is of a largely structural nature and is connected with the knowledge and skills acquired over many centuries by Indian traders, which offered them a competitive advantage in the international marketplace. The second is more cyclical and is connected to specific opportunities that opened up in the international economy in the 1850–1939 period. Before considering both these perspectives, it is useful to review the precolonial participation of traders from the Indian subcontinent in international trade.

This participation has a long history, which I here take up from the late medieval period. In the fifteenth century, Gujarati traders from the port of Cambay established a kind of thalassocracy that had come to dominate the Indian Ocean by the time the Portuguese arrived from the Atlantic in 1498. The best description of the Gujarati network is contained in a famous sixteenth-century Portuguese text, the *Suma Oriental* of Tomé Pires. Pires reported, memorably, that 'Cambay chiefly stretches out two arms, with her right arm she reaches out towards Aden and with the other towards Malacca',[6] thus conveying the extent of the Gujaratis' range. The arrival of the Portuguese and their capture of Malacca in 1511 did deal the Gujaratis a severe blow, but Albuquerque's failure to take Aden in 1513 allowed continued, albeit reduced, international trading operations. In the seventeenth century, Gujarati sea merchants, mostly Muslims belonging to the Shi'a Bohra community, operated from the port of Surat, which had replaced Cambay as a main base; they were actively involved in the sizeable trade between Mughal India and Yemen. While the Gujaratis dominated India's maritime trade with the western Indian Ocean, other Indian merchants traded across the Bay of Bengal with Arakan, Pegu, Tenasserim (located in what is now Burma) and Siam – these merchants were based in the ports on India's east coast, the most active of which was Masulipatnam.[7] The equally important caravan land trade between northern India and Central Asia and Russia through Afghanistan and Iran, which flourished between the sixteenth and eighteenth centuries, was largely controlled by traders from the Punjab and

[6] Armando Cortesao (ed.), *The Suma Oriental of Tomé Pires, Volume I, An Account of the East, From the Red Sea to Japan, written in Molucas and India in 1512–1515* (London, 1944), 42.

[7] Kenneth Macpherson, 'Trade and Traders in the Bay of Bengal: Fifteenth to Nineteenth Centuries', in R. Mukherjee and L. Subramanian (eds.), *Politics and Trade in the Indian Ocean World: Essays in Honour of Ashin Das Gupta* (Delhi, 1998), 183–209.

Sindh known as 'Multani' or 'Shikarpuri'.[8] Although it may be an exaggeration to speak, as does Stephen Dale, of an 'Indian world economy',[9] this brief overview does point to the important involvement of Indian traders in international trade before the English East India Company (EIC) established growing dominance over India's foreign sea trade in the second half of the eighteenth century, both edging out its Dutch and French rivals and dealing a severe blow to the activities of Indian sea merchants.

Despite this increasing dominance over the sea lanes by British ships and British traders, Indian merchants remained active in some areas where they had firm roots while also finding new opportunities. In the western Indian Ocean and in the Persian Gulf, their trading was not strongly affected by the rise of the EIC before the 1830s. In contrast, in the Bay of Bengal Indian trade suffered from the establishment of complete British control over the sea routes after the annexation of Arakan and Tenasserim in 1826. Still, Tamil Muslim traders known as Marakayar or Chulia found new opportunities to the south of this area following the EIC's establishment in 1786 of a factory at Georgetown on Penang Island, to the north of present-day Malaysia. On the western coast, Gujarati Kapol *bania* merchants from the Portuguese port of Diu gained a dominant position in the ivory and cloth trade between India and Mozambique (Portuguese East Africa) in the second half of the eighteenth century.[10]

However, the most remarkable development was the role played by Parsi traders in the China opium and cotton trade from the 1740s onwards. As the EIC increased its purchases of Chinese tea, it needed to find products to sell to China so as to avoid having to transfer bullion on a large scale to pay for the tea. The company thus turned to Indian cotton and Indian opium, because there was a strong Chinese demand for both. The Parsis had been brokers to the EIC in Surat and had then moved to Bombay where they had established a naval shipyard; consequently, British merchants found them useful as partners in the opium trade. Because the trade was illegal in China, the EIC left it to private British traders, whose ships for the opium trade were often Parsi-owned

---

[8] Stephen F. Dale, *Indian Merchants and Eurasian Trade 1600–1750* (Cambridge, 1994) and Scott C. Levi, *The Indian Diaspora in Central Asia and its Trade, 1550–1900* (Leiden, 2002).

[9] Dale, *Indian Merchants and Eurasian Trade*, 1–7.

[10] Pedro Machado, *Gujarati Indian Merchant Networks in Mozambique, 1777–1830* (PhD dissertation, School of Oriental and African Studies, London, 2005).

or financed. Parsi traders from Bombay, some of whom had settled in Canton, thus earned a share of the enormous profits generated by the opium trade after 1770.

Between 1810 and 1840, they also played an important role in the trade in Malwa opium, grown in the states of central India and exported to China through Portuguese Indian ports in defiance of the East India Company.[11] In this manner, the fortunes accumulated in the opium trade propelled the Parsis into the front ranks of international traders from India in the first half of the nineteenth century; although their role declined after 1860, when they tended to redirect their operations towards real estate and the founding of cotton mills in Bombay, they remained significant operators until the 1930s. They were partly replaced in the opium trade by Gujarati Muslims belonging to the Khoja community, a Shi'a community of Western India whose members had moved in great numbers to Bombay in the decades after 1800.

Khojas were also amongst those contributing to the rise of a powerful Indian trading network in East Africa centred on the island of Zanzibar between 1840 and 1890. After the Omani sultans had transferred their seat from Masqat to Zanzibar in 1840, they encouraged clove growing on the islands of Zanzibar and Pemba to make up for a production shortfall due to the Malthusian policies of the Dutch, who limited production in the Indonesian spice islands. When in Masqat, the sultans had forged close links with Indian financiers, some of whom followed them when they relocated to Zanzibar; the sultans then relied on advances from these financiers for development of the new crop. As Zanzibar became a major trading hub for the entire East African coast, such Indian traders-financiers, some of whom had moved from Masqat and others from Gujarat and Bombay, extended the range of their operations both spatially and in terms of commodities covered.[12] Although they were not directly involved in clove cultivation, their credit underwrote the entire system.

Even European commercial firms in Zanzibar, which in an earlier period had often lent money to the Indians, became dependent on their

---

[11] See Carl Trocki, *Opium, Empire and the Global Political Economy: A Study of the Asian Opium Trade 1750–1930* (London, 1999); Amar Farooqi, *Smuggling as Subversion: Colonialism, Indian Merchants and the Politics of Opium* (New Delhi, 1998); and Claude Markovits, 'The Political Economy of Opium Smuggling in Early Nineteenth Century India: Leakage or Resistance?' *Modern Asian Studies*, 43, 1 (2009), 89–111.

[12] Abdul Shariff, *Slaves, Spices and Ivory in Zanzibar: Integration of an East African Commercial Empire into the World Economy, 1770–1873* (London, 1987).

advances. In 1890, when the British established their protectorate over Zanzibar and the northern section of the East African coast, leaving the southern section to the Germans, the Indians were so entrenched in the area, forming significant colonies in all the major localities, that both colonial powers had no choice but to use their services in their attempts to develop a commercial economy there. Both post-1840 Zanzibar and post-1842 China had 'semi-colonial' economies. There increasing British economic domination and political influence were manifest in the important role taken on by British consuls and the granting of extraterritorial rights to British subjects (British Indians became such subjects after India emerged in 1858 as a possession of the Crown, after abolition of the EIC). Yet this domination coexisted with continued formal sovereignty by local rulers, although in Zanzibar, by contrast with China, the British ultimately established a protectorate. This 'transitional' status generally tended to facilitate penetration by Indian commercial networks, which the colonialists found easier and more profitable to accommodate and instrumentalise than to destroy. Hence temporal sequence, manifest in an often staggered pattern of imperial expansion, is of some relevance in explaining how in the second half of the nineteenth century Indian traders were able to resist competition from European firms that were better capitalised, had access to a well-developed banking system, and benefited from close links with both the ruling colonial elites and the imperial government in London.

The Resilience of Indian Networks in the High Imperial Era, 1870–1914

Some Indian traders and financiers were able to make themselves indispensable partners in the colonial enterprise even when rule was imposed directly, without any 'transitional' phase. This was the case in Lower Burma, annexed by the EIC in 1852. The area, consisting partly of the fertile Irrawaddy Delta, was transformed in the following decades into the rice bowl for Southeast Asia and a major exporter of rice to India, Ceylon, the Dutch East Indies and Europe.[13] In this transformation, a subcaste of Indian bankers, generally known as Nattukotai Chettiars or simply Chettiars, played a major role. They had no previous connection to the area, coming to Lower Burma together with the British Army, which has

---

[13] Michael Adas, *The Burma Delta: Economic Development and Social Change on an Asian Rice Frontier, 1812–1941* (Madison, WI, 1974).

led to their being sometimes considered a group of typical 'compradore' capitalists (the Portuguese term signifies a native-born commercial intermediary). They certainly acted as intermediaries for the British, advancing funds to the Burmese peasantry mostly borrowed from British banks, thus sparing the banks the bother of obtaining collateral for loans granted to borrowers with few assets apart from small landholding and family labour. While acting as guarantors for these small borrowers vis-à-vis the banks, these Chettiar moneylenders naturally rewarded themselves handsomely by charging high interest rates on loans for which they used monies they had themselves borrowed at lower rates. They were operating at some risk because in case of default, their only recourse was to foreclose and seize land, and land was of no use to them because they did not control any labour. They covered themselves mutually for the risk taken, caste solidarity between Chettiars undoubtedly being one of the factors rendering the whole system viable.[14]

Despite being functional participants in the colonial project of developing commercial agriculture in Lower Burma, which ultimately served mainly British commercial interests and imperial policies, the Chettiars did not lack effective agency. Given the amount they borrowed each year from the British banks in Burma, a massive default by them would have resulted in serious trouble for the banks, which knew it and were therefore not in a position to squeeze them even if they had wanted to. In addition, each year the Chettiars transferred part of their profits to their South Indian homeland of Chettinad, where they bought real estate and built sumptuous palatial homes, some still extant. The world depression of the early 1930s led to a collapse of the system: with the fall in the price of rice ruining many peasant households, the Chettiars had to foreclose on defaulting borrowers on a large scale, thus finding themselves in possession of hundreds of thousands of acres of agricultural land for which they had no profitable use. Gradually disengaging themselves from Burma, they then started to invest in South Indian industrial enterprises, largely laying the basis for further industrial development in Tamilnadu, one of the most industrialised states in present-day India. Developing into industrialists is not a usual trajectory for compradores, and that the Chettiars did so casts doubt on such a view of their role. They did not limit their operations to Burma and South India, but expanded into other Southeast Asian countries, particularly French Indochina, British

[14] The point is strongly emphasised in David W. Rudner, *Caste and Capitalism in Colonial India: The Nattukottai Chettiars* (Berkeley, 1994).

Malaya, Thailand and the Dutch East Indies. In this way they emerged as something like global financiers on a reduced scale; between 1880 and 1930 they ran a system parallel but linked to that of the Western international banks.

The story of the Multanis or Shikarpuris was fairly similar. As mentioned, they started as financiers to the caravan trade between Northern India and Central Asia, which led them to extend their operations into Russia on one side and Afghanistan, Iran and Chinese Xinjiang on the other.[15] Ejected from Russian Central Asia in the early 1920s by the Soviet revolution, they relocated largely in West India and South India, where they specialised in the rediscounting of bankers' bills, including Chettiar bills, between India, Burma, Ceylon and Malaya.

The resilience of all these Indian traders and financiers in the face of the onslaught of Western capital (at first sight a hopeless situation) can partly be explained through their mastery of certain types of skill and knowledge, which rendered them indispensable to Western firms and states trying to establish domination over territories about which they generally knew little. Indian trading communities – and this is a fact broadly overlooked in the literature – were great storehouses of knowledge about markets and about people, a knowledge not easily acquired by Westerners, despite all that has been written about 'colonial knowledge'. Centuries of trading in the Indian Ocean region had helped the Indian traders develop a fine-tuned sense of the tastes and needs of consumers in that vast area, and as a result they were able to respond quickly to changes in demand. The close links they forged over time with suppliers in India, particularly with producers of cloth, were also useful. Hence the Kapol traders from Diu mentioned earlier were able to develop textile production specifically attuned to the demand of the Mozambique market.

Around a century later, in the second half of the nineteenth century, Indian traders also anticipated shifts in taste generated by imperial expansion itself. One case in point was the growing desire amongst the rising Western middle class for 'Oriental' goods. As John Mackenzie has convincingly argued,[16] the growing Western economic penetration of Asia brought with it a growing appreciation of objects produced by Asian craftsmen, whether Indian, Chinese or Japanese. Some Indian traders, in

[15] For a sketch of the history of the Multani-Shikarpuri network, see Claude Markovits, *The Global World of Indian Merchants 1750–1947: Traders of Sind from Bukhara to Panama* (Cambridge, 2000), 57–109.

[16] John M. Mackenzie, *Orientalism: History, Theory and the Arts* (Manchester, 1995).

particular the merchants from Hyderabad (Sindh) known as Sindworkies, responded by developing a trade in so-called curios; they specialised successfully in this niche after 1860, setting up a chain of warehouses and shops that by 1914 extended from Kobe in Japan to Panama in Central America.[17] At first they acquired these objects from small workshops in their native province, but as demand quickly outran supply, they started purchasing from other areas in India, mostly Benares, Kashmir and South India. One line of products they dealt in was silk goods, and Indian production being small, this led them to seek new sources of supply in China and Japan starting in the 1890s. Consequently, over a few decades the Sindworkies developed a truly international trading network linking the Far East and India, where they were wholesale purchasers of craft products of different kinds, with colonial territories in Asia and Africa (and even Latin American countries such as Panama, Chile and Argentina), where they sold those items in retail stores not only to a clientele of affluent European and North American travellers but also to white settlers and soldiers. Admittedly, the Sindworkies' range was wider than that of any other such subcontinental network, but Parsi and Khoja traders, to take but two instances, were themselves active from East Africa to Japan.

Elsewhere I have tried to estimate the size of the migration of Indian traders to various Asian and African colonial territories between 1830 and 1930.[18] According to my calculations, the number of such traders outside India grew from a few thousand in the 1830s to around 250,000 by 1930. Not all of them had been in trade when they left India – some departed as workers and then shifted to a commercial activity. The most interesting case is that of the few thousand workers (of a total of 40,000 workers originally hired) recruited on indenture in Gujarat and the Punjab in the 1890s to work on the construction of the Uganda railway; they stayed behind at the expiration of their indenture contracts and opened shops in the East African interior. They became the famous *dukawallas* who played a remarkable role in the development of the regional commercial economy.

Such large-scale migration of Indian traders was undoubtedly part of the process economists call 'international factor mobility', but it straddled the boundary between capital movement and labour migration; this

---

[17] On the history of the Sindworkies, see Markovits, *The Global World of Indian Merchants*, 110–55.
[18] C. Markovits, 'Indian Merchant Networks outside India in the Nineteenth and Twentieth Centuries: A Preliminary Survey', *Modern Asian Studies*, 33, 4 (1999), 883–912.

probably explains why the phenomenon has been neglected by historians of the world economy, who tend to like neat categories. Very few Indian capitalists left India during this period. To develop their business abroad, proprietors of trading firms based in different Indian localities relied mostly on agents, who were either junior partners in the business or salaried employees. At a later stage some of these agents created their own firms and became small capitalists on their own. Yet most remained employed by capitalists at home and returned at some point to India. What was involved here was more a process of circulation than of migration. Most of the circulating workers were either skilled, as in the case of managers, or semi-skilled, as in the case of the more numerous shop assistants, although unskilled domestic servants were also part of that stream.[19] It is important to note that there was not a large capital outflow from India, because most firms were small and operated at low cost. Capital gains repatriated into India are not easy to trace because they usually arrived in the form of 'native bills' and were often undistinguishable from remittances sent to families by Indian workers abroad.

As a result, although it is possible to quantify the circulation of men (very few women were engaged in the process, although wives sometimes joined their husbands in their travels), it is much more difficult to appraise its economic importance. Indian traders were mostly niche operators, taking advantage of specific opportunities in specific markets at specific moments, and keen on avoiding detection by official agencies – not necessarily because they operated outside the law (although there are cases of traders taking up smuggling), but because they thought, correctly, that keeping a low profile was the best policy for coloured people in the white-dominated world of international business. In view of the lack of reliable quantitative data, I focus on a few trades in which various Indian merchant groups played a conspicuous role.

In the nineteenth century, the most important such trade was still probably in opium. Usually conducted between India and China, it remained a significant factor until 1910. Many fortunes were made in the opium trade, by Parsis until 1860 and by Khoja merchants at a later stage. In this trade Indians were generally partners of big Western firms such as Jardine and Matheson in Hong Kong,[20] to which the bulk of the profits appear to

---

[19] Markovits, *The Global World of Indian Merchants*, 156–76.
[20] On the main Parsi partner of Jardine, Matheson, see M. Reid, 'Jamsetjee Jejeebhoy', in M. Keswick (ed.), *The Thistle and the Jade: A Celebration of 150 Years of Jardine, Matheson & Co* (Hong Kong, 1982).

have gone, but with enough remaining profit going to Indian partners for them to prosper. The cotton trade was also a field in which Indian firms were active, even if they lost ground to Europeans after 1860.[21] With the growth of a significant cotton textile industry in Bombay after 1854, there was a shift towards exporting cotton yarn rather than raw cotton, especially to China, where factory-produced yarn was in great demand by local weavers. Because of foreign exchange considerations the Indian product was increasingly preferred to Lancashire yarn: the Indian rupee was a silver currency like the Chinese tael, whereas sterling was of course a gold currency, and silver constantly depreciated in relation to gold after 1873.

While broadly losing ground to Europeans in India's foreign trade, Indian traders did retain areas of strength in some crucial commodities. In the tea trade, for example, which was largely controlled by a few Calcutta-based British firms that shipped to London, between 1880 and 1917 exports by land route to the markets of Central Asia and Russia – a small but profitable segment of the trade – were largely controlled by Peshawari Muslim traders, who formed a significant merchant colony in Russian Central Asia.[22] In both the oilseed and leather trade, two major export trades from India, some Indian merchants shipped directly to foreign markets.

In the global trade in various tropical agricultural commodities produced outside India, Indian traders acquired some clout because of their knowledge of both supply and demand factors. Hence in the large Burma rice export trade, a few Kutchi Memon firms (those run by Gujarati Sunni Muslims from the Kutch area) with branches in Rangoon captured a significant share of annual exports to India, Ceylon, Malaya and Mauritius, whereas British firms dominated exports to Europe and the Dutch East Indies. Evidence has also emerged of the role of Indian traders from the Kathiawar area of Gujarat in the export of Ethiopian coffee from the French port of Jibuti to Europe[23] and of the role of some Penang-based Indian traders in the rubber export trade from Malaya. Indian traders

---

[21] See the contribution of Christof Dejung in this volume.

[22] See the petition, dated 18 October 1910 of thirteen Peshawari traders to the deputy commissioner of the Peshawar district protesting harassment by the Russian authorities. Asian and African Collections of the British Library, London, India Office Records, Political and Secret Department Records, Departmental Papers: Political & Secret Separate (or Special) Files 1902–1931, File 947/1912, L/P&S/10/247.

[23] In 1937, during the Spanish Civil War, the republican authorities in the port of Malaga seized a shipment of Ethiopian coffee that had been sent to Spain by the Jibuti-based

generally occupied a strong position in the trade in gems and semi-precious stones from Ceylon and Burma.

The Institutional Framework for the International Operations of Indian Traders

Indian traders made selective use of the infrastructure built up by Western capital to support the spectacular development of international trade between 1850 and 1914. They did not rely on the big international banks to the same extent as did Western trading firms; rather, they continued to use informal channels to finance at least part of their trading operations. A number of explanations for this come to mind here. Was this reluctance to use Western banks due to their discrimination against non-Western traders, or to some 'cultural' preference for more informal methods of banking, or to a rational calculation of transaction costs? Concerning the first possibility, in studying the history of the Hyderabad Sindworkies, I have not located any example of a refusal of credit by Western banks to these merchants. Although in Southeast Asia in the 1920s and 1930s, Sindhi traders often used the services of Japanese banks such as the Bank of Taiwan to finance their operations, in Africa they do not appear to have had any particular difficulties obtaining finance from Barclays and other big British banks. One small Sindhi trader in Port Said had an overdraft arrangement with the local branch of Barclays, despite his financial situation not being particularly flourishing.[24] From the limited evidence available, it seems impossible to solidly conclude that there was a systematic pattern of discrimination against Indian traders by Western banks.

It appears, in fact, that transactions costs may have played a decisive role here, possibly interacting with a culturally grounded preference for using networks in trading activity. It has often been noted that, to finance their operations, Indian traders relied very much on the resources provided by relatives, members of the same caste and even fellow townspeople. If we accept a definition – general enough to encompass different kinds of linkages between merchants – of trade networks as structures 'through which goods, credit, capital and men circulate regularly across a given space',[25] and accord due weight to the circulation

Indian firm of Shah Jamadar Harakchand. See the correspondence regarding the shipment in India Office Records, Political & Secret Department Records, Political (External) Files, 'Spanish Civil War', L/P&S/12/210.
[24] Markovits, *The Global World of Indian Merchants*, 208.
[25] Ibid., 25.

of information and skills over time, in the course of their transmission from one generation to the next,[26] the emphasis on both space and time allows a certain distance vis-à-vis both caste and family often seen as the main foundations of Indian trading networks. The crucial factor this points to is credit: it is often assumed that Indian traders relied entirely on their caste and family networks to obtain credit, which was advanced at low rate and without a demand for collateral on the basis of bonds of trust between lender and borrower. Yet an examination of evidence from court cases involving Sindhi traders, particularly in Egypt, has led me to question the premise of such an automatic bond between traders within a given community. Indeed, *reputation* emerges as the main factor in generating trust in such contexts – a view aligned with the argument developed by Avner Greif regarding Maghribi traders' 'coalitions'.[27] Because there were limits to both trust and network resources, large Sindhi firms, facing a rapid expansion in their activities in the late nineteenth century, tended to use letters of credit from reputable international banks to finance their growing purchases in Western Europe and the Far East.[28] In contrast, smaller Sindhi operators, with no easy access to banks because of insufficient collateral, mainly used documentary credit provided by the larger firms.

Within most Indian trading networks, financial transactions were generally conducted through a particular instrument known as the *hundi*. The *hundi* system, better known at present under its appellation of *hawala*, has attracted a lot of attention from economists and law enforcement agencies since 11 September 2001, because it has been suspected of being used to finance terrorist activities. A recent article by Marina Martin[29] has underscored how poorly economists and banking regulators understood the *hundi/hawala* system, even before the connection was drawn

[26] Ibid.

[27] Avner Greif, *Institutions and the Path to a Modern Economy: Lessons from Medieval Trade* (Cambridge, 2006). For a critique of Greif's approach, see Robert Boyer, 'Historiens et économistes face à l'émergence des institutions du marché', *Annales Histoire Sciences Sociales*, 64, 3 (2009), 665–93.

[28] The case of the Sindhis seems to call into question an often-repeated assertion that non-Western traders had difficulties answering demands for documentation levelled by Western bankers, shippers and insurers; see for instance C. A. Bayly, '"Archaic" and "Modern" Globalisation in the Eurasian and African Arena, c. 1750–1850', in A. G. Hopkins (ed.), *Globalization in World History* (New York, 2002), 59. In the absence of detailed empirical studies of other comparable trading networks, I am unable to assess how exceptional or typical the Sindhi case was.

[29] Marina Martin, 'Hundi-Hawala: The Problem of Definition', *Modern Asian Studies*, 43, 4 (2009), 909–37.

with international terrorism, in their assessment of it as primitive, inefficient and open to all kinds of abuses. Part of the problem stems from the multifunctional nature of the document known in India since at least the seventeenth century as a *hundi,* which is generally translated into English as a bill of exchange, draft or promissory note. The document could be used in a wide range of transactions. In trade, it could serve as an equivalent of a letter of credit, especially the kind of *hundi* qualified as usance or fixed term, which matured in 30 to 120 days. However, it could also be used simply as an instrument for transferring funds between two places; this was particularly the function of the sight or *darshani hundi,* which was payable on presentation. In this case, it amounted to a kind of bearer's cheque. Yet it could also be used for currency exchange in cross-border transactions. One of the reasons the *hundi* often aroused suspicion was that it was generally scribbled in an Indian language in a hand illegible to anyone outside the community of bankers who produced it, thus having the appearance of a secret code. The description of a Shikarpuri *hundi* by Richard Burton, the famous Victorian explorer, in a book on Sind, may be helpful:

The Hundi, that rude instrument with which the Shikarpuri Rotschild works is a short document, in the usual execrable stenography, laboriously scribbled upon a square scrap of flimsy bank-note paper, and couched in the following form:

11/4 True is the deity Shri!

1 To the worthy in every respect. May you ever be in good health! May you always be fortunate! Our brother Jesumal.

2 From Shikarpur, written by Kisordas; read his compliments!

3 And further, sir, this Hundi of one thousand rupees I have written on you in numerals and letters, Rs 1000, and the half, which is five hundred, of which the double is one thousand complete: dated this... of the month... in the Era of Vikramaditya, to be paid after a term of... days to the bearer at Kabul; the money to be the currency of the place.

In the year of Vikramaditya, etc., etc., etc.

The document contains marks which effectually prevent forgery; they are known only to the writer and his correspondents.[30]

It is clear that the *hundi*'s 'secret code' was only meant to ensure the safety of the transaction. It is generally accepted that cases of such bills not being honoured were very rare, for one clear reason: the reputation

[30] Richard Burton, *Sind Revisited* (London, 1877), 252–53.

of any banker who defaulted would have been ruined. The key difference
between this system and the Western banking system was that sanctions
for default were 'social' rather than legal, but there is no evidence they
were less effective in ensuring payment. The outcomes of the two systems
were broadly similar, but the transaction costs for participants in the
hundi system were certainly on the whole lower. This low cost basically
explains the extraordinary durability of the system, which still provides
a great deal of credit to small-scale Indian entrepreneurs.

The *hundi* system was especially useful to Indian traders when they
were entering a new field and were not yet in a position to borrow
from Western banks, being unable to meet their demands for guarantees
of solvency and collateral. Using the *hundi* option, on the basis of the
reputation they had built up within their own network, these traders could
get credit with very little collateral; after they had operated successfully
for a while, they could go to the Western banks with a good chance of
success. In this manner, internal resources readily available to most Indian
traders could facilitate a transition to more generally recognised status. In
addition, in case of difficulties, it was always possible to return to the old
system: fellow townspeople would rarely refuse credit to a trader going
through a hard time and to whom the Western banks were not ready to
advance any more money. By drawing on two separate sources of credit
in various combinations, Indian traders increased their survival chances
in the tough world of international trading.

It will perhaps come as a surprise that Indian participation in the international economy did not start with Mittal's acquisition of Arcelor or
Tata's of Jaguar Rover, but of course there remains a question of scale.
In the 1850–1939 period, few if any Indian firms were even remotely
comparable in size to the truly large Western commercial firms. The
largest Indian firms were roughly comparable to middle-sized Western
firms. Still, through networking and the low transaction costs it entailed,
some groups of Indian traders were able to capture a significant share
of international trade in some commodities, although this cannot be precisely quantified. In comparison to other non-Western traders with a
similar role in the international economy – a group including Sephardic
Jews, Armenians, Lebanese and Chinese – the Indians had one particular advantage: after 1858, they were all either subjects of the British
Crown (the case for those living in British India proper) or British-
protected persons (the case for those living in the native states); in both
cases they were entitled to protection by British consular authorities and

benefited from the privileges of extraterritoriality granted British subjects in many formally independent states such as the Ottoman Empire, Morocco, China, Japan and Siam. The years between 1860 and 1880 marked a golden age for these traders, because protection by the British flag allowed them to travel more or less everywhere without documentation and without fear of being discriminated against or molested. The situation started to change in the 1880s with the adoption of anti-Asiatic measures by the United States and by the white settlers' colonies of the British Empire. By the time of the First World War, a passport had become a universal requirement to cross borders, but having one did not guarantee entry to Indians, especially in the 'white' dominions of the British Empire. The 1920s and 1930s saw many independent states and colonial territories adopt a tough stance towards immigration from Asia, resulting in growing difficulties for trade networks that relied on a constant circulation of personnel across borders. However, there is evidence that sometimes intervention by both British consuls and the Indian government helped Sindhi traders counter the effects of such restrictions.[31]

Indian traders were often in different kinds of partnerships with Western firms to exploit opportunities in different markets, and it is not clear they were always junior partners, although detailed empirical studies of such partnerships in this respect are lacking. In addition to low transaction costs, they had the advantage of being able to tap a pool of skilled personnel in India who demanded much lower salaries than did Western managers and were more ready to expatriate for long periods. Yet their greatest advantage was an unrivalled knowledge of non-Western markets, accumulated over centuries of commercial ties with many regions of Africa and Asia. In some cases, they even showed themselves capable of operating outside their 'traditional' zones. Starting in the late nineteenth century, Sindworkies thus developed a presence in the Canary Islands, North Africa, West Africa and Latin America – regions where no Indian trader had set foot before.

Such expansion into uncharted territory points towards an ability to acquire new knowledge, although little evidence has come to light about the way it was acquired and diffused by Sindhi merchants. In their own process of expansion, they made use of the basic infrastructure provided by Western capitalism, including steamships and telegraphs, but they also continued to use traditional instruments such as *hundis*. Their firms were

---

[31] Markovits, *The Global World of Indian Merchants*, 230–40.

overwhelmingly family-based partnerships between brothers or father and son or uncle and nephew, and although these firms could either remain informal or adopt the legal form of a partnership, they almost never were joint-stock companies. This in itself did not set them apart substantively from Western firms, many of which were themselves family-based. Perhaps the notion of 'hybridity', addressing an ability to straddle two commercial worlds, can be applied as a distinguishing mark of Indian international trading firms. Yet perhaps this ability was simply a sign that the two worlds were increasingly one, neither pure West nor pure East but a very un-Kiplingesque mix.

The Impact of the First World War on Indian Trading Networks

It is often asserted that the Great War put an end to the intensifying international economic integration that began in the mid-nineteenth century, instead ushering in an era stamped by a high level of protectionism and economic nationalism. The war is thus seen as having resulted in a shrinking of opportunities in the field of international trade. Although the real picture may have been more complicated and less uniformly bleak,[32] in our context it needs to be remembered that Indian international traders were mostly 'niche operators' on whose fate macroeconomic developments did not necessarily have a very direct impact. As a matter of fact, most Indian traders appear to have been on an upward rather than on a downward curve after 1918. The Sindworkies were clearly on such a curve in the 1920s; although severely affected by the depression of the early 1930s, they quickly overcame its effects, maintaining a good level of activity until the Second World War. Expansion was evident in the creation of new firms, the opening of new branches by established firms, and the addition of new products to the sales catalogues. In the 1920s, the Sindhis partly diversified out of the curio trade to become significant players in the global Asian textile trade,[33] and they successfully specialised in the sale of Japanese textiles to colonial territories in Asia (the Dutch East Indies and Malaya) and Africa, including British West Africa. They dealt in different kinds of silk, cotton, rayon and woollen goods, widely sourced (although Japan emerged as the main source) and

---

[32] For a fairly nuanced presentation, see Foreman-Peck, *A History of the World Economy*, 175–207.

[33] Rajeshwari Brown, *Capital and Entrepreneurship in South-East Asia* (London, 1994), 207–09.

sold to an increasingly varied clientele: no longer exclusively affluent Western tourists, but now including more middle-class 'natives'. Although no reliable data about profits are available, indirect evidence points to them remaining fairly high until the eve of the Great Depression.

Although no comparable research has been published on other Indian trading networks, evidence gleaned from various scattered sources suggests that most existing networks were likewise on a trajectory of expansion and that new entrants were part of this process. Two Gujarati Muslim trading networks that have already been mentioned, those of the Sunni Kutchi Memons and the Shi'a Khojas, appear to have increased the scale of their operations. The former took advantage of the new surge in Burmese rice production in the 1920s to increase exports from Rangoon, commissioning rice mills that allowed them to add value by exporting rice in processed rather than raw form. Other Memon traders based in Karachi took control of the substantial import trade in Java sugar into India and opened branches in Surabaya, the main sugar-exporting port in Java. Khojas expanded in a major way in East Africa and began to branch out from trade into the processing industries. New entrants included Hindu traders who with the exception of the Sindworkies and Chettiars had been less prone than Muslims to expatriate, perhaps partly because of the religious taboo on crossing the *kala pani* (the 'back waters' or ocean).[34]

Two groups in particular here merit attention. The Lohanas – Gujarati Hindus stemming like the Memons from the tiny native state of Kutch – had started their movement into East Africa before 1914, but in the 1920s it was intensified, so that they played an increasing role in the region's trade.[35] The Marwaris, originating from certain areas of Rajasthan, had come to occupy a dominant position in the commercial life of North India and East India between 1860 and 1914,[36] making Calcutta the main centre of their activities. The jute trade had been the mainstay of their expansion. Before 1914, they had been content to purchase the crop from cultivators and sell it to Calcutta-based British firms that shipped it abroad. After the war, some Calcutta Marwari firms ventured into direct export, and by the late 1920s one of these firms, Birla Bros., had become one of the largest exporters and a power on the Jute Exchange

[34] For a brief discussion of this point, see Markovits, *The Global World of Indian Merchants*, 27.

[35] See J. S. Mangat, *A History of the Asians in East Africa c. 1886 to 1945* (London, 1971) and H. S. Morris, *The Indians in Uganda* (London, 1966).

[36] T. A. Timberg, *The Marwaris: From Traders to Industrialists* (Delhi, 1978).

in London. Marwaris had also started opening branches outside India, first in neighbouring Burma and at a later stage in Singapore and Japan. In the 1930s, especially after the devaluation of the yen in 1932, Japan became very attractive to different kinds of Indian traders as a country where it was possible to cheaply purchase a variety of goods for export to India. Joining the Sindhis, Khojas and Parsis, who had opened Japanese branches starting in the 1890s, were Marwaris, Gujarati Hindus and South Indian traders. Kobé was the port where most Indian traders were based. In particular the Sindhis developed close links with Japanese firms, which were interested in profiting from the market expertise of Sindhi agents and therefore offered good terms; the relationship flourished until Japan's entry into the Second World War in 1941 and even beyond.

Although during the interwar period the Indian economy as a whole became more inward looking, with whatever growth there being tied to an expansion in the domestic market, some Indian traders gained a stronger foothold in both India's foreign trade and the global commodity trade. There was, however, a growing division between two business subsectors. One subsector was increasingly geared towards exploiting opportunities on the domestic market through development of import-substituting industries, under a regime of increased customs protection after 1932; the other, largely disconnected from domestic developments in India, increasingly sought participation in 'global' trading. The first subsector tended to align itself with the nationalist project of creating an independent India with few links to the world economy,[37] whereas the second subsector operated in a political vacuum, having largely loosened its links with a declining British Empire. During the Second World War, the growing sense of alienation by Indian expatriate traders from their British imperial connections came into the open when most such traders in Japanese-occupied Southeast Asia collaborated with the Japanese against the British, aligning themselves with Subhas Chandra Bose and his Indian National Army. The 'patriotism' thus displayed by Indian traders did not, however, earn them any goodwill from the government of independent India after 1947. Nehru made it clear that the new India would not defend the interests of its traders abroad, whom the local elites and broader local populations of the newly independent Asian and African states generally viewed as exploiters. A difficult period had thus begun for the expatriate Indian traders.

[37] C. Markovits, *Indian Business and Nationalist Politics 1931–1939: The Indigenous Capitalist Class and the Rise of the Congress Party* (Cambridge, 1985).

Conclusion

Having played a major role in the Indian Ocean area for centuries, Indian traders undoubtedly suffered from the massive intrusion of Western capital into the area; nevertheless, as argued in these pages, they were able to maintain a significant level of participation in international trade. In contradiction to the widespread view of the essential superiority of Western capitalist institutions over non-Western ones, Indian traders were able to both maximise some of their long-standing assets and minimise the liabilities tied, especially, to the relatively small scale of their operations. Their main asset, which did not depreciate, was an unrivalled knowledge of markets and of consumers' tastes in the vast area extending from East Africa to Southeast Asia. This knowledge helped them adapt to shifts in tastes, and they could 'trade' the knowledge with Western firms to form partnerships, where their role was not necessarily a subordinate one. They were also able to use networking to lower transaction costs and pool resources, thus partly offsetting the scale advantage enjoyed by Western firms. By making simultaneous use of the traditional *hundi* system of financing and of modern Western banking infrastructure, they increased their chances of survival in the world of international trading. Although generally adopting a low profile and often limiting themselves to 'niche operations', during the high imperial era between 1880 and 1914, this strategy helped them withstand the worst of the Western onslaught. In the 1920s, they could thus emerge more openly as a force in global commodity trading. In the 1930s, ties developed between some Indian networks and large Japanese firms – a clear sign that Asia in general was starting to develop as a site of capitalist expansion. After Indian independence, Indian capitalism became broadly more inward oriented, although some trading networks increased their international operations; as we have seen, one such network was constituted by the Sindworkies, the Sindhi Hindus from Hyderabad, who largely relocated to Bombay after the partition of India.

In the early 1990s, with the advent of liberalising policies, India sought to reintegrate itself into the international economy, in the process rediscovering in its own long-neglected trading diasporas a possible bridge toward the world. Although it had studiously ignored these diasporas for decades, the Indian government suddenly started to woo them; the diasporas' response was at best half-hearted. Yet even though Indian business diasporas certainly do not play a role within the Indian economy analogous to that of Chinese business diasporas within the Chinese economy, when the Tata company suddenly 'goes international' in a major way, it is reconnecting with an earlier Parsi narrative of participation in international trading largely lost since the 1920s. Whether big India-based Indian business will be as successful in the international arena as the trading networks of earlier years remains an open question.

9

The International Patent System and the Global Flow of Technologies

The Case of Japan, 1880–1930

Pierre-Yves Donzé

'The Japanese has always been a totally unscrupulous copier as far as trademarks and patents are concerned'.[1] This opinion, which was expressed in 1932 by a Swiss watch merchant living in India who found himself facing an upsurge in competition from Japan, reflects a state of mind widespread at the time in the West: Japan was viewed as a nation whose economic boom was predicated on an imitation of foreign products and that turned copying into a characteristic cultural trait of that country or even Asia.[2] In reality, imitation and copying are, of course, not specifically Japanese or Asian characteristics, but rather are strategies widely adopted by latecomers as part of their industrialisation and catching-up policies. The history of technology transfers since the Industrial Revolution is an excellent illustration of these strategies, with the policies for acquiring British technology in the textile and machine industries adopted by the major Western nations in the eighteenth and nineteenth centuries

---

[1] International Museum of Watchmaking, La Chaux-de-Fonds, archives of the Swiss Chamber of Watchmaking, letter from the West End Watch Co to the Swiss Chamber of Watchmaking, 9 September 1932.

[2] Rupert Cox (ed.), *The Culture of Copying in Japan: Critical and Historical Perspectives* (London, 2008) and Sheridan Tatsuno, *Created in Japan: From Imitators to World-Class Innovators* (New York, 1991).

I would like to thank Shigehiro Nishimura, Kouji Kubota and Hiroko Moriyama for their comments and kind help.

serving as prime examples.[3] However, with the appearance of multinationals in the second half of the nineteenth century, the questions of regulating the flow of technologies across the planet and of intellectual protection soon arose. Because they operated on a global scale – opening branches or joint ventures for localised manufacturing of their products – and due to the appearance of trademarks for exported goods sold throughout the world, companies required a legal framework that could guarantee their comparative advantage on the global market.

This was the backdrop for the establishment of an international patent protection system with the adoption of the Paris Convention in 1883. The institutionalisation of intellectual property protection at the global level was a major breakthrough insofar as neither individuals nor companies had hitherto been able to protect their inventions and trademarks at the international level. The ability to protect inventions did exist before 1883, but it was based on national or local legislation that granted industrial and commercial operating monopolies for various products and manufacturing processes on the domestic market. Since the Ancien Régime, there were examples of such protection in many countries, including Great Britain,[4] Italy[5] and Japan.[6] In Germany, the adoption of national patent protection legislation laws in 1877 followed unification and was largely driven by the multinational Siemens.[7] Nevertheless, these various bodies of law were limited to the domestic market. Consequently, the major change introduced by the Paris Convention and the unification of national legislation was protection of inventions and trademarks on a global scale, to the main benefit of multinational

[3] John R. Harris, *Industrial Espionage and Technology Transfer: Britain and France in the Eighteenth Century* (Aldershot, 1998); David J. Jeremy (ed.), *Transatlantic Industrial Revolution: The Diffusion of Textile Technologies between Britain and America, 1790–1830s* (Cambridge, 1981); Kristine Bruland, 'British Technology and European Industrialisation', in *The Norwegian Textile Industry in the Mid-Nineteenth Century* (Cambridge, 1989); and David J. Jeremy (ed.), *Technology Transfer and Business Enterprise* (Aldershot, 1994).
[4] Christine MacLeod, *Inventing the Industrial Revolution: The English Patent System, 1660–1800* (Cambridge, 1988).
[5] Marco Belfanti, 'Corporations et brevets: les deux faces du progrès technique dans une économie pré-industrielle (Italie du Nord, XVIe–XVIIIe siècle)', in Liliane Hilare-Pérez and Anne-Françoise Garçon (eds.), *Les chemins de la nouveauté: Innover, inventer au regard de l'histoire* (Paris, 2003), 59–76.
[6] Tetsuo Tomita, *Shijo kyoso kara mita chiteki shoyuken* (Tokyo, 1993).
[7] Rudolf Boch (ed.), *Patentschutz und Innovation in Geschichte und Gegenwart* (Frankfurt am Main, 1999).

companies. For such firms as Singer Manufacturing Company[8] and General Electric,[9] the institutionalisation of the intellectual property system helped drive worldwide expansion. Their patent management policies enabled them to gain control of the market for innovation, sue rivals who copied them, and open joint ventures and branches abroad without risk.

Nevertheless, although often focused on, this historical fact is merely one aspect of the impact exerted by the international patent system on the worldwide flow of technologies. Multinationals were not the only actors influencing the system. In countries that came late to industrialisation, both industrialists and states made special use of the system to promote technology transfers to national firms, thus reducing their dependence on foreign multinationals. In the case of Germany, Jochen Streb and Ralf Richter have shown that in the interwar period the German Patent Office took more time to examine patent applications submitted by American machine tool manufacturers than that taken for German applicants, a practice designed to let German industrialists use imitation to close the gap opened up during the war.[10] Moreover, some countries had intellectual protection systems, complementing patent law, that were aimed at promoting the introduction and imitation of foreign inventions inside the country. This was for example the case in Spain, which from the mid-eighteenth century until its entry into the European Union in 1986, operated a system called patents of introduction; these authorised the protection of foreign inventions within the domestic market by actors not holding the inventions abroad.[11] Likewise, despite having signed the Paris Convention, some small European countries such as Switzerland and the Netherlands, under pressure from their domestic industries, only belatedly adopted patent laws, in order to let their entrepreneurs continue copying foreign products.[12]

---

[8] Robert Davies, *Peacefully Working to Conquer the World* (New York, 1976).

[9] Shigehiro Nishimura, 'Foreign Business and Patent Management before WWI: A Case Study of the General Electric Company', *Kansai University Review of Business and Commerce* 11 (March 2009), 77–97.

[10] Jochen Streb and Ralf Richter, *Catching-Up and Falling Behind: Illegal Knowledge Spillover from American to German Machine Tool Makers*, paper presented at the XVth World Economic Congress, Utrecht, 3–7 August 2009 (session D-6).

[11] Patricio Saiz, *Patents of Introduction and the Spanish Innovation System during the 19th and 20th Centuries*, paper presented at the XVth World Economic Congress, Utrecht, 3–7 August 2009 (session D-6).

[12] Eric Schiff, *Industrialisation without National Patents: The Netherlands, 1869–1912, Switzerland 1850–1907* (Princeton, 1971).

Uses of the international patent protection system were thus highly differentiated depending on a country's degree of development and the size of its companies. There was a relatively flexible relationship between harmonisation of the various national laws on patents within the global system and a national autonomy that remained substantial and provided a certain amount of leeway, enabling both early industrialisers and latecomers to fit into the system. This chapter examines the case of Japan, a country occupying a special position characterised by a dual imperative: to open itself up to foreign multinationals and thus become a part of the global system, while at the same time supporting the growth and development of a domestic industry by acquiring foreign technologies through imitation. In this manner, Japan serves as an example for understanding how the establishment of an international patent system in 1883 (in the Paris Convention) affected technology transfer policies. Japan's entry into the convention in 1899 did not signify complete integration into a globalised technology market; indeed, until the 1930s, the country's technology transfer policy involved two distinct processes highlighting different uses of the global system. The first process took in technologies used in the Second Industrial Revolution and brought to Japan by Western multinational enterprises through patent agreements, as was the case in the electrical industry (in particular, with Tokyo Electric). The second process took in technologies copied without any patent agreement. This was specifically the case in the consumer goods industry and with products easily reproducible by reverse engineering, such as the watchmaking industry (in particular, Seiko).

The Paris Convention

The institutionalisation of an international patent protection system dates back to the world fairs organised between 1850 and 1880 – key venues for manufacturers from all over the world to present their products, as well as for awareness raising and discussion.[13] A first patent congress took place in Paris in 1878, in conjunction with the world fair being held there. The Paris Convention agreed on five years later was a result of discussions held at that congress.[14] The convention was

---

[13] Fritz Machlup and Edith Penrose, 'The Patent Controversy in the Nineteenth Century', *Journal of Economic History* 10 (1950), 1–29.

[14] Yves Palsseraud and François Savignon, *Genèse du droit unioniste des brevets* (Paris, 1983).

stamped by two major principles[15]: (1) equality between the nationals of one state signatory to the convention and those of another such state (previously many states had allowed only their own nationals to protect their inventions) and (2) a patent's automatic six-month extension to all signatory states once it was registered in one of them.[16] The convention was signed in 1883 by eleven countries: eight European (Belgium, France, Italy, Netherlands, Portugal, Serbia, Spain and Switzerland) and three South American nations (Brazil, El Salvador and Guatemala). They were soon joined by Great Britain (1884) and Norway (1885) and later by Denmark (1894), the United States (1897), Japan (1899), Germany (1903), Australia (1907) and Austria (1909).[17]

Researchers generally view the Paris Convention as an essential phase in 'global patent-system integration'.[18] It allowed a globalised technology market to emerge, insofar as patents were no longer solely attached to monopolies for the industrial exploitation of inventions but became goods tradable worldwide. As such, these patents primarily benefited multinationals, facilitating their policies of expansion and international division of labour. Statistics compiled by the World Intellectual Property Organisation (see Table 6) highlight the different positions of the various states regarding internationalisation of patent protection and the fear of 'colonisation by foreign patent holders' expressed by some of them.[19]

The proportion of nonresidents among holders of intellectual property rights (covering patents, utility models, designs and trademarks) can largely be viewed as a reflection of the presence of multinationals. Hence it was no accident that the United States and Germany were among the three countries in which nonresidents accounted for less than one-third of all patent holders: these two countries hosted the most innovative enterprises, particularly in Second Industrial Revolution sectors such as electrical appliances, chemicals and automobiles.[20] Moreover, American and German multinationals managed to have their innovations patented

---

[15] Edith T. Penrose, *The Economics of the International Patent System* (Baltimore, 1951), 224.

[16] Here, the idea was to give the patent holder time to complete the necessary administrative procedures in other countries.

[17] Edith Penrose, *The Economics of the International Patent System* (Baltimore, 1951), 58–59.

[18] Eda Kranakis, 'Patents and Power: European Patent-System Integration in the Context of Globalization', *Technology and Culture* 48 (2007), 690.

[19] Ibid., 693.

[20] Alfred D. Chandler, *Scale and Scope: The Dynamics of Industrial Capitalism* (Harvard, 1990).

TABLE 6. *Proportion of Nonresidents
among the Holders of Patents Filed in
Certain Countries, as a Percentage,
1910–30*

	1910	1920	1930
Canada	83.4	84.8	88.8
France	53.9	49.1	53.1
Germany	30.6	–	26.7
Italy	64.5	46.2	68.5
Japan	8.8	10.2	8.3
Netherlands	–	70.6	82.6
Russia	71.3	–	–
Switzerland	58.0	50.2	49.0
United Kingdom	–	44.2	53.7
United States	10.6	10.2	13.5

Source: Statistics of the World Intellectual Protection Organisation (WIPO), www.wipo.int/
ipstats/en. For the United Kingdom, read 1921
instead of 1920; for Italy, read 1911 instead of
1910.

in other countries – because they had the means to implement this strategy
and because the strategy accompanied a policy of worldwide expansion.
The high proportion of nonresidents in other countries probably reflects
the policies of these American and German companies.

Japan was a special case because, although it was a late industrialiser
and was not particularly innovative during the first third of the twentieth century, it nonetheless featured a very low proportion of nonresidents among holders of intellectual property rights. This anomaly may
be explained by the way Japan used the international patent system. On
the one hand, the country's entry to the Paris Convention was aimed
at the earlier mentioned advantages that it offered: opening the country
to foreign multinationals and acquiring up-to-date technologies. On the
other hand, such affiliation with the international system was followed
shortly after by establishment of a system for protecting utility models
that by and large legalised pursuit of technological transfer via copying
and imitation.[21]

---

[21] For a history of the Japanese patent protection system, see *Tokkyo seido 70 nen shi*
(Tokyo, 1955); *Nihon sangyo gijutsu shi jiten* (Tokyo, 2007), 15–16; and *Kogyo shoyuken seido hyaku nen shi* (Tokyo, 1984–85), 3 vols.

Technology Transfer and Patent Protection in Japan

After being forced to allow access to international trade in the mid-1850s, Japan embarked on a policy of economic development with a specific goal: catching up with the West. In its quest for modernisation, technology naturally played a decisive role. Although there was hybridisation rather than a complete break with the technological culture of the Edo period,[22] imports of foreign technology played a key role in the Japanese economy. This basic pattern notwithstanding, the attitude of the Japanese authorities and industrial elite towards technology changed a great deal over time. Two major periods can be distinguished between 1860 and 1930.[23]

Technologies Without Capital (1868–1895)

The first phase covered the three decades stretching from the Meiji Restoration to the Sino-Japanese War (from 1868 to 1895), when Japan actively sought to acquire foreign technology while shutting out foreign capital. During this period the state played a key role, striving to set up an infrastructure and a capital goods industry (the main components being railways, mines, steel and machines) and to modernise traditional sectors (textiles, agriculture) with the help of foreign technology. The principal vectors of technological transfer were individuals, primarily foreign engineers hired by the Japanese authorities and Japanese engineers trained in the West, and objects imported to Japan and copied there. Foreign companies had very little impact on this process. The modest European direct investments in mines and railways during the 1860s were gradually taken over by the Japanese authorities after the Meiji Restoration.[24] Moreover, in 1881 the government banned imports of foreign capital, a restriction lasting until the Sino-Japanese War.[25] As a result, foreign direct investment (FDI) was virtually negligible until the late 1890s.

In this context, the authorities did not view the question of intellectual property as a priority, because they, as indicated, were primarily

---

[22] Tessa Morris-Suzuki, *The Technological Transformation of Japan: From the Seventeenth to the Twenty-first Century* (Cambridge, 1994) and Testuro Nakoka et al., eds., *Sangyo gijutsushi* (Tokyo, 2001).

[23] For a synthetic overview of Japanese economic history, see *Nihon keizai shi* (Tokyo, 1988–90), 8 vols.

[24] John McMaster, 'The Takashima Mine: British Capital and Japanese Industrialization', *Business History Review* 37 (1963), 217–39.

[25] Yoshio Asai, 'Nisshin sengo no gaishi donyu to Nihon kogyo ginko', *Shakaikeizaishi* 50 (1985), 655–75.

seeking to catch up with the West. Since the Edo period, however, Japan had had a monopoly system for commercially exploiting inventions, as could be found in the major European countries, but the Japanese system operated only at the provincial level and was closed to foreigners.[26] Consequently, Japan's opening to the West raised two questions: unification of intellectual property at a national level and foreigners' access to the system.

A consensus quickly emerged that it was necessary to protect inventions and trademarks for Japanese nationals; for their part, industrial circles soon expressed their opposition to reciprocal rights for foreigners. In the late 1860s, Japanese jurists began to disseminate information nationwide on Western systems for protecting inventions and trademarks, leading in 1870 to a public debate on the need to adopt such systems. Because there were no foreign multinationals in the country, the question of whether to guarantee patent protection for such firms did not arise. Nevertheless, chiefly at the state's urging, Japan proceeded to adopt an active policy of technology transfer, mainly in the fields of arms, shipbuilding, textiles and machines. During the 1860s and 1870s, the bulk of such technology was channelled through foreign engineers employed by various public and private firms.[27] However, because it cost the firms a great deal to employ these engineers, they successfully lobbied the state to protect the acquired innovations, enabling them to hold on to the comparative advantage the innovations conferred in the domestic market.[28] These firms' main contact in the administration was a key figure in Japan's industrialisation, Eiichi Shibusawa (1840–1931), considered the father of Japanese capitalism.[29] Along with a career in private industry, between 1869 and 1873 Shibusawa headed the Office of Reform at the Ministry of Finance, where he promoted the idea of patent laws to protect inventions acquired from foreigners.[30] A centralised system for granting monopolies over inventions came into force between 1871 and 1872, then was suspended until 1884. In the meantime, the regional authorities (prefectures) resumed their practice of granting these monopolies,

---

[26] Tetsuo Tomita, *Shijo kyoso kara mita chiteki shoyuken* (Tokyo, 1993).
[27] Ardath W. Burks (ed.), *The Modernisers: Overseas Students, Foreign Employees and Meiji Japan* (Boulder, 1985); Hoshimi Uchida, 'Gijutsu itten', in Shunsaku Nishikawa and Takeshi Abe (eds.), *Nihon keizaishi* (Tokyo, 1990), vol. 4, 265–72.
[28] *Kogyo shoyuken seido hyaku nen shi*, 16–17; Toshio Tamura and Nobuo Suzuki, 'Nihon tokkyo seido gaishi', *Tokkyo kenkyu*, 23–24 (1997), 49–50.
[29] Masaru Udagawa (ed.), *Nihon no kigyokashi* (Tokyo, 2002), 15–28.
[30] *Kogyo shoyuken seido hyaku nen shi*, 17.

but only at the local level. Because such local monopolies were of limited interest in a country undergoing economic unification, only 326 applications were submitted during this period.[31] On the national level, during the 1870s and early 1880s, trademarks, not inventions, were seen as a legislative priority, owing to several disputes between Western exporters and Japanese merchants who copied unprotected trademarks pertaining to consumer goods (beer, soap and drugs).[32] These conflicts resulted in a law on the protection of trademarks and designs, which came into force in 1884.

The question of national patent laws surfaced again after Japan adopted the Paris Convention. Even though FDI to Japan was not authorised, the state sought integration into the international system in order to work together with foreign companies and benefit from new technologies. A first draft bill, submitted by the Ministry of Agriculture and Trade in 1883, was meant to secure such integration. It reflected the state's very open attitude towards multinationals, but ran afoul of independent entrepreneurs seeking to protect their infant industries. As a result the Japanese parliament, in which industrialists' interests were well represented, vetoed this initiative. Legislation on the patenting of inventions was passed in 1885, but it only granted rights to Japanese nationals.[33] However, the law did contain several limitations, including a ban on patenting medicine, a fifteen-year time limit on maximum protection, and the annulment of patents if militarily necessary.[34] A new law on the protection of intellectual property was passed in 1888 to cover inventions, trademarks and designs with a single legislative instrument.

Statistics for patents on inventions registered between 1885 and 1898 illustrate how the Japanese used this instrument (see Table 7). Most patents were granted for traditional industrial sectors (textiles and agriculture) and for everyday objects. A quantitative approach does not make it possible to distinguish between pure innovation (Japanese invention) and hybridisation (the copying or adaptation of a foreign technology), but it shows that limiting protection of intellectual property to Japanese nationals had a major consequence: new technologies were not widespread. Among the modern sectors represented, there were some objects imported from the West, for which imitations were patented. This was

[31] Ibid., 20.
[32] Ibid., 35–36.
[33] *Nihon sangyo gijutsu shi jiten* (Tokyo, 2007), 15–16.
[34] *Tokkyo seido 70 nen shi*, 44.

TABLE 7. *Main Categories of Patents Registered in Japan, Number of Cases, 1885–98*

Sector	N	%
Lamps	161	4.9
Stationery	125	3.8
Shoes	113	3.4
Paint	95	2.9
Measuring tools	87	2.6
Looms	78	2.4
Metal tools	73	2.2
Keys and padlocks	70	2.1
Loom parts	70	2.1
Sericulture	62	1.9

Source: *Kogyo shoyuken seido hyaku nen shi* (Tokyo, 1984–85), vol. 1, 113.

the case with electric batteries, patented by the engineer Sagizo Yai in 1893, and pocket watches, giving rise to a patent registered by Ichibei Takaki in 1895.[35] Yet, although the new Western technologies sometimes led to the filing of Japanese patents, these instances were rare.

FDI and Integration into the World Economy (1895–1930)
As a strategy for technology transfer, the restrictive FDI policy revealed its limits during the 1890s: it simply was not suited to the innovations tied to the Second Industrial Revolution, which relied on complex production processes and know-how owned by companies or groups of companies that thereby controlled their application and use – such know-how made it difficult to copy imported Western products without cooperating with these firms. To gain access to such innovations and as a result of Western pressure,[36] Japan opened itself up to foreign investment and the presence of multinational companies through a series of measures: in

[35] *Kogyo shoyuken seido hyaku nen shi*, 123.
[36] Ibid., 98–103. On Japanese acquisition of the new technologies, see Katsu Udagawa, 'Senzen Nihon no kigyō keiei to gaishikei kigyō', *Keiei Shirin*, 24, 1–2 (1987), 15–31 and 29–40; Kozo Yamamura, 'Japan's Deus Ex Machina: Western Technology in the 1920s', *Journal of Japanese Studies*, 12, 1 (1986), 65–94; Hoshimi Uchida, 'Western Big Business and the Adoption of New Technologies in Japan: The Electrical Equipment and Chemical Industries, 1890–1920', in Akio Okochi and Hoshimi Uchida (eds.), *Development and Diffusion of Technology: Electrical and Chemical Industries. Proceedings of the Fuji Conference* (Tokyo, 1980), 145–72.

1897, the country both placed the yen on the gold standard and entered into bilateral patent protection agreements with the United States and Great Britain;[37] in 1899, it adopted a new business code liberalising the economic activities of foreigners; and that same year it joined the international patent system by acceding to the Paris Convention. However, the country did not open its doors completely but instead banned or limited FDI in several key sectors including shipping, mines, insurance and banks[38] – a protectionist policy designed, among other things, to ensure that the internationalisation of patents was not accompanied by a flood of imports.[39]

After 1900, the number of patents registered grew steadily in any event, rising from 586 in 1900 to 4976 in 1930 (see Figure 3). Foreigners indeed helped drive this growth, averaging 30.7 per cent of all patents filed between 1899 and 1930.[40] The two main countries were the United States and Germany, which between them accounted for 49 per cent of all foreign patents in 1910, 37 per cent in 1920 and 53 per cent in 1930.[41] The First World War, during which the patents of enemy nations were suspended, did not really diminish Germany's importance.[42] Over the short run, the country's temporary disappearance from the Asian markets had a substantial impact on Japanese industry because it boosted exports in a number of sectors where Germany had been very present before the war, particularly in the manufacturing sector (the main industries being bicycles, clock making and glass). Yet after 1918, Japan remained broadly dependent on German technologies in the chemical and electrical sectors.[43] (In this respect, the colorant industry represented an exception, taking advantage of the German patent suspension to expand; this led to the establishment of the Japan Dyestuff Manufacturing Company [1916] and the diversification of Mitsui Mining into this sector.)

---

[37] *Tokkyo kara mita sangyo hatten shi ni kan suru chosa kenkyu hokokusho* (Tokyo, 2000), 2.

[38] Stark Mason, *American Multinationals and Japan: The Political Economy of Japanese Capital Controls, 1899–1980* (Cambridge, 1992), 25.

[39] *Tokkyo seido 70 nen shi*, 31–32.

[40] The difference between these and the WIPO figures (see Table 1) is due to the fact that WIPO takes into consideration not only patents of inventions, as described earlier, but also the protection of marks, designs and utility models.

[41] *Kogyo shoyuken seido hyaku nen shi*, 587.

[42] Ibid., 410–12.

[43] Akira Kudo, *Japanese-German Business Relations: Cooperation and Rivalry in the Interwar Period* (London, 1998), 36.

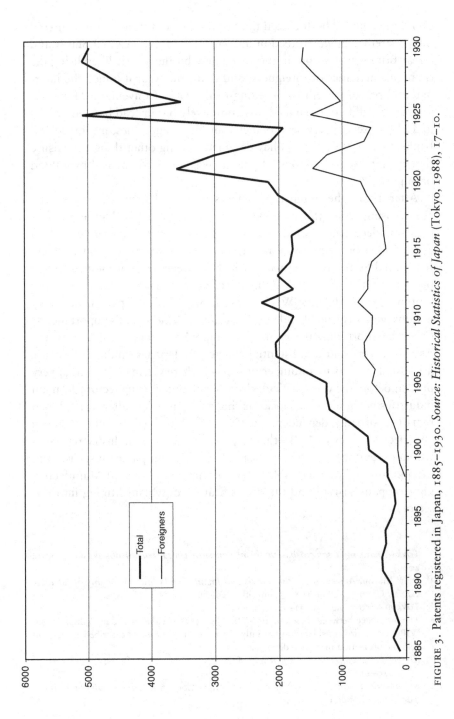

FIGURE 3. Patents registered in Japan, 1885–1930. *Source: Historical Statistics of Japan* (Tokyo, 1988), 17–10.

TABLE 8. *Main Sectors for Patents
Registered in Japan as a Percentage,
1900–30*

	1900	1910	1920	1930
Machines	28	31	35	26
Electricity	3	6	15	22
Chemicals	10	16	22	27
Other	59	47	28	25

Source: *Kogyo shoyuken seido hyaku nen shi*
(Tokyo, 1984–85), vol. 1, 590.

The machinery, electrical and chemical industries represented the three main sectors active in the Second Industrial Revolution (see Table 8). These sectors accounted for a significant and growing share of patents registered in Japan – more than half of all those registered in 1910 and three quarters in 1930. They were also the sectors preferred by foreign patent holders, constituting more than 95 per cent of all foreign patents registered in 1930.[44] That statistic, together with the massive presence of American and German patent holders in this group, points to the decisive role of multinationals in the Japanese patenting process.

There was thus a sharp dichotomy between the sectors in which Japanese and foreigner patent holders were concentrated (see Table 9). The statistics for 1905 show that the Japanese continued to focus on innovations relating to traditional sectors (textiles and agriculture) and everyday objects, whereas non-Japanese patent holders were concentrated in sectors tied to the Second Industrial Revolution.

In response to the dichotomy, in 1905 the Japanese authorities rounded out their legislative arsenal with a new law on the protection of utility models, based on the German system: under this law, the difference between a patent and a utility model was based on the degree of technological progress provided by an innovation, with fundamental inventions placed in the first category and practical improvements in the second. Japan's particular definition of utility models – they were distinguished less sharply from patents, the categorisation being based on the degree of inventiveness as established by the patent registry office[45] – allowed it to protect products that were not innovations per se but that

[44] *Kogyo shoyuken seido hyaku nen shi*, 593.
[45] John Richards, 'Petty Patent Protection', *Proceedings of Fordham University International Intellectual Property Law & Policy* (1998), vol. 2, ch. 47.

TABLE 9. *Main Categories of Patents Registered in*
1905, According to Nationality, Number of Cases

Inventions (Japanese)		Inventions (foreigners)	
Agricultural tools	53	Guns	37
Various machines	51	Various machines	28
Lamps	47	Carriages	25
Stationery	38	Chemical products	25
Looms	37	Steam-powered machines	23
Sericulture (tools)	32	Various appliances	19
Various tools	27	Boats	18
Cereal farming	23	Electrical appliances	18
Footwear	23	Electrical tools	17
Woodworking tools	22	Steam-powered devices	16

Source: Kogyo shoyuken seido hyaku nen shi (Tokyo, 1984–85), vol. 1, 217.

featured a new form or structure.[46] In this way the authorities sought to encourage technological development even in cases where goods and procedures were insufficiently novel to be registered as patents. Such cases usually involved imitations of foreign products, thus making it possible to legalise technological hybridisation and even straight-out imitation.[47]

Broadly speaking, patents were used to protect the capital goods industry, production processes and high-tech goods, whereas utility models protected ordinary consumer goods such as typewriters, galoshes, and plugs and sockets, all of which were imitations of imported products.[48] Utility-model rights, as indicated, were mainly held by Japanese nationals. Between 1905 and 1930, 140,699 utility models were registered, of which only 629 were filed by non-Japanese (0.5 per cent of the total), primarily the Germans and Americans.[49] During the same period, the number of registered patents was 67,782, of which 46,766 were held by the Japanese, who thus registered three times as many utility models as patents. There were also more disputes tied to utility models than to patents: between 1905 and 1930, there were 2562 of the former sort and 1958 of the latter. The disputes around utility models mostly related

---

[46] *Tokkyo seido 70 nen shi*, 72.
[47] Models are sometimes confused with designs. A design is a new product, whereas a model is a new application of an existing product. *Tokkyo kara mita sangyo hatten shi ni kan suru chosa kenkyu hokokusho* (Tokyo, 2000), 4.
[48] Ibid., 12 and *Kogyo shoyuken seido hyaku nen shi* (Tokyo, 1984–85), vol. 1, 342.
[49] *Historical Statistics of Japan* (Tokyo, 1988), 17–10.

to smaller companies, especially in respect to consumer goods such as bicycles, furniture, beauty products and cameras.[50]

The path that Japan followed enabled it to develop its industry in two major successive phases: an initial phase marked by a technological leap made without foreign input (1860–1895) and a second phase marked by integration into the international system and the admission of Western multinationals into the country (1895–1930). In this context, Japan's signing of the Paris Convention can be understood as announcing integration into a globalised technology market, for the sake of catching up in the chemical, electrical equipment, machinery and similar fundamentally important sectors. To be sure, this shift to a policy of technological transfer based on cooperation with Western multinationals was not unilateral. There was a persistent tendency to acquire technologies and know-how via traditional vehicles, a process taking place on the fringe of the international patent protection system and the operations of multinationals. It was concentrated in the consumer goods industry, which relied less on complex technologies than did industries such as electrical equipment.

The Technologies of the Second Industrial Revolution: The Case of Electrical Equipment

In the interwar period, technology transfers connected to Second Industrial Revolution sectors were controlled by either cartels or multinationals. Tetsuo Tomita has shown that, in both the Japanese electrical and chemical industries, a new approach to patenting foreign innovations emerged in the 1920s and 1930s, when the Japanese themselves began to submit applications to protect inventions held by foreign multinationals.[51] This new approach was, of course, a sign that the Japanese market was becoming truly integrated into the world market – a process exemplified by developments in the Japanese electrical industry.

The limits of Japan's traditional technology transfer policies first became manifest in the electrical sector. Before 1900, the Japanese managed to build simple electrical appliances. For example, seven patents were filed between 1885 and 1900 for electric batteries, three for lightbulbs, and nine for telephones.[52] Yet, because of an insufficient mastery of production processes, the overall number of patent applications remained

---

[50] *Tokkyo seido 70 nen shi*, 399.

[51] Tetsuo Tomita, *Shijo kyoso kara mita chiteki shoyuken* (Tokyo, 1993), 101–11.

[52] *Tokkyo bunrui betsu somokuroku* (Tokyo, 1958).

low, with copies of imported products unable to compete with the original items in either cost or quality. Electrical technologies were controlled by a handful of multinationals including General Electric, Westinghouse, AEG and Siemens, and could only be acquired through cooperation,[53] a factor leading, as suggested, to both liberalisation of FDI and patent protection. Nine foreign-backed electrical companies were founded in Japan between 1899 and 1930;[54] most were joint ventures involving American multinationals that had been developing production and distribution networks worldwide since the last quarter of the nineteenth century. The only non-U.S. companies were Siemens, based in Germany, which was instrumental in the establishment of three companies, and Columbia, based in Great Britain, which helped set up a phonograph factory in 1927.

The main U.S. company investing in Japan after 1900 was General Electric (GE).[55] At the outset of the investment process, it split its operations into two joint ventures. The first was in the domain of consumer goods and small electrical equipment. Founded in 1890, Tokyo Electric was a small Japanese firm that produced lightbulbs, but was unable to compete with imported German bulbs, which were both less expensive and longer lasting. In the early 1900s, Tokyo Electric's chief engineer had travelled to the United States seeking technical assistance in exchange for a stake in the firm; a contract handing a majority interest in the firm to GE was signed in 1905. The patent policy implemented by GE through the joint venture with Tokyo Electric was aimed at controlling the sale and production of electric lightbulbs in Japan.[56] GE's strategy here was simple: controlling the production of lightbulbs by holding on to the rights to their manufacture, thus limiting the activities of its main rival, the famous German company Allgemeine Elektrizitäts-Gesellschaft (AEG). That strategy was effective, forcing AEG to cut a deal with Tokyo Electric in 1914. Moreover, between 1910 and 1918, GE and Tokyo Electric sued all of the small-scale Japanese manufacturers producing lightbulbs under various patents not held by GE. The courts subsequently annulled the registration of these patents, which were very similar to those

---

53 Chandler, *Scale and Scope*.
54 *Nihon ni okeru gaikoku shihon* (Tokyo, 1948) and Katsu Udagawa, 'Senzen Nihon no kigyo keiei to gaishikei kigyo', *Keiei Shirin*, 24, 1–2 (1987), 18–20.
55 Shigehiro Nishimura, *GE sha no kokusai tokkyo kanri* (PhD dissertation, Kyoto University, 2005).
56 Shigehiro Nishimura, 'General Electric's International Patent Management before World War II: The 'Proxy Application' Contract and the Organisational Capability of Tokyo Electric', *Japanese Research in Business History*, 21 (2004), 101–25.

held by GE, leading to the eventual concentration of Japanese domestic production of lightbulbs under Tokyo Electric.

GE's second joint venture in Japan was in the domain of heavy electrical equipment. In 1909 it invested in the Shibaura Manufacturing Company, which had been producing telegraphs, turbines and motors copied from GE models but had run into the same problems as those facing Tokyo Electric. In the early 1900s, the Mitsui *zaibatsu* (family-controlled conglomerate) that owned Shibaura was thus considering closing the company when GE initiated negotiations that would save it. In exchange for a 25 per cent stake and a right to 1 per cent of royalties on Shibaura's sales, GE made available both its patents and research and development information to the company and began to train Japanese engineers in U.S. plants. In this way the joint venture allowed Shibaura to move from copying to developing products. In this respect, let me note a subsequent chapter in this company's history: in 1939, a shakeout led to a merger of Tokyo Electric and Shibaura Manufacturing to form Tokyo Shibaura Electric – the company that continues to be known as Toshiba.

Clearly, such joint ventures were crucial for technology transfer to Japan. However, holding a patent was only part of the story. As can be seen in the case of GE, a patent conferred power in the Japanese market, making it possible to eliminate rivals that were producing copies. Yet holding a patent did not in itself involve the transfer of know-how and the subsequent development of competitive firms, which instead resulted from ongoing practical training in the U.S. and German plants of multinational companies and from visits to Japan by American and German engineers. Nishimura has shown how this knowledge acquisition led to a different form of partnership in patent management: in 1919, GE transferred full responsibility for such management in the Japanese market to Tokyo Electric. From then on, the Japanese joint venture received all patents registered in the United States, deciding which would require protection in Japan according to its industrial and commercial policies. All told, Tokyo Electric registered more than 400 GE patents in Japan between 1919 and 1930.[57]

The Consumer Goods Industry: Watch and Clock Making as an Example

The technologies of the Second Industrial Revolution were not the only drivers of modernisation in the Japanese economy during the first third

---

[57] Ibid., 121.

of the twentieth century. Changing ways of life during the Meiji period resulting from acculturation, urbanisation and economic growth were accompanied by the emergence of companies specialising in the manufacture of new products targeting Japanese consumers (beer, chocolate, umbrellas, bicycles, musical instruments, cameras, etc.). The shift from importing these consumer goods to producing them stemmed from a technological transfer process differing from that affecting sectors of the Second Industrial Revolution in that it mainly took place without the cooperation of Western partners, because patents were not being used to control domestic markets or technological transfer. When it came to consumer goods, not only were innovations copied and adapted from the West sometimes registered as utility models, but the focus was often simply on protecting trademarks,[58] whose marketing, rather than the production of the goods themselves, was what really mattered. In this regard, the Japanese watch- and clock-making industry is a good case in point.

In Japan, this industry developed within the traditional pattern of technology transfer, which involved the establishment of an import-substitution industry.[59] Clocks and watches were imported into Japan from the 1860s onwards, with the market being dominated by Swiss, American and German manufacturers until the century's end. Starting in the second half of the late 1880s, Japanese manufacturers made various attempts to establish a domestic watch industry. The main industrial enterprises set up at that time were Aichi Clock (1893) and Meiji Clock (1895) in Nagoya, and Hattori in Tokyo (1892). In the early twentieth century Hattori became the leading Japanese watch-making company, marketing its products under the Seiko brand: by 1910, it was producing 42 per cent of all clocks and 86 per cent of all watches manufactured in the country.[60]

The boom in the Japanese watch-making industry resulted from an independent development policy based on a strategy of technological transfer with no input from foreign firms. Between 1890 and 1910, the main means to acquire needed technologies were to import Swiss and American machine tools and to send young Japanese engineers to Swiss

---

[58] *Kogyo shoyuken seido hyaku nen shi*, 133.

[59] For the beginnings of the Japanese watch-making industry, see Hoshimi Uchida, *Tokei sangyou no hattatsu* (Tokyo, 1985) and Pierre-Yves Donzé, 'Le Japon et l'industrie horlogère Suisse: Un cas de transfert de technologie durant les années 1880–1940', *Histoire, Economie et Société* (2006), 105–25.

[60] Figures from Hirano Mitsuo, *Seikoshashi hanashi* (Tokyo, 1968).

watch-making schools and study tours in Europe and the United States. These strategies, combined with a protectionist customs policy that penalised imports, boosted the new consumer goods sector to the extent that domestic production ended up outstripping imports – in 1899 for clocks and in 1930 for watches.[61]

However, until the Second World War, the watches and clocks manufactured in Japan were imitations of Swiss or American products. Under these conditions, the patent protection policy in force took on a different dimension from that in the electrical industry. With Japanese manufacturers focused on copying or adapting foreign products, there was a strong tendency to register utility models rather than patents. Moreover, a majority of these (732 utility models, or 52% of the total) related to simple items such as watch cases and bracelets. The electric clock, which had appeared as a key technological innovation in the interwar period, was not really a factor (accounting for 7.2% of all registered utility models).

The Japanese recorded far fewer patents in the same domain (261), mainly in the electric clock sector (132, or 50.6%) and after the First World War: from 1919 to 1930, electric clocks accounted for 73.6 per cent of all patents registered (see Figure 4). Although a few companies emerged as rights holders in this sector, they were not Hattori or other watch and clock makers but rather electrical appliance companies engaged in intense diversification (Fuji Electric, Hitachi); in the end they did not go ahead with the production of electric clocks, a field that was marginal at the time.[62] For the most part, rights holders were people who were above all interested in protecting innovations relating to clocks (64 patents, or 24.5%) and watch cases (40 patents, or 15.3%). When it came to watch mechanisms – which posed the main technological transfer challenge in the watch-making industry – only three patents were filed (1.1%). The technological development policy of Hattori, the main watch-making enterprise, was consistent with this general trend. Although Hattori had registered thirty-four ownership titles by 1930, only three were patents, and they concerned elements secondary to the firm's development (two concerned alarm clocks and one a chromium-plating process). The thirty-one utility models involved copied elements (for the most part cases

[61] Takao Shimano, *Shohin seisan yushutsunyu butsuryo ruinen tokeiho 1871–1960* (Tokyo, 1970), 595–98.
[62] In 1930, the Japanese watch-making industry produced 11,699 electric clocks, representing a mere 7.3% of overall production value. Hirano Mitsuo, *Seikohanashi* (Tokyo, 1968).

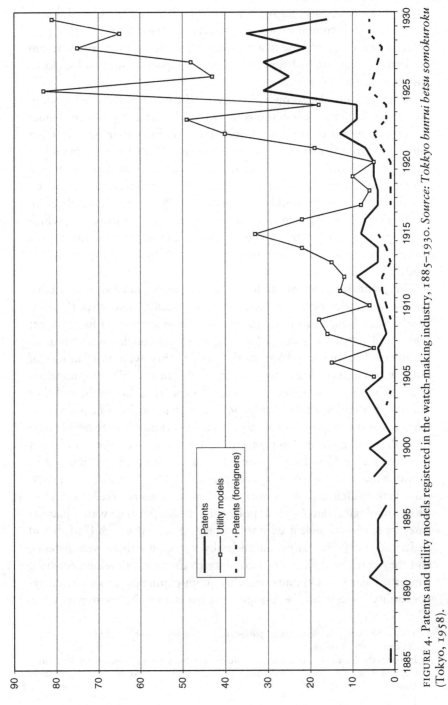

FIGURE 4. Patents and utility models registered in the watch-making industry, 1885–1930. *Source: Tokkyo bunrui betsu somokuroku* (Tokyo, 1958).

and straps). Furthermore, Hattori did not acquire any foreign patents during this period.

The lack of technical cooperation between Hattori and Western watch-making firms did not prevent the latter from protecting some of their innovations within the country. In all, 65 patents were registered by non-residents, primarily individuals from Switzerland (23 patents, or 35.4% of all foreign patents), the United States (18 patents, or 27.7%), Britain (7 patents, or 10.8%) and France (6 patents, or 9.2%).

The filing of foreign patents was itself generally viewed as a protectionist gesture. There were two phases in this process, tied to the evolutionary development underway in the Japanese watch- and clock-making industry. In the initial stage, which lasted until the First World War, the first Japanese watch- and clock-making companies mainly produced clocks. Accordingly, the Western exporters of these products filed patents to prevent copies from being made. For the most part the twenty-one foreign patents registered up until 1918 mainly concerned clocks (fifteen patents) and were held by the countries dominating the trade (the United States, the United Kingdom and Germany). During this period, only a single patent was registered by a Swiss citizen – an electric clock maker named David Perret (patent No. 6643, 1903). Then during the 1920s, non-Japanese watch makers became interested in protecting pocket watches, which both Hattori and various workshops for assembling Swiss watches had begun producing. Swiss watch makers filed twenty-two watch patents between 1919 and 1930. Even though the vast majority of these individuals wished to protect their products and prevent technology transfer, there was one exception: the Tavannes watch company, one of the main Swiss watch factories, which operated an assembly workshop in Tokyo from the 1910s onwards. The four patents registered by this company during the 1920s (nos. 41866, 1922; 44451, 1923; 61691, 1924; and 65224, 1925) concerned the most complicated watch parts (winders and springs), which were difficult to copy and doubtless reflected the transmission of more complex know-how, as manifest in the electrical industry as well.[63]

The second major challenge posed in the 1920s was to the electric clock industry: although several Western companies filed patents in Japan to protect their products (including the International Time Recording Company of New York, Landis & Gyr SA and Kienzle Uhrenfabrik), there

---

[63] Nevertheless, the reassembly workshop with which Tavannes Watch worked without recourse to FDI failed and was bought in the mid-1920s by an alarm clock manufacturer.

was also a policy of technology transfer through patents. For example, the watch- and clock-trading firm Tenshodo acquired the rights to the electric clocks of two French companies, Les Ateliers Blier Frères (no. 71838, 1927) and Léon Hatot (no. 79401, 1928), and Tokyo Electric bought two patents belonging to an American engineer in 1929 (nos. 81601 and 83482). However, neither of these firms succeeded in manufacturing Japanese electric watches.

Conclusion

In Japan between 1880 and 1930, Second Industrial Revolution sectors and the consumer goods industry followed different developmental paths in which patents played different roles. In the former case, as exemplified by the electrical appliances industry, the technologies involved relatively complex production processes and were controlled by powerful international actors. At the end of the nineteenth century, multinationals in the electrical industry adopted a strategy of global expansion in which the circulation of technology and know-how was viewed as a key element. For these multinationals, patents were instruments for furthering growth. As can be seen in the case of General Electric, the chief value of patents for the Japanese market was legal: they enabled multinationals to eliminate competition by asserting the primacy of their rights. In this case technology transfer dovetailed with the legal framework formed by the international patent system; cooperation between Western and Japanese partners allowed the latter to acquire the necessary technological know-how to develop a domestic industry.

In the case of the consumer goods industry as exemplified by watch making, what was involved, in contrast, was the emergence of a new industrial sector based on an active policy of technology transfer – a sector that, however, emerged on the fringe of the international patent system and was shaped by independent firms. Japanese industrialists were not facing powerful, organised partners: the Swiss watch-making industry was fragmented among hundreds of small firms, and there was no international cartel in the sector. Intellectual property rights were not widely applied and did not in any way define the framework for the transfer of technology. Japanese manufacturers acquired foreign know-how through a traditional mode of copying and adaptation, without the consent of the relevant Western firms.

In this manner the example of Japan helps us understand the exact role played by the international patent system in the emergence of a global technology market at the end of the nineteenth century. Granted, the Paris Convention introduced a fundamental break in 1883, insofar as patents could no longer be considered as furnishing a monopolistic right to industrial exploitation of an innovation at the national level. Thereafter they applied to the entire world and thus became instruments of power whose primary role was to regulate and negotiate technology transfer at an international level. Yet because of their international organisational structure and vast financial resources, it was mainly multinationals and cartels that relied on patent law to control the technology market.[64]

Nevertheless, as can be seen from the evolution of the Japanese watch-making industry, the international patent system did not regulate the flow of all technologies. Because there was no sufficiently powerful partner, technologies and know-how continued to circulate, be traded and acquired by more conventional vehicles. Consequently, the globalisation of specific markets such as the technology market was not solely a result of the desire by states to unify their national markets. Rather, it was a consequence of multinationals' tendency to instrumentalise international institutions, such as the Paris Convention, remaining a work in progress, at least up until the Second World War.

[64] Penrose, *Economics of the International Patent System*, (Greenwood, 1973) 232.

PART III

THE FIRST WORLD WAR AND THE
CONSEQUENCES FOR ECONOMIC GLOBALISATION

PART II

10

Transnational Cooperation in Wartime

The International Protection of Intellectual Property Rights during the First World War

Isabella Löhr

Until recently intellectual property rights were not a widely discussed topic. This situation has changed dramatically during the last decade with the rise of computer technology and the Internet, which allow ordinary users to reproduce and redistribute copyrighted material such as books, computer programmes and works of music without a great expenditure of time and energy. In the debates that have broken out as a result, the basic argument centres on the cultural, social and economic role that intellectual property rights play in modern societies. The goal is to arrive at a compromise concerning how to rebalance the relationship among copyright holders, the various cultural industries, the public and the interest that states have in using copyrighted material for the promotion of education and science.

Current debates on how to handle these rights on a national level have been strongly shaped by international organisations such as the World Trade Organisation, the World Intellectual Property Organisation, UNESCO and the European Union. These organisations face the challenge posed by one problem in particular: national copyright laws stop at national borders, whereas trade with cultural goods crosses political boundaries and breaks through national copyright monopolies. At the end of the nineteenth century, states, intellectuals, the cultural industries and lawyers were already arguing for the establishment of specialised international organisations for building a reliable structure of intellectual-property-rights governance on a global scale. The overall aim was a multilateral copyright regime taking in as many states as possible and centralised in an international organisation – one focused on implementing, monitoring and adjusting copyright rules to contemporary technical,

economic, political and cultural developments. In 1886, the major
European book-trading countries founded the Berne Union, the first
international organisation for governing cross-border trade in cultural
goods.[1] The Berne Union is of special historical importance, because it
was not only an instrument for regulating the transnational trade activity
of the cultural industries but also a tool for balancing public and private
interests; reconciling political, economic and cultural policy concerns;
and closing the gap between national interests and international law.

Yet what happens to such an international organisation, based in
a fundamental way on principles of mutual and peaceful cooperation
between states and actors from civil society, when a conflict such as the
First World War transforms its major member states into enemies? In
this chapter I argue that, through the Berne Union, the European book
trade was embedded in social, political and legal institutional structures
that could resist the restrictive trade policies and wartime propaganda
of the European states. Contrary to what has often been maintained, the
First World War did not mark a watershed for Europe's cultural industries, dividing a prosperous phase of global trade from another phase
of decreasing economic interaction and cooperation.[2] Rather, coalitions
emerged between publishers, authors, legal experts and the Berne Union
to keep war out of the Berne Convention – thereby paving the way
for a global extension of Western copyright standards in the following
decades.[3] This discussion focuses on literary and artistic property, leaving
aside the history of both patent rights and trademarks. Whereas copyright law acknowledges the benefit of individual creativity for society by
granting exclusive rights that combine the economic right to use a piece of
art, for example, with the moral right to forbid any nonauthorised alterations of this work, patent rights were set up as an instrument of economic
policy. Their task is thus to promote technical and economic progress:

---

[1] Christopher May and Susan K. Sell, *Intellectual Property Rights: A Critical History*
(Boulder, 2006), 107–32; Sam Ricketson, *The Berne Convention for the Protection of
Literary and Artistic Works, 1886–1986* (London, 1987).

[2] Such a view is held for instance in the following works: Knut Borchardt, *Globalisierung
in historischer Perspektive* (Munich, 2001); Robert Boyce, 'The Collapse of Globalisation
in the Inter-War Period: Some Implications for Twentieth-Century History', in Gabriele
Clemens (ed.), *Nation und Europa. Studien zum Internationalen Staatensystem im 19.
und 20. Jahrhundert* (Stuttgart, 2001), 121–32.

[3] Isabella Löhr, 'Intellectual Cooperation in Transnational Networks: The League of
Nations and the Globalization of Intellectual Property Rights', in Mathias Albert (ed.),
The Communicative Construction of Transnational Political Spaces and Times (Frankfurt
am Main, 2009), 58–88.

inventors receive a temporally limited monopoly over their invention under the condition that they must disclose its technical details so that competitors can base their future work upon already existing knowledge.[4]

The Propertisation and Internationalisation of Culture in the Nineteenth Century

Intellectual property rights were established between 1750 and 1850 in the European, North American and South American states and then spread worldwide in the course of the late nineteenth and twentieth centuries. Modern intellectual property law is a bundle of individual rights developed in a secular, market economy and liberally organised societies. This law was meant to guarantee and standardise the rights of authors, publishers, performing artists, the public and the state to engage in scientific, cultural and social competition and provide a secure contractual foundation for cooperation in the production, dissemination and reception of culture and knowledge.[5] Crucial to the codification of intellectual property rights was the rapidly intensifying consumption of and trade in books, works of art and music during the nineteenth century – developments brought about by growing literacy within broad sections of the population, the emancipation of the middle classes, and new technical opportunities to produce and reproduce cultural works. As a consequence modern liberal societies increasingly had to deal with questions involving ownership of goods that were at once cultural, political and mercantile, as well as entitlement to publish, use and receive works of a literary and artistic nature.

To understand the apparently inexorable rise of intellectual property rights since the late eighteenth century and the enormous political stability of the international copyright system even in extreme political crises such as the First World War, we need to turn our attention first to theories of property and then to the networks and organisations within which international copyright law became embedded starting in the late nineteenth century. Economic theory has stressed the importance of property

---

[4] For further reading see Florian Mächtel, *Das Patentrecht im Krieg* (Tübingen, 2009); Margrit Seckelmann, *Industrialisierung, Internationalisierung und Patentrecht im Deutschen Kaiserreich* (Frankfurt am Main, 2006).

[5] Lionel Bently and Brad Sherman, *Intellectual Property Law* (Oxford, 2008); Hannes Siegrist, 'Geschichte des geistigen Eigentums und der Urheberrechte: Kulturelle Handlungsrechte in der Moderne', in Jeanette Hofmann (ed.), *Wissen und Eigentum. Geschichte, Recht und Ökonomie stoffloser Güter* (Bonn, 2006), 64–80.

rights regimes for modern market-based societies. Whereas economists like Douglass C. North have set out the role played by relevant institutions in reducing uncertainty and thus promoting market activities,[6] social scientists and historians have rather ignored the formative impact of property and property relations in the course of the twentieth century in particular, instead emphasising power relations and social inequality.[7] This, however, has changed in the last few decades, when a deepening discussion of intellectual property rights has in turn sparked debate on the complex relationship between culture, knowledge and information, and property and its role in the constitution of modern societies.

The concept of the propertisation of culture and society has been developed in the social sciences to explain the rise in the modern period of property rights regimes. The concept interprets property rights, and particularly intellectual property rights, as a fundamental vehicle for artists and those using their art to extend their initial rights to copy and publish literary works. Due to the intent of authors and publishers to protect their interests and market access as much as possible, intellectual property became the main legal category for handling and regularising culture and knowledge in the course of the late eighteenth and nineteenth centuries. Yet the presence of such a process does not necessarily indicate the prevalence of a liberal and individualistic approach to property and property rights regimes. Rather, the concept of propertisation acknowledges the immaterial character of cultural goods, which means the presence of a heterogeneous set of actors (creative artists, users of artworks, the public and the state) and a fundamentally different legal framework for intellectual property rights as compared to material property (for example, in the temporal limitations at work in the former category). For this reason the concept underscores the embeddedness of intellectual property rights in a wider institutional and sociocultural framework. Once established as a legal, social, economic and also aesthetically reflected category, such rights provided an ordering principle for the construction of knowledge regimes; they would also determine the way societies set up their cultural institutions, rules and norms, in a process involving the restriction of access rights and assignation of a range of roles and functions to relevant actors in culture and society.

---

[6] Douglass C. North, *The Rise of the Western World: A New Economic History* (Cambridge, 1980).

[7] Volker Heins, 'Die Rückkehr der Eigentumskritik', *WestEnd. Neue Zeitschrift für Sozialforschung* 5 (Frankfurt, 2008), 44–67.

Hence crucial for the management of culture and knowledge was not only a certain property rights regime but also a linkage with alternative institutions that sometimes weakened the individual and exclusive rights of authors or publishers in favour of interests of the public or state, including the state's interest in maintaining its educational and cultural policies; the interest of professional organisations in restricting access to the reproduction of cultural goods; and the interest of people with education, wealth, appropriate social background or cultural capital (for example, in the case of authorship) in maintaining exclusive property rights or access to professional positions. Propertisation thus conceptualises intellectual property rights as a fundamental category contributing decisively to the shaping of modern society by integrating a complex ensemble of social, cultural, political, economic and legal institutions, relationships and values.[8]

Yet to explain the stability of the Berne Union between 1914 and 1918, we also need to look more closely at international politics and ask how propertisation strategies were connected to strategies for internationalising intellectual property rights. Legislators in various European states needed not only to draw up laws to protect these rights but also to set up international regulations for distributing and handling cultural goods (at the time this meant books and other printed works), once these goods began to be exchanged in significant quantities between different states and different legal and linguistic areas.[9] An early attempt to solve this problem involved bilateral trade agreements, which since the mid-nineteenth century prevented reprinting within different European states. However, implementation of such bilateral and multilateral agreements was uneven, with some also being restricted to the short term. It thus became increasingly necessary to introduce long-term, universal legal standards in Europe covering the largest possible area.[10]

---

[8] Hannes Siegrist, 'Strategien und Prozesse der "Propertisierung" kultureller Beziehungen. Die Rolle von Urheber- und geistigen Eigentumsrechten in der Institutionalisierung moderner europäischer Kulturen', in Stefan Leible, Ansgar Ohly and Herbert Zech (eds.), *Wissen, Märkte, geistiges Eigentum* (Tübingen, 2010), 3–36; Hannes Siegrist, Isabella Löhr, 'Intellectual Property Rights between Nationalization and Globalization: Introduction', in *Comparativ* 21 (2011), 7–28.

[9] Miloš Vec, 'Weltverträge für Weltliteratur: Das Geistige Eigentum im System der rechtssetzenden Konventionen des 19. Jahrhunderts', in Louis Pahlow and Jens Eisfeld (eds.), *Grundlagen und Grundfragen des Geistigen Eigentums* (Tübingen, 2008), 107–30.

[10] Stephen P. Ladas, *The International Copyright Protection of Literary and Artistic Property in Two Volumes* (New York, 1938), 44–68; Catherine Seville, *The Internationalisation of Copyright Law: Books, Buccaneers and the Black Flag in the Nineteenth Century* (Cambridge, 2007), 41–77.

Hence starting in the 1860s, main European book-trading countries such as Great Britain, France, Germany, Switzerland and Belgium pushed for an international agreement acknowledging the rights of publishers and authors on the European continent. In 1886, these efforts resulted in the Berne Convention, the first multilateral treaty for the legal protection of literary and artistic works.[11] From then on, each citizen of one of the convention's member states who published his or her works in another member state had equal legal standing with that state's authors. Through a harmonisation of national and international law offering both authors and holders of rights of usage binding rights covering distribution and reception in the entire territory of the Berne Convention, cross-border trade was meant to become more calculable.[12] In this manner, while states expanded the scope of their citizens' legal rights, they also handed over part of their function in institutionalising and nationalising culture to a specialised international organisation.

The Berne Convention was embedded in a union of states called the Berne Union, one of several such organisations established in the second half of the nineteenth century to oversee the technical, legal, social and economic tasks resulting from the increasing cross-border movement of people, goods and ideas.[13] The general intent of these organisations was to provide a framework for rules not only governing transnational trade but also minimising transaction costs and spurring commercial-industrial, cultural and social activities among states and world regions.[14] Well-known international public unions, some of which are still in existence, were the International Telegraph Union (founded 1865), the Universal Postal Union (1874), the Paris Convention for the Protection of Industrial Property (1883), the International Union for the Publication of Customs

[11] Jacques Secretan, 'L'évolution structurelle des unions internationales pour la protection de la propriété intellectuelle', in Bureaux internationaux réunis pour la protection de la propriété intellectuelle (eds.), *Les unions internationales pour la protection de la propriété industrielle, littéraire et artistique, 1883–1963* (Geneva, 1962), 15 f.

[12] Bénigme Mentha, 'Berne Convention', in H. L. Pinner (ed.), *World Copyright: An Encyclopedia* (Leyden, 1953), 1029–70.

[13] Rüdiger Wolfrum, 'International Administrative Unions', in Rudolf Bernhardt (ed.), *Encyclopedia of Public International Law*, vol. 2 (Amsterdam, 1995), 1041–47.

[14] Wolfram Fischer, 'Die Ordnung der Weltwirtschaft vor dem Ersten Weltkrieg: Die Funktion von europäischem Recht, zwischenstaatlichen Verträgen und Goldstandard beim Ausbau des internationalen Wirtschaftsverkehrs', *Zeitschrift für Wirtschafts- und Sozialwissenschaften* 1 (1975), 289–304; Carl Strikwerda, 'Reinterpreting the History of European Integration: Business, Labor, and Social Citizenship in Twentieth Century Europe', in Jytte Klausen and Louise A. Tilly (eds.), *European Integration in Social and Historical Perspective: 1850 to Present* (Lanham, 1997), 55.

Tariffs (1890) and the Central Office of International Railway Transport (1890).[15]

Recent research has stressed the significantly new elements introduced by these unions into national and international politics from the 1860s onwards.[16] The most important innovation in our context was the implementation, with the Berne Union, of an institutional and organisational infrastructure allowing both state and nonstate actors to cooperate in a field that took in not only private groups such as publishers, intellectuals and lawyers but also the states' cultural and educational policies.[17] Moreover, in providing these groups with the means to influence the handling and propertisation of cultural goods beyond their own national territory, the Berne Union made it possible for state delegates, the cultural industries and intellectuals to introduce, in terms of property, the regulation of culture and knowledge into international politics.[18]

States generally viewed the other international public unions the same way they viewed the Berne Union: as a means to expand their sphere of influence across national borders. States signed international conventions that prescribed binding technical, legal and social rules for their own interaction and that of both private persons and companies. To institutionalise the rules, the conventions were anchored in the international unions, dedicated to one or another relevant international activity; all signatory states had to be members of the unions. These unions' permanence was ensured through continuous conferences for revising the treaties and through international offices, in most cases located in small or neutral states such as Switzerland and Belgium. The offices, in fact, turned out to be a key element for the unions' maintenance and development, because they provided a staff of civil servants exclusively loyal to the unions and responsible for surveying the application of the rules and their

---

[15] Craig N. Murphy, *International Organization and Industrial Change: Global Governance since 1850* (Cambridge, 1994), 46–49.

[16] Madeleine Herren, *Internationale Organisationen seit 1865: Eine Globalgeschichte der internationalen Ordnung* (Darmstadt, 2009); Akira Iriye, *Global Community: The Role of International Organizations in the Making of the Contemporary World* (Berkeley, 2004).

[17] For the institutional and political innovations of the public unions see Gerold Ambrosius, *Regulativer Wettbewerb und koordinative Standardisierung zwischen Staaten: Theoretische Annahmen und historische Beispiele* (Stuttgart, 2005); Miloš Vec, *Recht und Normierung in der Industriellen Revolution: Neue Strukturen der Normsetzung im Völkerrecht, staatlicher Gesetzgebung und gesellschaftlicher Selbstnormierung* (Frankfurt am Main, 2006).

[18] Sam Ricketson, *International Copyright and Neighbouring Rights: The Berne Convention and Beyond* (Oxford, 2006), 41–83; Vec, 'Weltverträge', 107–30.

continuous calibration with technical advances.[19] In this manner, despite being dependant on agreements between governments of various states, the unions significantly transformed conventional interstate diplomacy, offering a stable institutional basis for the political, economic and social infrastructure of international cooperation emerging in the second half of the nineteenth century.[20]

Through their regulations, international public unions played a central role in reinforcing the rights of a range of affected parties – in the case of the Berne Union, this group took in authors, composers, artists, publishers, booksellers, lawyers and the consuming public. From its beginnings the international protection of authors' rights had two dimensions. On the one hand there was the basic cooperation between nation-states needed to inaugurate international conventions. In this respect the nation-state continued to serve as the central managing institution for regulating cross-border trade with cultural goods, its main function being to territorialise law through national legislation. On the other hand, the Berne Union owed its existence in large part to the initiatives of experts and interested professionals[21] – enterprising and politically aware publishers, authors, musicians, scientists, artists and lawyers who were strongly aware of the need to internationally align their individual authorial and publishing rights. Organised in national and international interest groups and trade associations, they held congresses and campaigned for cross-border acknowledgement of copyright rules starting in the 1850s, with states actively including them in negotiations and international legislation. Because their everyday production, dissemination and receipt of cultural goods endowed them with a consistent role in connecting various national legal systems, cultures and publishing industries, these experts and professionals were naturally a target group for the project of internationalising authors' rights.[22]

---

[19] Hartwig Bülck, 'Verwaltungsgemeinschaften, internationale', in Karl Strupp and Hans-Jürgen Schlochauer (eds.), *Wörterbuch des Völkerrechts*, vol. 3 (Berlin, 1962), 564–77; Wolfrum, *International Administrative Unions*, 1041–47.

[20] Madeleine Herren, 'Governmental Internationalism and the Beginning of a New World Order in the Late Nineteenth Century', in Martin H. Geyer and Johannes Paulmann (eds.), *The Mechanics of Internationalism: Culture, Society, and Politics from the 1840s to the First World War* (Oxford, 2001), 121 f.

[21] Hannes Siegrist, 'Geistiges Eigentum im Spannungsfeld von Individualisierung, Nationalisierung und Internationalisierung: Der Weg zur Berner Übereinkunft von 1886', in Rüdiger Hohls, Iris Schröder and Hannes Siegrist (eds.), *Europa und die Europäer. Quellen und Essays zur modernen europäischen Geschichte* (Wiesbaden, 2005), 52–61.

[22] Ricketson, *International Copyright*, 41–83.

The participation of experts and professional associations was one of the essential features of the international public unions, with states considering these transnational actors to be fulfilling an important function: contributing[23] to a fundamental reform of both national and international politics. The unions themselves embodied the possibility of adapting intergovernmental politics to societal initiatives, the states thus acknowledging an incapacity to independently manage cross-border economic, legal, technical and cultural interaction. As a result, the national legislative monopoly was subsumed in this context into a system of global governance linking national policy, intergovernmental agreements and transnational business activities.[24]

The European Book Trade and the First World War

In the period between 1840 and the outbreak of the First World War, European book production increased significantly. The rise of the European book industries was one facet of the fundamental economical, social, cultural and political transformation of European societies expressed as a shift from primarily agrarian to primarily industrial production and a vast expansion of public administration.[25] Both basic skills in reading and writing and an expansion of higher education opportunities were self-evidently crucial to the process of constructing a secular, industrialised and liberal society based on a market economy. In turn, growing literacy rates and an upward valuation of education and culture strongly promoted the development of various cultural industries into an independent and – at least in Western Europe – wealthy branch of the economy.[26] The international office of the Berne Union documented the economic development of the worldwide publishing industries in statistical overviews, which it regularly published in its monthly journal between 1888 and 1952. Although the journal's editorial staff repeatedly

[23] Ambrosius, *Regulativer Wettbewerb*, 48; Tilman J. Röder, *Rechtsbildung im wirtschaftlichen 'Weltverkehr': Das Erdbeben von San Francisco und die internationale Standarisierung von Vertragsbedingungen, 1871–1914* (Frankfurt am Main, 2006), 42 f.

[24] Michael Zürn, 'Global Governance', in Gunnar Folke Schuppert (ed.), *Governance-Forschung. Vergewisserung über Stand und Entwicklungslinien* (Baden-Baden, 2005), 127.

[25] Wolfram Fischer, 'Wirtschaft und Gesellschaft Europas 1850–1914', in Wolfram Fischer (ed.), *Handbuch der europäischen Wirtschafts- und Sozialgeschichte, Vol. 5: Von der Mitte des 19. Jahrhunderts bis zum Ersten Weltkrieg* (Stuttgart, 1985), 1–207.

[26] David Vincent, *The Rise of Mass Literacy: Reading and Writing in Modern Europe* (Cambridge, 2000).

underscored that the data's reliability could not always be validated, the figures are the only source we have to at least gain an idea of the growth rates of global book production. In this regard, Figure 5 compares the book-trading countries at the head of international book production until the mid-twentieth century: France, Germany, Great Britain, Italy, Japan, Russia/the Soviet Union, Spain and the United States.[27]

The information presented in Figure 5 is indeed not detailed enough to inform us of, for example, the number of translations included in the annual publication rates or rates of imports and exports. In this discussion, I therefore neither closely examine Figure 5 nor use it to illuminate the development of particular national book markets;[28] however, the production rates it points to offer an impression of the increasing vitality of this economic branch between 1890 and 1913, together with the negative impact of the First World War on the European publishing industries. What conclusions can we draw, then, regarding the war's impact on the Berne Union and the cross-border trade with copyrighted material?

First Figure 5 shows that, except for the United States and Russia/the Soviet Union, the majority of the nation-states with flourishing book industries were members of the Berne Union.[29] Second, in contrast to Japan, where the decrease in book production rates only set in at the start of the 1920s as a result of economic crisis, the European and North American publishing industries were strongly affected by the war and suffered great losses. Third, the figures mirror the shift from peacetime to wartime economies, as marked by a concentration of industrial capacities, resources (for example, the introduction of rationing measures for paper) and human labour on the production of goods essential to the war effort.[30] In this regard, in all belligerent countries the book industry was seriously affected by governmental economic restrictions meant to finance the war. Yet if we convert the figures and set an index (1900 = 100%),

[27] *Le Droit d'Auteur: Organe mensuel du bureau international de l'union pour la protection des oeuvres littéraires et artistiques, Statistique intellectuelle* (Berne, 1890–1953).

[28] For further reading see Reinhard Wittmann, *Geschichte des deutschen Buchhandels* (Munich, 1999); Frédéric Barbier, *Histoire du livre* (Paris, 2000); John Feather, *A History of British Publishing* (London, 2006); Gerhard Menz, *Der europäische Buchhandel seit dem Wiener Kongreß* (Würzburg, 1941).

[29] Ladas, *The International Copyright Protection*, 97.

[30] Roger Chickering, *Imperial Germany and the Great War, 1914–1918* (Cambridge, 1998), 32–46; Hans-Peter Ullmann, 'Kriegswirtschaft', in Gerhard Hirschfeld, Gerd Krumeich and Irina Renz (eds.), *Enzyklopädie Erster Weltkrieg* (Paderborn, 2009), 220–32.

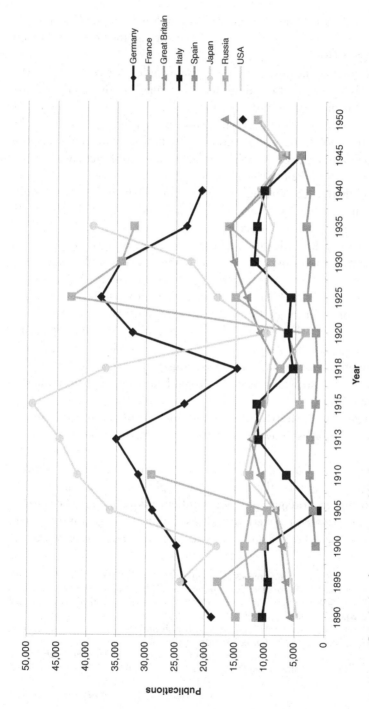

FIGURE 5. International comparison of book production, 1890–1950. *Source: Le Droit d'Auteur: Organe mensuel du bureau international de l'union pour la protection des œuvres littéraires et artistiques, Statistique intellectuelle* (Berne, 1890–1953).

it becomes clear that most of the publishing houses needed a relatively short time to recover from the war or even surpass the book production rates of 1913 (see Figure 6).

In addition to indicating that the publishing industry recovered quickly, Figure 6 also shows that it did not have to struggle in the interwar years with long-lasting structural deficits that could be traced back to the war economy – which sheds critical light on the present-day discussion of the 'crisis of the book trade' said to have been experienced by publishers and intellectuals at the end of the 1920s in face of the rise of radio and cinema as serious rivals to the book market.[31]

Finally, there is the question of the extent to which the major book-trading countries such as Great Britain, France and Germany intentionally used the war to restrict competition by foreign enterprises. The Trading with the Enemy Amendment Act passed in 1916 authorised the British government to act against any company in the United Kingdom suspected of being associated with or cooperating with the enemy.[32] Although this law also covered the publishing industries, neither the publishers' association files nor governmental sources consulted in the German and French cases offer any hint that copyright laws were broken intentionally during the war.[33] Rather, the absence of any complaints in the sources indicates that copyright agreements were not seriously affected – except for one case discussed next, which, actually strengthened rather than weakened the Berne Union.

In August 1916, shortly after enacting the Trading with the Enemy legislation, the British government decided to freeze the copyright entitlements of citizens belonging to enemy states and put them under public trusteeship.[34] Although this initiative was ostensibly aimed at German publishers and authors, the government explained that it was actually meant to protect foreign copyright entitlements in Britain, because in wartime no private or governmental institution could guarantee adherence to copyright laws; a public trusteeship was thus the only way of

[31] Catherine Bertho, 'Les concurrences', in Henri-Jean Martin, Roger Chartier and Jean-Pierre Vivet (eds.), *Histoire de l'édition française. Vol. 4: Le livre concurrencé, 1900–1950* (Paris, 1986), 22–35; Stephan Füssel, 'Das Buch in der Medienkonkurrenz der zwanziger Jahre', *Gutenberg-Jahrbuch* 71 (1996), 322–40.

[32] John McDermott, 'Trading with the Enemy: British Business and the Law during the First World War', *Canadian Journal of History* 32 (1997), 201–20.

[33] See the documents concerning the First World War and intellectual property rights in the archives of the French and German foreign ministries, of the Börsenverein des Deutschen Buchhandels and of the Société des Gens de Lettres.

[34] For a report on the British law, see *Le Droit d'Auteur* 29 (1916), 119.

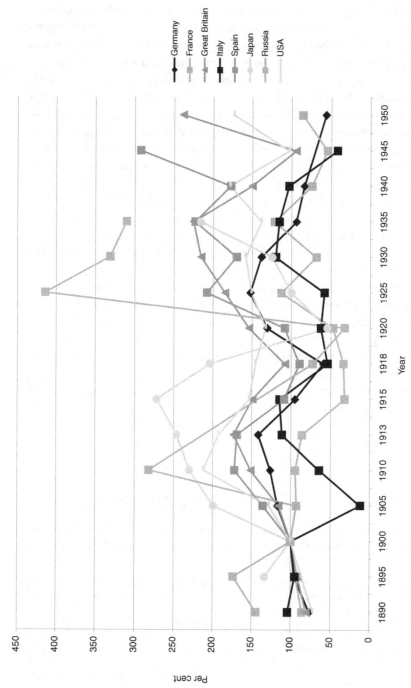

FIGURE 6. International book production rates, 1890–1950. *Source: Le Droit d'Auteur. Organe mensuel du bureau international de l'union pour la protection des œuvres littéraires et artistiques, Statistique intellectuelle* (Berne, 1890–1953).

maintaining the relevant agreements.[35] The law only applied to cultural
works produced or published after the war's outbreak, and foreign rights-
holders were guaranteed adequate compensation; the law in any event was
repealed with the Versailles Treaty. Nevertheless, authors and publishers on both sides of the front strongly attacked the British government
for violating the rules of the Berne Union.[36] Considering the fact that
I cannot find any complaints in German and French governmental or
private institutional sources concerning the deprivation of rights caused
by the British initiative during or after the war, and taking account of
the British decision not to repeat the policy during the Second World
War,[37] it appears that intellectual property rights were broadly excluded
from economic warfare strategies during the First World War. After Versailles, although the European publishing industries had to initially deal
with severe financial losses and a production decrease, they recovered
very quickly, with the union's legitimacy not having been called into
fundamental question.

The remarkable continuity manifest here perhaps partly stemmed from
the minor importance of book production for the war effort when compared to other economic sectors, although empirical evidence in this
regard is lacking. For a more firmly grounded explanation, we need to
direct our attention towards the economic and social networks present
in the field of intellectual property rights, as established before 1914 and
institutionally centralised in the Berne Union. With help from the concept
of propertisation, we can see that both the internationalisation of a certain notion of culture and knowledge and that notion's embeddedness in
professional networks served as a strong basis for maintaining copyright
law during the First World War.

The Berne Union in Legal Theory and Legal Practice, 1914–1918

At the beginning of the war, the question arose of whether the Berne
Union should continue to exist, rooted as it was in nineteenth-century

35 Francesco Ruffini, 'De la protection internationale des droits sur les œuvres littéraires
   et artistiques', in *Recueil des cours de l'Académie de Droit International de La Haye*
   (Paris, 1926), 462 f.
36 Léon Malaplate, *Le droit d'auteur dans les rapports franco-étrangers* (Paris, 1931),
   139.
37 Bénigme Mentha, *La guerre et les unions internationales pour la protection de la propriété industrielle et des œuvres littéraires et artistiques* (Zurich, 1943), 25 f.; Kurt Runge,
   'Die Revidierte Berner Übereinkunft zum Schutze von Werken der Literatur und Kunst in
   Kriegs- und Nachkriegszeit', *Gewerblicher Rechtsschutz und Urheberrecht* (henceforth
   GRUR) 50 (1948), 33.

internationalism and economic cooperation[38] – principles clearly conflicting with the bellicose nationalism prevailing on various home fronts
since August 1914. There was not even any clause in the Berne agreement
regulating its application in wartime, so that its validity in this period
would only be confirmed by legal experts as it were retroactively, after
the war's end[39] – the multilateral convention's indissolubility forming a
contrast with traditional bilateral treaties, which indeed ceased to exist
with the war's outbreak and had to be explicitly reinstated with peace.[40]
Described more precisely, as long as some member states remained neutral, it was agreed that the rules of the convention would continue to be
in force among all member states, even those at war with each other.[41]
Legal experts saw only two ways to annul such conventions – resignation
by individual members or concerted self-dissolution by the signatories.

Although these experts exchanged their arguments only after the peace
settlement, having already experienced the convention's continuity until
1918, national jurisdictions had faced the delicate task of deciding on the
status of the Berne Convention while the war was proceeding. It appears
that only one legal judgment was made regarding the convention in the
1914–18 period. In July 1917, a music publishing house based in Milan
sued another such house in Hamburg for having illegally copied and
distributed two Verdi operas. The Hamburg Oberlandesgericht (higher
regional court) decided in favour of the claimant, stating that, although
the Italian-German bilateral copyright agreement of 1884 had been can-
celled with the war's outbreak, all rights granted in the framework of the
Berne Convention before 1914 were still in force.[42]

A close look at the bulletin of the international office of the Berne Convention, *Le Droit d'Auteur*, and the periodicals of the German and French
professional associations of authors and publishers – the *Börsenblatt
des Deutschen Buchhandels* and the *Bibliographie de la France*, respectively – confirms the widespread absence of copyright piracy between
1914 and 1918 within the territory of the Berne Union.[43] This is all
the more remarkable in that it appears that publishers, legal experts and

---

[38] Martin H. Geyer and Johannes Paulmann, 'Introduction: The Mechanics of Internationalism', in Geyer and Paulmann (eds.), *The Mechanics of Internationalism*, 1–25.
[39] Marcel Plaisant, *La création artistique et littéraire et le droit* (Paris, 1920); Mentha, *La
guerre*.
[40] Runge, *Die Revidierte Berner Übereinkunft*, 31.
[41] Malaplate, *Le droit d'auteur*, 133; Mentha, *Berne Convention*, 1068.
[42] A report on the verdict: *GRUR* 23 (1918), 130–32.
[43] For ongoing documentation see *Le Droit d'Auteur* 1914–18; for a summary, see
Malaplate, *Le droit d'auteur*, 134 f.

members of national governments had great difficulty in receiving any information about how international copyright rules were being handled in other European countries. In January 1915, the board of the German publishers' association (the Börsenverein des Deutschen Buchhandels) sent an inquiry to the Chamber of Industry and Commerce in Leipzig asking how to deal with foreign copyright entitlements. In response the chamber apologised for not being able to offer reliable information. There would be no experts' consensus on this complicated issue, with even the German Foreign Ministry remaining in the dark.[44] The Société des Gens de Lettres faced comparable problems. In 1916 its board considered preparing a booklet about the translation rights of French authors abroad. Some board members argued that such a booklet would make little sense because no one knew if the Berne Convention was still in force, whereas other members insisted that nothing indicated the convention had been dissolved. The booklet was issued, but only took account of French allies and neutral states.[45]

Although there was substantial insecurity regarding the theory, practice and politics of international copyright law, the documentation does suggest general support for the Berne Convention within national governments and among legal experts and transnational actors from the commercial and cultural spheres. What, then, was the basis for sparing international copyright law in the war's nationalist propaganda effort and not sacrificing it to a preference for a purely nationalistic copyright policy? I offer a tentative answer to this question in the next section.

The International Office in Berne: Institutional Permanence and Informal Networks

One of the international public unions' distinctive features was their representation by various permanent international offices, staffed by individuals committed to furthering their unions' aims, but, crucially, in close collaboration with national governments and the various specialists and professional organisations. In the domain of international copyright law, the international office of the Berne Union thus remained uniquely

---

[44] Letter of the Börsenverein to the Chamber of Industry and Commerce in Leipzig, 15 January 1915 and the Chamber's reply, 17 March 1915 (Staatsarchiv Leipzig: Bv I, 21765/91, 56).

[45] Registre des procès-verbaux du comité de la Société des Gens de Lettres, Comité du 4 décembre 1916, vol. 19, 29.

free of any war-related legal or ideological conflicts, its director thus arguing in October 1914 for strict observance of the Berne Convention, complications tied to the war notwithstanding.[46] In maintaining this standpoint over the following years, the office underscored the union's role as a mediator tying the convention to national war legislation.[47] Through its strong dedication to the convention and concomitant willingness to instruct both governmental and private actors regarding what it felt was the proper way to proceed – which is to say, as an *accord typiquement pacifique* – the international office emerged as a moral authority, thus contributing significantly to dissolving legal and jurisdictional uncertainty in the wartime context. It did so in awareness not only of the convention's role as a major achievement of nineteenth-century internationalism but also of its status as an essential element in the future reconstruction of Europe.[48]

In any event the office's impact was only possible because of support by the professional associations, which adopted two strategies in this regard: making internationally announced proclamations in favour of the convention and engaging in concerted action against any infringement of international copyright law. In September 1916, the board of the Börsenverein thus agreed to reject any action meant to revoke foreign copyright claims, arguing that the war did not affect national or international copyright rules;[49] this decision confirmed a statement already published in the organisation's bulletin in September 1914. The fact that the organisation moved past the national framework was symbolically important: in 1915, the international office published the statement in its internationally distributed bulletin *Le Droit d'Auteur*.[50] Professional associations in other countries published similar appeals; for instance the Società italiana degli autori ed editori,[51] the British Publisher's

[46] Ernst Röthlisberger, 'Das Schicksal der Literarverträge und Literar- sowie anderer Rechtsschutzunionen im Kriege', *Schweizerische Juristen-Zeitung* 11 (1914), 74–78; *Le Droit d'Auteur* 28 (1915), 5–6.

[47] 'Les rapports unionistes pendant la guerre', *Le Droit d'Auteur* 28 (1915), 5–6; 'Les unions internationales et la guerre,' *Le Droit d'Auteur* 30 (1917), 118–19; 'La solution des questions concernant la propriété intellectuelle dans les accords intervenus entre les belligérants au commencement de 1918', *Le Droit d'Auteur* 31 (1918), 113–17.

[48] Mentha, *La guerre*, 5; Malaplate, *Le droit d'auteur*, 132 f.

[49] Minutes of the Börsenverein's board meeting on 20 September 1916 (Staatsarchiv Leipzig: Bv I, 21765/91).

[50] 'Allemagne. De la traduction d'œuvres étrangères en temps de guerre', *Le Droit d'Auteur* 28 (1915), 6–7; 'Les rapports unionistes pendant la guerre', *Le Droit d'Auteur* 28 (1915), 117.

[51] Ruffini, *De la protection internationale*, 459.

Association at the beginning of 1915[52] and the Syndicat français de la
propriété intellectuelle in 1916.[53]

The most important role of these associations was, however, to
respond in the rare cases of international copyright infringement during the war. The most prominent case was the so-called *édition de guerre*,
an unauthorised reprint of French composers by the German publisher
Johannes Platt. The international office, the Börsenverein, and other associations started a concerted and eventually successful campaign to end the
reprint's distribution[54] – a campaign that was exemplary in its arrangement of an out-of-court settlement to the infringement issue. Crucial
to the campaign were coordinating efforts by the international office,
involving detailed reports on both appeals by publishers' associations in
Switzerland, Germany and the Netherlands not to buy or sell the *édition
de la guerre*[55] and the reaction of German publishers: after discussing the
matter, the German association of music publishers asked the Ministry
of Justice to take measures against the reprinting.

The international office rightly considered Johannes Platt's succumb-
ing to this pressure as a major success.[56] In the few cases of copyright
infringement after the campaign against that publisher, the same model
was applied: publication of detailed reports and appeals to boycott the
illicit products.[57] In 1920, the office assessed the situation in light of
the previous war years as follows: 'Thanks to all these combined efforts,
the literary union might be the one international union, among all the
others, which has suffered least from the global conflict in regards to
its standing and practical efficiency. Its reputation is so solidly anchored

[52] *Le Droit d'Auteur* 28 (1915), 9.
[53] *Le Droit d'Auteur* 29 (1916), 131.
[54] Summarising this cooperation: 'Le bilan de la guerre mondiale en matière de propriété
intellectuelle', *Le Droit d'Auteur* 33 (1920), 37–41.
[55] 'Effondrement, sous la pression commune, d'une entreprise de contrefaçon musicale, dite
édition de guerre', *Le Droit d'Auteur* 29 (1916), 11–12; 'Suppression, en germe, d'une
nouvelle entreprise de contrefaçon musicale, dite édition de guerre', *Le Droit d'Auteur*
(1916), 36; summarising the case: Mentha, *La guerre*, 18 f.
[56] 'Effondrement, sous la pression commune, d'une entreprise de contrefaçon musicale,
dite édition de guerre', *Le Droit d'Auteur* 29 (1916), 12.
[57] 'L'organisation de la lutte contre la piraterie internationale pendant la guerre', *Le
Droit d'Auteur* 30 (1917), 39–42; 'Allemagne. Lutte contre une nouvelle entreprise
de contrefaçon musicale', *Le Droit d'Auteur* 31 (1918), 130–31; 'Allemagne. Lutte
contre une nouvelle entreprise de contrefaçon musicale', *Le Droit d'Auteur* 32 (1919),
45; extensively reporting the case: Malaplate, *Le droit d'auteur*, 134–37; Ruffini, *De
la protection internationale*, 459; 'Les rapports unionistes pendant la guerre', *Le Droit
d'Auteur* 28 (1915), 116 f.

that one can, with confidence and without deluding anyone, supply it with new recruits'.[58]

The Paris Peace Treaties and the Return to Prewar Copyright Law

In 1919 the two multilateral conventions aimed at protecting intellectual property rights, the Berne Convention and the Paris Convention for the Protection of Industrial Property, were part of the Paris peace negotiations. The inclusion of the Berne Convention in the reorganisation of Europe's political, social and economic landscape triggered controversy among European publishers, authors and jurists: based on their own recent experiences, they were highly uneasy at the idea of approaching intellectual property rights as a war issue with relevance to the peace treaties. Clause 306 of the Versailles Treaty, stipulating the renewed validation of the international property conventions on grounds that they had not been in force after 1914, caused particular unease.[59] Other details of the clause also sparked intense controversy by pointing in the opposite direction than the initiatives by authors, publishers and the international office to preserve the convention during the war. The clause partly overlooked rules contained in the Berne Convention, declaring German authors and publishers unauthorised to sue for any compensation for reprints published illegally between 1914 and 1918. Instead, sale of such publications was to be allowed until the summer of 1920.[60]

The response to these regulations was a striking consensus against any effort to politically interfere with an intellectual property rights regime seen as having maintained its efficiency throughout the war.[61] To preserve such autonomy in the face of efforts to both punish Germany and reorganise postwar Europe economically, politically and socially, the international office found itself again compelled to seek support from the national interest groups,[62] especially through a mobilisation of informal

---

[58] 'L'Union internationale en 1920', *Le Droit d'Auteur* 33 (1920), 6–7; for a detailed overview of the legal, social and economic consequences of the war for the cultural industries, see 'Le bilan de la guerre mondiale en matière du propriété intellectuelle', 33 (1919), 37–41, 50–55, 66–70.

[59] Runge, *Die Revidierte*, 33.

[60] Ibid., 31.

[61] Georges Chabaud, *La propriété industrielle, littéraire et artistique et les traités de paix* (Nancy, 1921); Malaplate, *Le droit d'auteur*, 141; Mentha, *La guerre*, 24; Plaisant, *La création artistique*, 100 ff; Ruffini, *De la protection internationale*, 466.

[62] The international office openly asked which states or groups would take the initiative in reestablishing the prewar conditions of the Berne Union: 'Le premier traité de paix

networks; the result was a gradual general agreement in both legal theory
and jurisdiction, in the course of 1920 and 1921, that the Berne Convention had not been suspended during the war and thus lay outside the
Versailles Treaty's sphere of influence.

One particular clause in the treaty, clause 310, seemed wholly incompatible with international copyright law. It classified all copyright treaties
between German and foreign publishers as licences – the licensing concept
normally only being applied to industrial property rights.[63] German publishers in particular feared this clause because it included regulations
that could be interpreted wholly to their detriment. The clause granted
German publishers six months to reinstate agreements with foreign publishers after the Versailles Treaty's signing, and after that time, all contracts that had not been renewed were to be annulled.[64]

German publishers were particularly concerned by 'licence' notion: if
the notion were retained, they would run the risk of either fully losing
their legal rights abroad by refusing the 'licence' as inappropriate or seeing their copyrights downgraded to licence status.[65] The Börsenverein's
board instructed its lawyers to commission reports on possible interpretations of the notion.[66] Yet the board remained uncertain regarding
what to recommend to its members,[67] thus sending a representative to
the Berne international office for advice. After initially abstaining from
any comments on the practical effects of the 'licence' stipulation in light
of the political framework,[68] the office faced up to the need to issue a
recommendation: to the effect that the Börsenverein should ignore the
time frame for renewing the 'licences', giving Berne Union law priority
over the Versailles Treaty's politically initiated regulations.[69] From both

conclu avec l'Allemagne et la protection de la propriété intellectuelle', *Le Droit d'Auteur*
  32 (1919), 83.
[63] For a survey of the discussion see Mentha, *La guerre*, 24 f.; Malaplate, *Le droit d'auteur*,
  140 f.
[64] Ruffini, *De la protection internationale*, 466.
[65] Letter of the Börsenverein to the Verlegerverein, 16 September 1919 (Staatsarchiv
  Leipzig: Bv I, 21765/199).
[66] For example: 'Willy Hoffmann, Verlagsverträge im Friedensvertrag', *GRUR* 25 (1920),
  108–09; report of the Councillor of Justice Dr. Hillig on Paragraph 310 in a letter to Dr.
  Georg Paetel, member of the board of the Börsenverein, 16 September 1919 (Staatsarchiv
  Leipzig: Bv I, 21765/199).
[67] Letter of the Börsenverein to Albert Osterrieth, 25 March 1920 (Staatsarchiv Leipzig:
  Bv I, 21765/199).
[68] Report of Gustav Kirstein on behalf of the Börsenverein (Staatsarchiv Leipzig: Bv I,
  21765/199).
[69] Letter of the Börsenverein to Albert Osterrieth, 25 March 1920 (Staatsarchiv Leipzig:
  Bv I, 21765/199). Because the files of the international office are not extant, it is not
  possible to give reasons for the office's change of strategy.

Le Droit d'Auteur and the files of the Börsenverein, we can see that no private or public organisations instituted legal proceedings against German publishers after the six-month period at issue was up, in July 1920. The international office and the professional groups it worked with could then devote themselves to the most urgent task on their agenda: preparations for the next Berne Union conference, scheduled for 1928.[70]

Conclusions

To understand both the general continuity of the Berne Union during the First World War and the capacity of its member states to differentiate between national war aims and their obligations towards the multilateral copyright regime, we need to take account of three distinct features leading to an intertwining of national legislations, cultural and educational policies, and the book trade on a European level. First, the effectiveness of national copyright law – the legal protection of authors and publishers against illegal reprints at home and abroad – was mainly dependent on the effectiveness of international copyright rules, so that the Berne Convention provided valuable instruments for regulating and controlling the cultural industries on a national scale. Second, for this reason the convention provided considerable economic and cultural returns for authors, publishers and national administrations. Consequently, the concerned actors from the cultural, economic and political spheres had a strong interest in maintaining and optimising the Berne Union. Third, to achieve this aim the convention was institutionally anchored in an international organisation, guaranteeing permanence and the ability to adapt the multilateral regulations to technical, economic, cultural and political change.

The far-reaching consequences of this institutionalisation and standardisation of the rules for the regulation of cross-border trade of cultural goods became clear during the First World War. The international office of the Berne Union turned out to be the central managing institution for offering clear instructions to both state and nonstate actors on how to behave in an exceptional situation. Crucial to the union's ability to orient and stabilise international copyright law during the war was its institutional structure. It facilitated effective transnational cooperation among the national publisher associations, engaged in for the sake of dissolving the legal incertitude prevailing during and after the war. The

---

[70] Letter of the French Minister of the Interior to the Foreign Minister, 19 August 1921 (Archives Diplomatiques Nantes: Ministère des Affaires Etrangères/ Sous-direction des unions internationales/ 2ème tranche/ C/ 18).

international office's regulative power stemmed from its neutrality, the expertise of its employees, and its mandate to urge member states to adhere to the convention regardless of the political climate. By giving the convention's multilateral law priority over national law and expressing a moral commitment to it, and with the strong support of the national publishers' associations, the office developed considerable normative power. In creating a clear hierarchy, it offered orientation to state and nonstate actors deeply involved in war events and incapable of overseeing the status of international jurisdiction and legal theory.

Yet why did national governments and publishers' associations follow the guidelines of the international office – which, after all, was only a managing institution for a multilateral contract between sovereign states? The establishment of the Berne Union was part of the multilateralisation of international relations during the second half of the nineteenth century. As emphasised earlier, this process was by no means restricted to the realm of interstate relations;[71] recent research on the international organisations involved emphasises their generative power and their legitimation through competence to regulate international trade, caution member states to obey the convention rules, and address both state and non-state actors.[72] Accordingly, Michael Barnett and Martha Finnemore have approached these international organisations as having an independent role in world politics, their task being not only to conserve international regulations but also to apply them to such actors.[73] Their policies, the authors indicate, put 'emphasis on both agency and structure' underlining the organisations' 'ability to constitute or construct new actors in world politics, create new interests for actors, and define shared international tasks'.[74]

In view of the continuity regarding intellectual property in the First World War period, such policies point to the weight of the organisational structure of international trade relations. Although from the beginning of the war, foreign trade with cultural goods decreased significantly, organisations such as the Berne Union, rather than diminishing cooperation

---

[71] Madeleine Herren and Sacha Zala, *Netzwerk Außenpolitik: Internationale Kongresse und Organisationen als Instrumente der schweizerischen Außenpolitik, 1914–1950* (Zurich, 2002), 12.

[72] See, e.g., Iriye, *Global Community*.

[73] Michael Barnett and Martha Finnemore, 'Political Approaches', in Thomas G. Weiss and Sam Daws (eds.), *The Oxford Handbook on the United Nations* (Oxford, 2007), 48.

[74] Ibid.

among states, made all the greater efforts to protect authors' rights in an extreme situation. For publishers, authors and national governments, the international regulations in play provided the only effective mechanism for strengthening their national cultural industries in the framework of international competition – because cross-border trade of cultural goods was incapable of being completely controlled, securing at least a minimal return flow of investment activity was of common interest. At the same time, the international office of the Berne Union turned out to be a highly independent player, intent on actively mobilising the institutional and social networks anchored in the Berne Convention. It did so, as indicated, by appealing to both the union's normative aims and the convention's political value, and by building immediate coalitions with private actors likely to profit most from an efficiently working international copyright regime. In this way the office contributed decisively to a differentiation between the Berne Convention's focus and the national imperatives of military conflict. The continuity of these coalitions immediately after the war underscored the union's status as more than a mere executive unit. It was in effect the embodiment of an idea: the endurance of a set of fundamental rules in the face of even drastic political and cultural change.

The Resilience of Globalisation during the First World War

The Case of Bunge & Born in Argentina

Phillip Dehne

Historians have tended to view the First World War as a pivotal moment in the history of global economic integration. First the war shredded the fabric of globalisation, and then the uncertain peace that followed left transnational business unsteadily twisting in the breeze for the next three decades. Yet the history of Bunge & Born, one of the world's most powerful multinational grain trading firms throughout the twentieth century, brings into question this portrayal of the war as year zero for business. Instead, the development of Bunge & Born in Argentina during the First World War highlights that company's ability to retain its prewar place in the local grain economy while setting itself up for continued successes postbellum. Bunge & Born proved resilient despite a marked wartime decline in the availability of transatlantic shipping and communications, and despite being targeted as the most 'enemy' of companies by the feisty Britons in charge of their empire's economic war in Argentina. Bunge & Born's wartime successes highlight the complexity of the structure of world trade in grain in the early twentieth century. Even as implementing the economic war augmented the powers of the British state in relation to British business, attempts to hurt this company exposed the inadequacies of British power, particularly the great difficulty of controlling markets in neutral countries. Despite Bunge & Born's long-term focus on dominating the movement of grain from South America to overseas markets, it was the depth and breadth of Bunge & Born's integration into local markets in South America that made the company surprisingly nimble in finding ways to outfox its British opponents.

Argentina's Grain Trade Before the War

Bunge & Born held the largest slice of the lucrative export trade in Argentine wheat and other grains during the first decades of the twentieth century. In the 1880s, wheat, corn and linseed came under intensive cultivation across the pampas, so that between 1909–13 Argentina trailed only Russia as the top grain exporter in the world.[1] European-based commercial partnerships built large export companies in Buenos Aires and Rosario, branches that by 1914 had in many cases become their de facto world headquarters.[2] At the turn of the century, the so-called Big Four firms commanded the entire structure of the Argentine wheat trade, with the largest company, Bunge & Born, controlling at least a quarter of the market.[3] Argentine farmers called Bunge & Born 'the Octopus', its tentacles reaching through all steps in the trade. Bunge & Born controlled the supply of credit needed by purchasing agents and, through them, by farmers in the pampas. It also exploited an information gap: their expert and immediate knowledge of international prices and market conditions enabled Bunge and the other of the Big Four exporters to limit the prices they paid to the uninformed and often desperate *acopiadores* and farmers strung across the pampas. Bunge & Born's estimated capital of £2 million in 1910, built from virtually nothing over the previous three decades, may have been the largest of any grain merchant in the world.[4] To supplement that capital, it had access to wide varieties of credit from British and European banks and the Banco de la Nación that did not loan money directly to farmers.[5] Indeed most of Bunge's profits probably came from speculation and transactions using borrowed money.[6]

---

[1] Osvaldo Barsky and Jorge Gelman, *Historia del Agro Argentino: Desde la Conquista hasta fines del siglo XXU* (Buenos Aires, 2001), 162.

[2] On the tendency of transatlantic European companies to adopt very flexible management models, with 'evidence of both centralizing and decentralizing approaches', see Robert Greenhill, 'Investment Group, Free-Standing Company or Multinational? Brazilian Warrant, 1909–52', *Business History* 37 (1995).

[3] James R. Scobie, *Revolution on the Pampas: A Social History of Argentine Wheat, 1860–1910* (Austin, 1964), 92–93. In an extremely rare interview of a Bunge & Born executive, Jorge Born estimated in 1910 that Bunge & Born, Dreyfus, and Weil together controlled 80% of Argentine grain; see Jorge Schvarzer, *Bunge & Born: Crecimiento y diversificación de un grupo económico* (Buenos Aires, 1989), 18–19.

[4] Stanley Chapman, *Merchant Enterprise in Britain from the Industrial Revolution to World War I* (Cambridge, 1992), 205, 318.

[5] Barsky and Gelman, *Historia del Agro Argentino*, 190.

[6] Chapman, *Merchant Enterprise*, 208.

There was a time when British grain markets and British merchants ruled the overseas transit of new world grains. Indeed, experts from the London Corn Trade Association in the 1880s advised the founders of the Argentine grain exchange on best rules and practices when the export trade there was just getting underway.[7] Yet by 1914 it was apparent that the ever-rising torrent of Argentine grains would not pass through the hands of British companies. Although there has always been disagreement as to their nationality, the Big Four –Bunge & Born, Dreyfus, Weil Brothers, and Huni & Wormser – were definitely not British.[8] The nationality of Bunge & Born was particularly impossible to pin down. The economic historian Stanley Chapman has variously described Bunge & Born as 'a German partnership who operated mainly in Argentina', as a 'leading British-based investment group', and as a firm run by Ernesto Bunge, the Belgian 'court Jew' of King Leopold II.[9] Amazingly, such characterisations are not necessarily contradictory: Bunge & Born provides perhaps the ultimate example of a belle époque multinational corporation.[10] Like the most successful investment groups, it had modest capital in its European branches 'concealing a massive and increasingly diversified overseas operation'.[11] Bunge & Born appeared to be international in management and partnership, with large contingents of both Belgian and German capital and nominally headquartered in Antwerp,

[7] Morton Rothstein, 'Multinationals in the Grain Trade, 1850–1914', *Business and Economic History* 12 (1983), 93.

[8] Roger Gravil explains that 'the grain trade was primarily in German hands', relying for this assessment of nationality on characterisations by Britons during the war. Gravil, *The Anglo-Argentine Connection*, 40. Eager to demonstrate the overall weakness of British economic penetration in Argentina and the ability of the Argentines to rule their own house, D. C. M. Platt claims that the 'Big Four' were Argentine: Platt, 'Economic Imperialism and the Businessman: Britain and Latin America before 1914', in Roger Owen and Bob Sutcliffe (eds.), *Studies in the Theory of Imperialism* (London, 1972), 300. Yet no one in Argentina seemed to believe that Bunge & Born or others were 'Argentine'. For example, Consul Hugh Mallet in Rosario in 1904 explained that 'there are several British firms engaged in shipping grain, but the bulk of this trade is in the hands of foreigners, principally Germans'. Report for the year 1903 on the Trade and Commerce, &c., of the Consular District of Rosario, No. 3157, P.P. 1904, xcvii, Cd. 1766–91.

[9] Stanley Chapman, 'British-Based Investment Groups before 1914', *Economic History Review*, 38, 2 (May 1985), 248. Chapman, *Merchant Enterprise*, 206, 292.

[10] Although there has never been a standard model of a multinational corporation; Brian Roach, 'A Primer on Multinational Corporations', in Alfred D. Chandler Jr and Bruce Mazlish (eds.), *Leviathans: Multinational Corporations and the New Global History* (Cambridge, 2005), 24.

[11] Chapman, 'British-Based Investment Groups', 238.

TABLE 10. *Trading Companies and Their Market Share in Argentina*

Companies	Market share (in % of Argentine total)
Bunge & Born	23
Dreyfus	22
Huni & Wormser	10.5
Weil Brothers	10
General Mercantile Co.	9.5
Hardy & Mühlenkamp	7
H. Ford & Co.	7
Sanday & Co.	6
Procter, Garrett, Marston, & Co.	3
Others	2

Source: Harold Ford of Ford & Co. to Tower on 27 Oct. 1915 (Tower to FO No. 345 of 27 Oct. 1915, F.O. 181525 of 30 Nov. 1915. FO 368/1207, National Archives, Kew). Also, Tower's annual report for 1913, CP 10379, in Kenneth Bourne and D. Cameron Watt (eds.) *British Documents on Foreign Affairs* (Frederick, MD: University Publications of America, various dates), part I, D, vol. 9, paragraph 177.

but the managers and partners of the flagship Buenos Aires branch held such authority that the true centre of power in the company was never obvious.[12] Wherever their headquarters, in 1914, all of the Big Four grain companies in Argentina were led by men such as Alfredo Hirsch, the General Manager of Bunge & Born, who identified themselves as German, socialized together regularly at the Deutscher Klub, and provided leadership for other local institutions of the German émigré community.[13]

Critics and competitors accused these big grain firms of collusion in the international marketplace, in the options markets of Rosario and Buenos Aires, and in purchasing from farmers along the railway lines (see Table 10). They successfully gained control not only of the newly developing export trade but also made their presence felt in the domestic trade that, until the reorganisation of futures trading in the Bolsa do Comercio during the first decade of the century, had been run by the *acopiadores* and other independent merchants of the Bolsa de Cereales. By 1914, Bunge & Born's vertical expansion into flour mills in Buenos Aires stimulated the centralisation of the milling trade in the capital, to the extreme

[12] On the ambiguity of the relationship between Bunge & Born in Argentina, Bunge SA in Antwerp and related companies, see Raúl H. Green and Catherine Laurent, *El Poder de Bunge & Born* (Buenos Aires, 1988), 55–60, 69–76.

[13] Ronald C. Newton, *German Buenos Aires, 1900–1933: Social Change and Cultural Crisis* (Austin, 1977), 15.

detriment of provincial mills.[14] According to Sir Reginald Tower, the British minister to the Argentine Republic, the Big Four 'constitute practically a trust', one without British members.

Not a few Britons saw this as unfortunate, especially considering the fact that the bulk of these grains, at least 44 per cent of Argentine grain exports between 1900–05, went to the United Kingdom.[15] The failure of British grain companies to grab hold of the trade went hand in hand with the general decline of British merchants in South America. The historian Desmond Platt has described the withering of once dominant Anglo-Argentine merchant houses as the result of the rational relocation of British businesses to the more easily exploitable markets of the British Empire.[16] However, there remained quite rational reasons for British observers to decry the failure of British entrepreneurs to move into the exploding grain trade. Minister Tower warned the Foreign Office in 1913 that the Big Four had a potential stranglehold over goods vital to feeding the United Kingdom. Between the years 1909–13, more than 11 per cent of the total wheat supplies of the United Kingdom came from Argentina.[17] Because most Argentine grain was available in January and February, a moment wedged between the autumnal European harvests and the rise of North American spring wheat, the timing of Argentina's trade appeared particularly critical for the continuous feeding of the loaf-a-day consumers of the United Kingdom.[18]

Yet before 1914 other British-owned businesses refused to help nurture British grain exporters in Argentina. The London-based railways in Argentina continued to tie themselves to the Big Four by granting rebates to companies willing to ship exclusively with their line. British merchant shipowners followed similar practices.[19] To British banks, life without the German-run grain exporters became unimaginable, and they fretted whenever it appeared that they might lose any of the Big Four as customers. In early 1914, the head of the London and River Plate Bank in Buenos Aires worried that if Bunge & Born asked for facilities to exchange more

[14] Scobie, *Revolution on the Pampas*, 111–12.

[15] Ibid., 110.

[16] D. C. M. Platt, *Latin America and British Trade 1806–1914* (New York, 1972), 137–39, 306–07.

[17] Frank Surface, *The Grain Trade during the World War: Being a History of the Food Administration Grain Corporation and the United States Grain Corporation* (New York, 1928), 23.

[18] Dan Morgan, *Merchants of Grain* (New York, 1979), 108.

[19] Gravil, *The Anglo-Argentine Connection*, 44–54.

than £150,000 at a time, the conservative practices pushed by their home office in London might lead the bank to refuse the business. The bank manager feared that an offended Bunge & Born might no longer use the bank for any transactions.[20] Everyone knew that the grain giant had ready credit all over town.

The British War on Bunge & Born

Yet despite its links to British shipping and banking, when the First World War began in August 1914, Bunge & Born immediately acted in a pro-German manner, and the British of Argentina labelled the company as an enemy. As the British naval blockade halted the wheat, corn and linseed headed directly to German ports during the opening months of war, shipments to the neutral nations surrounding Germany ballooned. A special deputation of ship brokers and exporters from the British Chamber of Commerce in Buenos Aires complained to Sir Reginald Tower that over the seven weeks before October 28, at least twenty-two ships with more than 100,000 tonnes of cereals sent by Bunge & Born and Weil Hermanos had left for Scandinavian ports. Over the same period the previous year, there had been no such shipments.[21] Once in Stockholm or Copenhagen, this grain was easily transhipped to Germany, because the minimal presence in the Baltic Sea of the submarine-fearing British navy did not constitute an effective blockade.

Most upsetting to the Anglo-Argentine community was the fact that British ships often carried these suspect goods. Estimating that local German grain firms held contracts controlling 85 per cent of the British tonnage available in Buenos Aires, Consul-General Horatio Mackie argued that by allowing Germans to use these British ships, local agents of the British lines failed to act 'up to the spirit' of existing Trading with the Enemy laws.[22] The British Chamber of Commerce in Buenos Aires suggested that the British Government withhold war risk insurance from shipowners who allowed their vessels to carry goods for German firms.[23] There were also a flurry of calls to ban the practice, common in the grain trade, of shipping 'for orders' to St Vincent or Las Palmas. Under this

[20] Letters of 24 Apr. and 28 May 1914, from Harry Scott to Thurburn, private. Box D76/2, BOLSA Archives, University College, London.
[21] Executive Committee Minutes, Vol. 1, meeting of Fri., 30 Oct. 1914. Also, Tower to FO tel. No. 31 Com'l, 29 Oct. 1914. FO 118/337.
[22] Mackie to Tower, 7 Oct. 1914. FO 118/342.
[23] Tower to FO tel. No. 31 Com'l, 29 Oct. 1914. FO 118/337.

practice, vessels would steam to one of these mid-Atlantic island destinations. By the time they arrived, the owners of the cargo would know where in Europe they wanted to send the goods, send a telegram, and the ships would head where they were directed. 'For orders' increasingly meant for Germany, via Scandinavia. Consul-General Mackie suggested that the British government try to control cargoes transported by British shipping by making British ships present their bills of lading and insurance documents for the endorsement of British consuls at each port they steamed in or out of around the globe, enabling the government to trace transactions from departure to destination.[24] Such regulations aimed not to scare away British shipping from servicing the South American ports, but rather to make it more difficult for German importers and exporters to continue their business with Europe and the United States. Those regulations could be used to manipulate British-flag shipping to cripple local German merchant houses, while also aiding British firms whose access to the increasingly scarce shipping would give them a significant competitive advantage over the Germans.

There was significant resistance among British shipowners and the Board of Trade to any changes to the system. Yet Hirsch and other German businessmen were known among the Britons of South America as the primary suppliers of the German cruisers that plagued British shipping in the South Atlantic during the first months of the war. Tower had no doubt that these 'Jewish pro-German firms' were profiting hugely through suspicious trades.[25] And the lure of controlling the grain markets was tremendous both for British merchant houses in Buenos Aires and Rosario, and for their allies in the British government, who hoped to build up permanent British control of the business.

After significant bureaucratic infighting in the corridors of Whitehall, victory went to the proponents of war against these distant Germans in neutral lands. These economic warriors devised as their weapon the Statutory List, a published blacklist of companies designated by the British government as enemies and thus banned from using the British services that connected them with the rest of the world, including shipping, coal, telegraphy and banking. The Foreign Trade Department (FTD), a

---

[24] Mackie to Tower, 7 Oct. 1914, in Tower to FO No. 268 Com'l, 16 Oct. 1914, FO No. 71594, 16 Nov. 1914. FO 368/928. Also, Dickson to Tower No. 41, 14 Oct. 1914. FO 118/342.

[25] Tower to FO No. 257, 14 Sept. 1915 (received 11 Oct. 1915). FO 833/18.

new branch of the Foreign Office, was created to administer this new blacklist.[26]

The first Statutory List for South America was issued on 16 March 1916. Subsequent lists targeted Germans in a variety of other trades, particularly German merchandise importers and wool and hide exporting companies. However, this first blacklist targeted simply, and not surprisingly, wheat exporters, including Bunge & Born, Weil Hermanos and E. Hardy & Co.[27] Bunge & Born initially panicked. The English-language newspapers of Buenos Aires reported rumours that the company would fire all of its German employees.[28] The firm's lawyer, R. C. Aldao, came to the legation to ask Tower if the company could be removed from the list if it dismissed Hirsch. However, the initial fear quickly faded, and the company's self-defence soon grew cannier. In April, another lawyer explained that both George Born and Ernest Bunge were Belgians, who, through no fault of their own, found themselves living in German-occupied Antwerp. This lawyer also argued that Hirsch had proven his allegiances when he founded the Belgian Relief Commission in Argentina, that the company did not sell goods to enemies of Britain, and that it had dismissed all of its German employees.[29] Yet Tower stood unmoved. Buoyed by his hopes for building British business and certain that Bunge & Born was a fundamentally pro-German company in personnel, activities and intents, he told the company's lawyers that even 'documentary proof of death-bed repentance' would not lead British authorities to take the firm off the Statutory List.[30]

Tower could be so cocky because through the early months he believed that being on the Statutory List was really hurting the company.[31] Indeed, initially the export trade of Bunge & Born and Weil Brothers was tremendously curtailed. Yet enlisting allies in the war against Bunge & Born was not without difficulties. The Belgian minister in Argentina resisted attempts to destroy the grain-trading monolith and worked to

---

[26] For more on the economic war in South America, see Phillip Dehne, *On the Far Western Front: Britain's First World War in South America* (Manchester, 2010).

[27] 'TWTE (Neutral Countries) Proclamation, 1916. Additions and alterations of S/L in neutral countries – Argentina, Morocco, Netherlands, Persia, Portuguese East Africa, and Sweden' (signed 16 Mar.). *Board of Trade Journal*, 92 (1916), 848–50.

[28] *Buenos Aires Herald*, 31 Mar. 1916, 28.

[29] Tower to F.T.D. No. 90, 11 Apr. 1916. FO 118/390.

[30] Tower to F.T.D. No. 62, 24 Mar. 1916. FO 118/390.

[31] Tower to F.T.D., No. 89262, 30 Sept. 1916. FO 833/16. Also, Tower to F.T.D. No. 169, 29 May 1916. FO 118/390.

'rehabilitate' the firm by relaying information to Tower that placed Bunge & Born as a Belgian company, while advocating the ejection from the company of its 'German element'. Tower refused to back down even after the Belgians in February 1917 published a blacklist identical to the British one except for the omission of Bunge & Born. He could easily ignore the Belgian minister, whose country was occupied, in a country where Belgian trade had never been dominant.

Tower found that a much more difficult problem in attacking Bunge & Born was the variety of guises used by the company. Blacklisted firms began to conduct trade not in their own names, but rather through middle-men. No one had fully anticipated this problem in March 1916 when the first Statutory List hit South America. Such intermediaries became known as 'cloaks' because they enabled listed companies to disguise their activities. People and companies agreed to work on behalf of firms on the Statutory List by allowing their names to be used in shipping manifests and bills of exchange so that goods on British ships could reach them. Others stored the goods of listed firms in their warehouses, sold to listed firms goods that they had imported themselves, or allowed their addresses to be used to bypass British censors. Many cloaks were true straw men, individuals (often of local nationality) who were unlikely to conduct any trade other than as cloaks. Straw men throughout South America who helped to circumvent the Statutory List did so from some mix of fearlessness of the consequences of being listed, desire for potentially easy profits, and either a pro-German or disinterested position towards the war in Europe. Tower suggested in a letter to the FTD that the cloak problem revealed 'the facile and complaisant character of the Latin American generally', with his constant friendliness and desire to please easily abused 'by the German tempter', a phrase perhaps most revealing of Tower's wartime paranoia about the insidiousness of the German threat.[32] When the names of the listed firms did not appear in shipping documents, cables and mail, their business conduct was inscrutable, at least from the perspective of London.

At first, the British on both sides of the Atlantic did not appreciate the seriousness of the cloak problem, and believed it could be dealt with through informal local measures. Initially, when British firms learned that Tobino and Arvigo sold along grain that had once been owned by Bunge & Born, outraged British grain dealers pledged to refuse further

---

[32] Tower No. 377 of 30 June 1917, No. 140701 of 22 Aug. 1917. FO 833/17.

dealings with the company.[33] Yet despite this threat, a variety of people in South America remained willing and able to act as cloaks, helping listed firms send and receive goods and thereby continue their lucrative international trade. It had been hoped that such cloaks would cower in fear of being themselves placed on the Statutory List. Yet the British consulates, legations and local Chamber of Commerce could only determine who worked as a cloak through constant, close inspection of intercepted communications and shipping manifests and by nurturing informants in the ports and customs houses. When discovered, some cloaks were placed on the Statutory List. However, by the middle of July 1917, British officials understood that there was a virtually inexhaustible supply of potential cloaks and that placing them on the Statutory List was, in Tower's words, 'like pouring water into the sea'. 'The 'cloak' system is my despair', he lamented.[34]

Understanding how Bunge & Born operated during the First World War must be accomplished from outside the company. Bunge & Born has never been particularly accommodating to journalists or historians; determining its annual profits or losses, or even basic facts about how it makes its money, is largely guesswork.[35] However, by using the extensive British diplomatic and consular archives some of the company's wartime transactions can be traced. At least fourteen Bunge & Born related companies and individuals eventually reached the Statutory List, but undoubtedly many more were never placed on this official list. The company also eluded the blacklist by spinning off a variety of companies during the war. Hirsch and other managers of Bunge & Born formed the Sociedad Financiera é Industrial Sud-Americana in August 1915; some real estate holdings were spun off into a firm called La Inmobiliaria, a company that had nominally existed earlier but did not begin active operations until March 1916, at the moment when Bunge was placed on the Statutory List. The Sociedad Financiera entered the Statutory List three months later. Local Britons denounced another company, the Société Anonyme des Minoteries et d'Elevateurs a Grains, as owned by Bunge

[33] Tower to F.T.D. No. 319, 14 Aug. 1916. FO 118/391.
[34] Tower private to Ronald Macleay (Deputy Controller of the F.T.D.), 21 Jul. 1917. FO 118/433.
[35] On the difficulty of understanding Bunge & Born's business model, see Philippe Chalmin, *Traders and Merchants: Panorama of International Commodity Trading* (Char, 2nd edn. 1987), 181–84, 198–200. Schvarzer attempts to create aggregate statistics of the capital assets and profits of the various Bunge & Born related companies, but he recognises they are sketchy and incomplete; Schvarzer, *Bunge & Born*, 27.

& Born. Yet after Hirsch resigned from his managing position at that company, and Tower failed to unearth conclusive proof that its shares were held by any of the directors of Bunge & Born, Tower decided that he could not recommend the firm for the Statutory List.[36] Likewise the trade of a number of farms and cattle ranches owned by Bunge & Born or Alfredo Hirsch were 'purely local in character' and thus unlikely to be hurt by the Statutory List regulations focusing on foreign trade.[37]

The multiplicity of Bunge & Born's guises made it a difficult target. The lumbering Statutory List always seemed a step behind, taking months to come into effect. Tower recommended Pels & Lakatos, a company of ex-employees of Bunge & Born, for the Statutory List on 5 January 1917, but the company was only listed on 11 May.[38] Tower proved that Jorge Engelhard imported specialised milling machinery from Switzerland through an Italian in Argentina, Antonio Battilana, who upon receiving it had been instructed to transfer it to Bunge & Born.[39] Engelhard entered the Statutory List, but only three months later, far too late to stop the shipment.

Tower hoped the British government would succeed in promoting British grain firms to take Bunge & Born's place. However, a disappointed Tower found himself scolding British firms for being more interested in sparring among themselves than cooperating for their mutual benefit. Within days of the publication of the first Statutory List in March 1916, the British company Sanday & Co. claimed that purchases of huge quantities of wheat by a compatriot, Ross Smyth & Co., had triggered a rise in prices, hurting both Argentine wheat on the world market and Sanday's position within Argentina. The British Chamber of Commerce supported this claim that prices were artificially high due to such purchases, which they correctly assumed were financed by the British government. Tower grew annoyed both at the bickering British grain firms and at the British government for not informing him that they were purchasing through Smyth & Co. at prescribed, above-market rates.[40]

---

[36] Tower to F.T.D. No. 251, 12 July 1916. FO 118/391.
[37] For example, the 'Estancia La Pelada', the 'Explotacion de campos y montes del Rio Bermejo', and the 'Belga Americana'. Tower to F.T.D. No. 239, 23 Apr. 1917, and Tower to F.T.D. No. 259, 1 May 1917. FO 118/432.
[38] Tower to F.T.D. No. 10, 5 Jan. 1917. FO 118/432.
[39] Tower to F.T.D. No. 468, 9 Aug. 1917. FO 118/433.
[40] Tower to FO No. 140 Com'l, 30 Mar. 1916, No. 80318 of 28 Apr. 1916. Letter from Powell-Jones of the Chamber of Commerce of 24 May, in Tower to FO No. 202, 26 May 1916, No. 125796 of 29 Jun. 1916. FO 368/1478.

And instances continually arose of even these reliable Allied grain exporters inadvertently buying stocks of grain from Bunge & Born. Tower persuaded the Allied grain houses to set up a 'disapproved list' of firms thought to be intermediaries locally for Bunge & Born, in the hopes of making it easier for British companies to avoid indirect transactions with enemy firms on the local futures market.[41] Yet the grain houses were split over whether to stop all options operations: Ross Smyth & Co. opposed any ban. Tensions among the British grain brokers grew when Sanday & Co. accused Dreyfus & Co. of dealing with Bunge & Born.[42] Yet soon thereafter, Sanday & Co. itself received 1800 tonnes of oats from Bunge & Born, which had arrived in Sanday's hands very indirectly. It had made a contract with the Buenos Aires firm Mellado & Bridger for grain to be delivered in Bahia Blanca. Mellado & Bridger bought the grain from Mauricio Zuckerberg in a contract stamped 'allied'. Zuckerberg bought the grain in the option market from J. P. Baas Jr, who as it turned out was actually just a straw man for Bunge & Born. When Sanday & Co. discovered the chain of exchanges, it refused to take the shipment, but Zuckerberg appealed to the Cereal Exchange. The board of the exchange reminded Sanday that, as a marketplace in a neutral country, it did not recognise any significance to the 'allied' stamp on the contract and therefore according to the rules of the exchange, Sanday must accept the oats. Tower reluctantly accepted that Sanday had no other option.[43]

The options markets in both Buenos Aires and Rosario allowed Bunge & Born a tangled mass of transactions through which it could find intermediaries to launder its grain. Bunge & Born easily outwitted the British throughout the buying season in early 1917, bidding slightly higher for grain when purchasing from *acopiadores* and farmers, then profiting handsomely through resales when it turned out that the harvest produced far less than expected.[44] In the end, of course, all the grain available was purchased by the hungry Allies, who particularly relied on Argentine grain in the early months of the year when northern hemisphere suppliers awaited the spring.[45] Tower rued that Bunge & Born was 'enriching

---

[41] Tower to F.T.D. No. 333, 22 Aug. 1916. FO 118/391.
[42] Tower to F.T.D. No. 46, 20 Jan. 1917. FO 118/432.
[43] Tower to F.T.D. No. 158, 17 Mar. 1917. FO 118/432.
[44] Tower to F.T.D. No. 285, 14 May 1917. FO 118/432.
[45] According to statistics compiled by Frank Surface, 32.5 million of the 40.1 million bushels of wheat exported from Argentina in 1917 went to the three western Allies: the

themselves at our expense'.[46] Once again, Bunge & Born's information advantage, which stretched from its close connections with farmers and merchants in the countryside to its understanding of the grain markets of the capital, allowed the company to continue to profit from the grain export trade even while on the Statutory List.

By the middle of 1917, the British government lost faith in the ability of British firms in Argentina to sort out their differences. The Royal Commission on Wheat Supplies, the buying agency for all wheat coming into Britain, undertook a massive amount of business in Argentina, purchasing more than 9,000,000 tonnes of cereals there from its creation in October 1916 until the end of the war. It initially made purchases in Argentina through British-controlled cereal firms. Yet after the first year or so of the battle against the German wheat firms, the Commission decided that the British firms were not capable of making the massive purchases needed during the 1917–18 season and appointed a Wheat Commissioner in Argentina. The Commission purchased that season's crop by converting eight Allied cereal firms into buying agencies, allowing them to make some profit from fixed allowances and brokerage fees, while the price offered by the Commission was made known to farmers and thus could not be manipulated for the profit of the middlemen. During that season, the Wheat Commission purchased 45 per cent of the unprecedentedly large Argentine wheat crop, nearly 12 million quarters (units of 480 lbs.) of the total 26.7 million quarter Argentine crop.[47] Yet despite the existence of the Wheat Commission and its seeming hold over the bulk of Argentina's internationally traded grain, firms on the Statutory List such as Bunge & Born still operated on a tremendous scale. The Wheat Commission attempted to purchase grain exclusively from nonblacklisted firms, but it remained difficult to determine whether a given firm was a cover for one of the blacklisted giants or even whether one of the Allied firms had intentionally or inadvertently bought its grain from a listed firm.

With the failure of the Statutory List to shut down the cloaks, intermediaries and subsidiaries of Bunge & Born, locally directed measures against the enemy grain company intensified. One way was to ratchet up control of jute bags. The British Empire held a near monopoly over the

United Kingdom, France and Italy. Surface, *The Grain Trade during the World War*, 22–23.

[46] Tower to F.T.D. No. 285, 14 May 1917. FO 118/432.

[47] First Report of the Royal Commission on Wheat Supplies, P.P. 1921., xviii, Cmd. 1544, appendix 5 and appendix 7.

supply of jute, most of which came from India. Jute bags were vital to the shipment of the grain crops, at least from the farms to train depots, and the lack of grain elevators in Argentina meant that shipment in bags remained the norm even on many trains and merchant ships.[48] In early 1916 Tower appointed a 'jute commission' that compiled an approved list of jute importers.[49] Companies looking to enter the approved list often came calling at the British Legation, one more example of how the duties of economic warfare increasingly taxed Tower's staff.[50] Yet despite the staff's efforts throughout 1917, much jute leaked to firms on the Statutory List. In January 1918, in a further measure designed by Tower to prove to the two hundred businesses in Argentina that dealt in raw jute and jute bags the 'uncompromising attitude of H[is] M[ajesty's] G[overnment] in regard to trade with the enemy', the jute commission made inclusion in the list of approved importers in Buenos Aires contingent on a firm's signing a guarantee that it would abstain 'from all dealings *whatsoever* with (Statutory) listed firms'. Even most bag traders not implicated in trade with Germans would be placed initially on a restrictive 'list B', with Consul-General Mackie issuing individual certificates.[51]

Yet in January 1918, Bunge & Born mailed a circular to many firms telling of the 750,000 new jute bags that its own factory just produced and advertising its plans to sell many of these bags on the open market, thus flaunting British attempts at control.[52] Tower soon learned how one of Bunge & Born's employees purchased 500 bales of raw jute from a bag factory owner named Manuel Fuente, who approached an intermediary named Casteran, who arranged with a broker to purchase jute from an approved British importer, Hardcastle & Co. via a legitimate dealer, Portalis & Co. Sending the jute between Hardcastle and Bunge involved at least five intermediaries, none of whom necessarily knew the final destination of the goods.[53] After interrogating a number of the participants and reviewing an array of documents, in August Tower proved that Juan Casteran had received letters from Bunge & Born that held it responsible for payment to Fuente. Casteran obviously knew he was delivering British goods to enemy firms and should have been placed on the

[48] Scobie, *Revolution on the Pampas*, 91–92.
[49] Tower to F.T.D. No. 231, 28 June 1916. FO 118/390.
[50] Tower to F.T.D. No. 417, 30 Sept. 1917. FO 118/391.
[51] Tower to F.T.D. No. 37, 15 Jan. 1918. FO 118/468. Also, First Report of the Royal Commission on Wheat Supplies, P.P. 1921., xviii, Cmd. 1544, appendix 31.
[52] Tower to F.T.D. No. 65, 30 Jan. 1918. FO 118/468.
[53] Tower to F.T.D., No. 83, 14 Feb. 1918. FO 118/468.

Statutory List. However, he was never blacklisted, and in November, Tower took heated criticism from both British businessmen and the Italian press for the way that the situation was handled. The British Chamber of Commerce demanded that all the companies involved be placed on the Statutory List, for fear that to do otherwise would give the impression locally that any guarantees that companies signed with Britain 'may be broken with impunity'. The Italian newspaper *L'Italia del Popolo* asked why the British jute controllers had not done anything about Portalis. The paper had discovered that Casteran & Co. had in fact been a virtual subsidiary of Portalis, which had probably known about the trade with Bunge & Born. In addition, the Briton involved in the transaction, P. A. Hardcastle, should have known better. Tower called Hardcastle in for a harsh lecture, explaining that it should have been obvious that, because neither Portalis nor Casteran were bag manufacturers, Hardcastle should never have sold them so much raw jute.[54] Did Hardcastle know it was going to Bunge & Born? Tower doubted he could ever get the truth.[55] For Tower, the case was 'illustrative of what is doubtless going on all through the country and which seems unavoidable'.[56]

After much reluctance to join this difficult economic war that had made Britain quite unpopular among many Argentines, the United States finally began to publish its Enemy Trading List in late 1917; at the same time it began to circulate to New York shipping lines a list of cloaks who should not be consigned any goods from the United States. At least ten of the fifty-one names on the first provisional cloaks list for Argentina were targeted because of their connections to Bunge & Born.[57] Even so, throughout 1918 Bunge & Born continued to use cloaks and shift its resources to evade British scrutiny while still making profits. Its involvement in Argentine flour milling likely expanded during the war; Jorge Engelhardt was blacklisted for importing new milling machinery from Switzerland for Bunge & Born. Its trade in grain and flour with Brazil, begun with its investment in a Brazilian flour mill in 1905, also remained strong throughout the war. In a February 1918 report, Tower passed along from the local British Chamber of Commerce twelve names of companies and individuals working for Bunge & Born in the 'general merchant business' with Brazil, particularly in trade from Argentina to Brazilian

---

[54] Tower to F.T.D. No. 537, 8 Nov. 1918. FO 118/469.
[55] Tower to F.T.D. No. 568, 2 Dec. 1918. FO 118/469.
[56] Tower to F.T.D. No. 83, 14 Feb. 1918. FO 118/468.
[57] F.T.D. to Tower, No. 338 of 11 Oct. 1917. FO 118/426.

flour mills.[58] In addition, the company found new ways to invest its capital, including granting short-term loans to the Argentine government.[59] Finally, Bunge & Born also continued its operations in the Argentine countryside. In June 1918, British censors described an intercepted letter written by one of Bunge & Born's competitors to a correspondent in Rotterdam, which reaffirmed the continued inestimable importance of Bunge & Born across the grain-growing pampas, where many farmers remained deeply indebted to the grain giant.[60] In short, much of the grain sloshing through the Argentine marketplace, ultimately destined for the stomachs of British, French and Italian civilians and soldiers, was initially purchased from farmers by the enemy company Bunge & Born.

When the creation of the Cloaks List proved insufficient to stop Bunge & Born's trade, in January 1918 Tower asked the Foreign Trade Department to place on the Statutory List companies 'whose business operations have hitherto been regarded as on too small a scale to justify their inclusion'.[61] A British government agent in Argentina suggested that Tower himself should be given 'full discretionary powers' to immediately place names on the Statutory List.[62] However, by the middle of 1918, because the machinery of the Statutory List still chugged along too slowly in London, Tower came to favour a new blacklist created by the Chamber of Commerce, the 'Undesirable List'. Malefactors could be hurt more quickly by immediately being placed on the 'Undesirable List', while also printing their names under the heading of Bunge & Born on copies of the Statutory Lists that were published for use by Allied partisans in Argentina.[63] Tower had come to realise that changes in blacklisting had to happen more quickly and be accompanied by more local publicity for boycotts against a broader array of German companies.[64] These efforts might succeed by maximizing unity with the other Allies and their supporters, which was not so difficult to achieve when it came to the French and Italians, but was a problem when it came to the United States.[65]

---

[58] Tower to F.T.D. No. 114 of 25 Feb. 1918. FO 118/468.
[59] Tower to F.T.D. No. 423, 16 Aug. 1918. FO 118/469.
[60] WTID weekly bulletin No. 135, 13 Jun. 1918. ADM 137/2919.
[61] Tower to F.T.D. No. 56, 23 Jan. 1918. FO 118/468. One of the names placed on the first cloaks list, Mauricio Marx, was placed on the Statutory List along with his company and his associate Sigismundo Jacobi on September 6, 1918.
[62] INF 4/6.
[63] Tower to F.T.D. No. 367, 14 Jul. 1918. FO 118/469.
[64] Tower to Chamber of Commerce, Executive Committee meeting, Mon. 10 June 1918.
[65] On the continued inefficacy of a great power using economic sanctions without allies, see Jerry Guo, 'Buying American in Tehran', *New York Times*, 2 Sept. 2009.

For by August 1918 it had become apparent that Bunge & Born had
gained influential North American supporters. In August, the U.S. commercial attaché, Robert Barrett, suggested to Tower that it was in the
interest of the Allies to get the company on their side after the war. Barrett proposed that a Belgian businessman, Casimir de Bruyn, be approved
as the new manager of a reconstituted Bunge & Born. Tower saw through
the wily scheme, which actually had been suggested to Barrett by Hirsch's
lawyer and also reflected the desires of U.S. chargé d'affaires Robbins,
who was married to the daughter of de Bruyn. Tower knew that de Bruyn
presently ran Molinos Harineros y Elevadores de Grano, a supposedly
Belgian-owned mill that the British Wheat Commission had purchased
grain from in 1917, but that was increasingly suspected of operating in
secret accord with Bunge & Born.[66] He also noted that Barrett's proposal to rehabilitate Bunge & Born would still allow Hirsch to own a
third of the capital of the new company. Tower could never agree to such
terms.[67]

In September 1918, Tower fretted, 'It is impossible to exaggerate the
serious consequences of that organisation [Bunge & Born] remaining
intact'[68] after the war, which suddenly ended two months later. After the
Armistice, Allied grain traders desperately hoped to maintain sanctions on
their German competitors. They telegraphed British prime minister David
Lloyd George in February 1919, pleading for him to bar Bunge & Born,
Weil Hermanos and General Mercantile Co. from competing in Allied
markets and from chartering Allied tonnage. With virtually all of the
world's shipping under Allied control, this would have meant maintaining
the Statutory List restrictions.[69] Yet instead restrictions were soon lifted
from these companies, and once-enemy firms quickly retook the River
Plate grain trade. It quickly became apparent that the blacklisting of
German-tainted grain firms during the war had done nothing to limit
their abilities to conduct business, nor did the war help British shippers
to gain predominance. It would certainly be wrong to conclude that
the Statutory List had 'drastically reduced' German involvement in the
Argentine grain trade.[70]

---

[66] On the 1917 wheat purchase, Tower to F.T.D. No. 377, 30 June 1917, para. 40. FTD
140701, 22 Aug. 1917, 52963. FO 833/17.
[67] Tower to F.T.D. No. 403, 7 Aug. 1918; Tower to F.T.D. No. 472, 18 Sept. 1918. FO
118/469.
[68] Tower to F.T.D. No. 472, 18 Sept. 1918. FO 118/469.
[69] Tower to F.T.D. No. 36, 15 Feb. 1919. FO 118/507.
[70] Gravil, *The Anglo-Argentine Connection*, 121.

Conclusion: The British War on Bunge & Born

In 1914, Bunge & Born appeared a ripe and ready target for British economic warfare. Rolling up Bunge & Born and other German grain exporters ranked as probably the primary goal of the British trade war in South America. The UK government and British businessmen controlled transatlantic shipping, transoceanic cable and mail traffic, international financial instruments and other facilities ordinarily assumed to be critical to the continued functioning of a multinational enterprise like Bunge & Born. The British government also fostered its own national champions that it hoped could step into Bunge & Born's shoes. Yet despite incessant efforts to harpoon the 'Octopus', Bunge & Born eluded Britain's economic war.

Rather than bringing an end to the integration of this huge Argentine company into the global marketplace for food, the First World War proved to be a time of continued prosperity for the firm. Its managers evaded difficulties that arose due to Britain's economic warfare and to general wartime dislocations of global and local marketplaces. They changed its corporate structure, increased the enterprise's focus on its Argentine rather than Belgian offices, and expanded investment and integration into local Argentine and South American markets both in grains and in other enterprises. By using connections to individuals and companies in various countries, Bunge & Born nurtured a steady supply of surreptitious intermediaries quite willing to help it continue its transatlantic trade. The quasi-black market it created in avowedly neutral Argentina greatly limited the effects of Britain's war against the company.

For far too long it has been falsely assumed, even by those awestruck by the company's continuous diversification and profitability, that the First World War was a rough time for Bunge & Born.[71] It is closer to the truth to say that it emerged unscathed, in a strong position from which to profit from the postwar global economic boom. Unsurprisingly, considering the successes of diversification during the war, the company continued these efforts both in Argentina and abroad. Investments in Brazil continued to expand after the war, and in 1920 the company associated with P. N. Gray & Co. in New York and Chicago. Three years later this entity officially became the Bunge Corporation in the United States. By 1921 it was already marked as one of the top three U.S. exporters, a dominant

---

[71] Green and Laurent, *El Poder de Bunge & Born*, 35–38.

position the company has largely maintained in the U.S. market through the present day.[72]

Within Argentina, Bunge & Born continued to enhance its dominance both in the grain markets and more broadly within the Argentine economy. Bunge & Born flourished in Argentina for many decades after the war, profiting greatly from the speculation in wheat futures that proliferated immediately after the declaration of peace, and further diversifying within Argentina by building paint factories and textile mills. Bunge & Born enlarged its financial domination of the countryside, continuing to advance to farmers and agents the funds to buy their seeds, a practice that allowed the firm to establish the prices of the crop. The ubiquity of the firm overwhelmed Argentine farmers after the war, who rued that 'Bunge gives the farmer his credit, sells him his seed, and buys his grain. And when the crops are in, Bunge sells the farmer the rope to hang himself'.[73] In his report after leading a high-level official economic mission to South America in 1929, Lord d'Abernon called for increased participation by British firms in the grain trade between Argentina and Britain, because the entire trade remained in the hands of 'continental' European shippers.[74] Yet the trend would not change, because British firms remained unable or unwilling to do the crucial work of integrating transactions back to the sources of supply in the pampas.[75] In 1931, Bunge & Born handled 43 per cent of the wheat exported from Argentina, a significant increase over its already dominant prewar percentage.[76] In perhaps the most painful blow to Anglo-Argentines, their wartime archenemy, Alfredo Hirsch, became the company's president in 1927. Until his death in 1956, Hirsch guided the giant global grain firm in its continued expansion and diversification into other businesses, creating what *Time* magazine described in 1962 as 'the mightiest trading company south of the Equator'.[77]

Forever secretive (a trait undoubtedly augmented by the usefulness of subterfuge during the war), Bunge & Born in Argentina long remained as it was during the First World War – an opaque linkage of the family interests of the Hirsch and Born families owning assets from hotels to

[72] Mira Wilkins, *The History of Foreign Investment in the United States, 1914–1945* (Cambridge, 2004), 160–61, 220–21.
[73] Morgan, *Merchants of Grain*, 38–40.
[74] FO to BT, 29 Mar. 1930, A1911/77/51 (D.O.T. 26538/1930). BT 60/26/2.
[75] Chapman, *Merchant Enterprise*, 228.
[76] Carl Solberg, *The Prairies and the Pampas: Agrarian Policy in Canada and Argentina, 1880–1930* (Stanford, 1987), 143.
[77] 'The Beneficent Octopus', *Time*, 19 Oct. 1962.

ranches in Argentina, 'a major trader *cum* industrialist, the most stateless of the stateless groups', with equity of at least $1 billion in 1979.[78] When Jorge and Juan Born were kidnapped in Buenos Aires by leftist rebels in September 1974, the company easily pulled together an astonishing $60 million ransom payment and bought their freedom.[79] Unsurprisingly their families immediately moved to the relative safety of Brazil, their easy statelessness mirroring the mobility of the multinational they controlled. Despite such wide-ranging investments and expenses, Bunge & Born's continued focus on the global grain trade gave this privately run company perhaps $10 billion of annual turnover by 1979, when it remained one of the top five global grain companies and among the largest trading firms in the world.[80] Even after the grain trade was largely nationalised by Juan Perón in the late 1940s, Bunge & Born maintained tremendous economic power in Argentina. It would later even expand its influence in Argentine politics and policy, when the government of the Peronist Carlos Menem brought in two Bunge & Born executives to serve as Ministers of the Economy in the early 1990s.[81] Bunge Argentina is now a subsidiary of Bunge Limited, headquartered in White Plains, New York, and its continued dominance in the Argentine economy is mirrored by its power globally. In 2001 Bunge became a publicly traded company, but the role of the families of its early leaders remains significant (as of this writing, Jorge Born Jr is deputy chairman, with other family members serving on the board of directors). The corporation's globalisation has continued to bring tremendous profits; in 2008, net income for the first time topped $1 billion.[82]

From this longer-term perspective, it is astonishing to consider that Bunge's many subsequent decades of profitability grew from fertile roots nurtured during the turmoil of the First World War. Nearly a century ago, this multinational Leviathan discovered that the networks of its trade could not be destroyed even by a war waged by a resource-hungry hegemonic power like the United Kingdom.[83] Instead, the distant war bred

---

[78] Chalmin, *Traders and Merchants*, 175, 198.
[79] Jonathan Kandell, 'Argentine Ransom Is Put at $60 Million', *New York Times*, 21 June 1975, 3.
[80] Chalmin, *Traders and Merchants*, 153–54, 175.
[81] Javier Corrales, 'Do Economic Crises Contribute to Economic Reform? Argentina and Venezuela in the 1900s', *Political Science Quarterly* 112, 4 (Winter 1997–8), 628.
[82] Bunge 2008 Annual Report, at http://216.139.227.101/interactive/bg2008/.
[83] On the use of the term 'Leviathan' to describe modern multinational corporations whose penchant for innovation can enable them to challenge 'the power of the nation-states', see Chandler and Mazlish, *Leviathans*, 1–2.

capitalist innovations and diversification on the periphery of the world economy.[84] The global power of Bunge & Born was deeply rooted in local structures of trade that proved impermeable to the seemingly powerful British. Rather than seeing the First World War as the end of fin-de-siècle globalisation, the case of Bunge & Born highlights the transformations and overall resilience of such company-level globalisation before, during and after the war.

[84] For another example of this phenomenon, see Sven Beckert, 'Emancipation and Empire: Reconstructing the Worldwide Web of Cotton Production in the Age of the American Civil War', *American Historical Review* 109 (Dec. 2004), 5.

Global Economic Governance and the Private Sector

The League of Nations' Experiment in the 1920s

Michele d'Alessandro

Global economic governance proved a far more complicated matter in the 1920s than it had been in the decades before 1914. The common desire of most policy makers throughout the world to return to a sustainable international economic order resembling that of the classical gold standard was eventually frustrated by the early 1930s. Rebuilt in the mid-1920s, the international monetary system only had an ephemeral, fragile existence before collapsing into three distinct currency areas. Moreover, its operation in the second half of that decade produced highly uneven effects on the countries adhering to the system, adding deflationary pressure to the world economy.[1] The situation of the world trading system was even worse: a set of shared principles and norms among the major trading countries could not be reestablished until the late 1940s, and the system's overall performance remained extremely weak throughout the interwar years.[2]

Barry Eichengreen has explained the difficulties of global economic governance in the 1920s in terms of both a loss of credibility in governments' commitment to the rules of an international order, and the drastic

---

[1] Barry J. Eichengreen, *Golden Fetters: The Gold Standard and the Great Depression, 1919–1939* (New York, 1992).

[2] Charles H. Feinstein, Peter Temin and Gianni Toniolo, *The World Economy between the World Wars* (New York, 2008), 12.

I am particularly grateful to Christof Dejung, Jürgen Osterhammel and Niels P. Petersson for their insightful comments on an early draft of this chapter. I wish to express thanks as well to the other conference participants for their useful remarks.

decrease of international cooperation even as it was most required.[3] These developments were themselves the result of three factors: (1) the altered structure of political systems in many countries – where the extension of the voting franchise to the middle and lower classes had produced weak governments with little capacity to impose restrictive economic policy measures, as required by external constraints whenever the country suffered a loss of reserves; (2) a system of international relations poisoned by unresolved contentious issues such as German reparations and inter-allied debt; and (3) the divergent conceptual frameworks used by policy makers from different countries to interpret past and present economic and financial developments, making it hard for governments to reach multilateral agreement on how best to stabilise the world economy.[4] Overall, to paraphrase Jeffry Frieden, in the 1920s the domestic political support for governments supportive of a rules-based global economy was in decline.[5]

Against this backdrop, there was perhaps little that even the best designed and most effective international organisation could achieve, and the League of Nations' Economic and Financial Organisation (EFO) was neither well designed nor effective.[6] It came into existence with little previous planning and against the resistance of important League member countries; it lacked the official support of the United States, the world's most powerful economy – even though President Woodrow Wilson was the League's most ardent proponent, the country rejected membership in 1919; it was not entrusted with executive powers enabling it to adopt, let alone enforce, binding decisions; and finally, some of the most venomous issues in international financial affairs, most notably war debts and

---

[3] Eichengreen, *Golden Fetters*, 9, and, in greater detail, ch. 7. Although Eichengreen's analysis is basically concerned with the international monetary system, his arguments can easily explain the difficulties encountered by efforts at reconstructing an international economic and trade regime through the 1920s.

[4] Ibid., 10–11 and 391–92.

[5] Jeffry A. Frieden, *Global Capitalism: Its Fall and Rise in the Twentieth Century* (New York, 2006), xvii.

[6] The standard text on the Economic and Financial Organisation is Martin Hill, *The Economic and Financial Organization of the League of Nations: A Survey of Twenty-Five Years' Experience* (Washington, 1946); the sharpest international law perspectives are provided by Victor-Yves Ghébali, 'Aux origines de l'Ecosoc: L'évolution des commissions et organisations techniques de la Société des Nations', *Annuaire français de droit international* 18 (1972), 465–511; Giorgio Conetti, *La costituzione delle organizzazioni tecniche nella Società delle Nazioni* (Milano, 1979). A recent, comprehensive review of the EFO's work and procedures is Patricia Clavin and Jens-Wilhelm Wessels, 'Transnationalism and the League of Nations: Understanding the Work of Its Economic and Financial Organisation', *Contemporary European History* 14 (2005), 465–92.

reparations, were carefully kept outside its remit. In this light, the EFO's accomplishments in the 1920s, most particularly in the field of finance, were actually quite remarkable. Contemporary perceptions in any case varied, and though many were sceptical about the chances of success of the organisation, one could count at least as many others holding sanguine expectations. On the one hand, EFO officials were naturally committed to an agenda of international economic cooperation and did their best to pursue it throughout the decade, looking for support amongst influential political leaders, interest groups and other international bodies.[7] On the other hand and reciprocally, politicians and private organisations whose economic programmes required international endorsement and coordination to be implemented at the national level, solicited the backing of the EFO.[8] All in all, the EFO, itself an embryo of modern multilateral economic organisation,[9] was meant to perform a few vaguely defined functions; yet given the stark differences between governments

[7] Ever since the early days of the League of Nations, many authors – from Schanzer and Monnet to Morley, Barros, Bussière, and Clavin and Wessels – have portrayed the secretariat as a highly influential body, one even enjoying a significant degree of autonomy. Other authors such as Ranshofen-Wertheimer, Siotis and Steiner take a more cautious view. Although the secretariat clearly exerted influence on the League's functioning and work, its actual autonomy seems to have varied over time as a result of changing attitudes by governments towards the League; it also seems evident that its ability to initiate policy was not independent of external support by governments, political leaders or powerful interest groups. See Carlo Schanzer, 'L'equivoco fondamentale della Società delle Nazioni', *Nuova antologia* 232 (1923), 3–16; Felix M. Morley, *The Society of Nations: Its Organization and Constitutional Development* (Washington, 1932); Egon F. Ranshofen-Wertheimer, *The International Secretariat: A Great Experiment in International Administration*, (Washington, 1945), 399–401; Jean Siotis, *Essai Sur Le Secrétariat International* (Genève; Paris, 1963); James Barros, 'The Role of Sir Eric Drummond', in *The League of Nations in Retrospect* (Berlin; New York, 1983), 31–41; Bussière, 'L'Organisation économique de la SDN et la naissance du régionalisme économique en Europe', *Relations internationales* 75 (1993), 301–13; Zara S. Steiner, *The Lights That Failed: European International History, 1919–1933* (Oxford, 2005); Clavin and Wessels, passim.

[8] This was most notably the case with policies concerning such issues as trade tariffs, industrial organisation and several international commodity markets. Beyond policies, there was also an attempt to establish reciprocal backing between international organisations and transnational movements, as Goethem notes in respect to the relationship between the International Federation of Trade Unions and the ILO. See Geert van Goethem, *The Amsterdam International: The World of the International Federation of Trade Unions (IFTU), 1913–1945* (Aldershot, 2006), 151.

[9] Louis Pauly has identified the two main bodies of the EFO, the Economic Committee and the Financial Committee, as forerunners of the General Agreement on Trade and Tariff and the International Monetary Fund. See Louis W. Pauly, *The League of Nations and the Foreshadowing of the International Monetary Fund* (Princeton, NJ, 1996). As far as the Financial Committee is concerned, much the same view is held by Harold James, *The End of Globalization: Lessons from the Great Depression* (Cambridge, MA, 2001), 25.

regarding international economic policy and their fierce reluctance to cede even trivial portions of their sovereign power, the actual extent of delegated authority was very limited.[10] The EFO thus enjoyed only a greatly restrained freedom of action, which made it extremely hard for the organisation to preserve both legitimacy and effectiveness. The route taken by its officials in the 1920s to cope with this situation was to mobilise the support of nongovernment actors.

It is the aim of this chapter to illustrate the new mode of global economic governance devised by the League of Nations' Economic and Financial Organisation in the second half of the 1920s, after it had become clear that the old mode was ineffective and was starting to threaten the organisation's legitimacy. The experiment in a new mode of governance was much akin to a route of last resort to escape the deadlock brought on by governmental influence over the work of the organisation, most particularly of its Economic Committee. This politicisation implied that the dispassionate, technical consideration of economic issues expected of the EFO was now superseded by overwhelming national interests championed by committee members acting as government representatives far more than as expert advisers for the League. As suggested, the new mode of governance adopted to counteract this development hinged on the active involvement in international economic policy making of business leaders, unions and consumers' associations. Interestingly, such actors not only came from nationally based associations but also from transnational movements and several international organisations such as the International Chamber of Commerce (ICC) and the International Labour Organisation (ILO).[11] In addition, acting as much more than mere policy advisers, nonstate actors were called on to serve as agents of policy change in the domestic arena.

However many hopes the EFO's new drive in global economic governance raised, it fell short of keeping its promise. In fact, nonstate actors turned out to be divided by conceptual, class and interest cleavages, which prevented them from agreeing on almost any set of international economic

---

[10] In modern international relations, governments usually delegate authority to an international organisation only after resolving their policy conflicts. When important divergences persist, as was the case with international economic policy in the 1920s, delegation becomes less likely. See Darren G. Hawkins, David A. Lake, et al., 'Delegation under Anarchy: States, International Organizations, and Principal-Agent Theory', in D. G. Hawkins, D. A. Lake, D. L. Nielson and M. J. Tierney (eds.), *Delegation and Agency in International Organizations* (Cambridge, 2006), 3–38.

[11] Because they were situated below, above and beside the state level, representing organisations of various natures, it seems most appropriate to refer to these actors collectively as 'nonstate actors'. However, I also make use of the term 'private actors'.

policies: not on trade liberalisation, nor on the method to address overcapacity in world commodity markets, and even less on the plan of French politician Louis Loucheur to organise and rationalise European industry by means of international cartels.

The private sector involvement in the EFO's new model of global economic governance differed in several ways from many pre–First World War instances of business-elite participation either in building the institutional underpinnings of a globalised world economy or in shifting the intra-trade balance in favour of one or another group. What was at stake in such instances was the ability of this elite and other nonstate actors to design and implement successful international schemes for self-regulation. By contrast, the engagement of private sector representatives in EFO activities had primarily an official character and gave rise to a complex, triangular interplay among the international organisation, member governments and nonstate actors. Second, the variety of nonstate actors was considerably wider. Third and more important, the role the EFO gave the private sector in the 1920s had a greatly enlarged public policy scope: the debates held in Geneva were concerned with vast issues such as international economic policy and the establishment of a new international economic order. This implied that private actors were supposed to represent far more general interests than those of a single industry. Finally, the scale of private sector official involvement was seemingly unprecedented.

Against this historical backdrop, this chapter, based on firsthand sources from the archives of the League of Nations and the private papers of the Italian industrialist Alberto Pirelli (a long-time economic and financial diplomat of the Italian government during the interwar years), is organised as follows. The first section reviews the procedures defining the EFO's work within the League's institutional setup and its mode of governance during the first half of the 1920s. This is followed by a description of the 1925–29 experiment with a new governance approach based on large-scale private actor involvement, reform of the Economic Committee (EC) and subsequent creation of the Economic Consultative Committee (ECC). The chapter ends with an overview of the international industrial cartel debate and a few observations by way of conclusion.

The EFO Within the League of Nations and its Early Mode of Governance

Like the other 'technical organisations' of the League of Nations, the Economic and Financial Organisation was an advisory body charged with

providing the League's political organs – its council and its assembly –
with advice on economic and financial issues and with assisting member
states in their projects of international cooperation.[12] It was made up of
two standing bodies – the Economic Committee, with which this chapter
is mainly concerned, and the Financial Committee – and of a series of ad
hoc committees and subcommittees serving on temporary terms.[13] Its only
permanent body was the Economic and Financial Section of the League's
secretariat, headed by Sir Arthur Salter until 1931. Despite the limited
functions it was entrusted with, the range of the EFO's activities kept
growing over time, as did its personnel, so that by the end of the 1930s it
was by far the largest technical organisation in the League of Nations.[14]
As is typical of international organisations, it provided global public
goods,[15] most systematically through the collection and publication of a
wide range of economic and financial statistical data.[16] Building on this
capacity and its unique 'habit of looking at problems from the point of
view of the world as a whole',[17] the EFO became the most prominent
international forum for monitoring, analysing and debating global economic policy issues and developments.[18] Financial stability was another
area in which the Financial Committee achieved significant results in the
1920s, designing and carrying out a number of monetary and financial
stabilisation schemes in Central and Eastern Europe. By contrast, the
accomplishments of the Economic Committee were much less impress-
ive. Although it succeeded in drawing up international conventions on

---

[12] See Hill, *The Economic and Financial Organization*, 5; Conetti, *La Costituzione Delle Organizzazioni Tecniche*, 98–100.

[13] Two other standing committees were added at a later stage: the Fiscal Committee (1929) and the Committee of Statistical Experts (1931).

[14] See Hill, *The Economic and Financial Organization*, 4.

[15] For a definition of global public goods see Inge Kaul, Isabelle Grunberg, et al., 'Defining Global Public Goods', in I. Kaul, I. Grunberg and M. A. Stern (eds.), *Global Public Goods: International Cooperation in the 21st Century* (Oxford, 1999), 2–19.

[16] See Alexander Loveday, 'Geneva as a Centre of Economic Information', *Index. Svenska Handelsbanken* 9 (1934).

[17] Internal memorandum prepared by the British Foreign Office in 1918 as a basis for the League of Nations' project. See Alfred Eckhard Zimmern, *The League of Nations and the Rule of Law, 1918–1935* (London, 1936), 196–208. The uniqueness of the EFO's point of view was also remarked on by Herbert Feis, *Research Activities of the League of Nations: A Report Made to the Committee on International Relations of the Social Science Research Council on the Methods and Progress of Research in the League of Nations and International Labour Organization, June, 1929* (Old Lyme, CT, 1929).

[18] See for instance Eric Bussière, 'L'Organisation Économique de la SDN'.

several trade-related issues of mainly legal character,[19] throughout its existence the EC largely failed to affect world economic and trade conditions. Probably most disappointing was its inability to satisfactorily address the issue – enshrined in the League's covenant and a major legal foundation of the EFO itself – of 'equitable treatment' for commerce between member countries in the League; it thus could not reestablish an international trade regime, whether based on a process of gradual trade liberalisation or on moderate protectionism.

Three interrelated factors stood behind the EC's poor performance. First, trade issues greatly exacerbated the distributional conflict between those who stood to win and those who stood to lose from a higher degree of economic openness. These issues stirred up domestic political debate and turned out to be very difficult for governments to treat – seemingly much more so than monetary issues, on which there was general consensus that countries should return to the gold standard as soon as possible. Second, in the course of the 1920s the belief that trade liberalisation was the best recipe for a fast return to sustained economic growth came to be increasingly questioned. As the head of the commercial agreements department of the French Ministry of Commerce, Daniel Serruys, observed, the years 1922–26 witnessed a paradigm shift from dogmatic free-trade orthodoxy to a more pragmatic view justifying a formidable array of protectionist measures to accommodate the great disparity among national economic conditions.[20] Right or wrong, the new view represented a serious impediment to a unified trade regime, not least because Serruys – who served on the Economic Committee from 1920 to 1930 – was himself one of its champions, and France both a major trading country and still one of the great powers. Third, internal procedures and decision-making rules exposed the EFO to national-interest politics likely to negatively affect its work to a high degree. This latter consideration warrants further analysis.

Although the EFO was free to set its own agenda and adopt recommendations, its committees were subject to political control by the council

---

[19] A list of successfully adopted treaties cover simplification of customs formalities (1923) protection of industrial property rights (1925), commercial arbitration (1927), economic statistics (1928), and the unification of laws concerning bills of exchange (1930 and 1931). Matters for which a convention could not be drawn up were a most-favoured nation clause and a customs standard nomenclature. In the second half of the 1920s, efforts to reduce trade tariffs, culminating in the 1930 conference aimed at concerted economic action for the sake of a tariff truce, failed dramatically. See Hill, *The Economic and Financial Organization*, ch. 4.

[20] See Daniel Serruys, 'L'œuvre économique de la S.D.N. – 2', *La revue des vivants* 3 (1929), 731–44.

and the assembly.[21] Even though the council's preemptive oversight in the early years of the organisation was soon relaxed, the assembly's Second Committee never actually gave up its right to shape the EFO's agenda both ex ante and ex post. This resulted in a degree of self-censorship on the EFO's part, with fear of potential criticism or disavowal conditioning its approach to politically sensitive matters.[22] There was, however, a second potent channel through which national politics crept into the EFO's committees and influenced its activities. Committee members were appointed by the League of Nations' council on suggestion of the secretariat. In principle, they would not be representatives of governments but experts working in their personal capacity, chosen on grounds of individual skills and technical competences, in conformity with the technical character of the functions they were expected to perform. In addition, they were formally held accountable only to the council. Yet despite insistent official emphasis on expertise, personal capacity and international cooperation, not only did patterns of national representation in the main committees reflect council composition,[23] but as noted by Arthur Salter, head of the Economic and Financial Section of the secretariat, appointments to the EC were 'always of persons ascertained to be acceptable to the Governments, and [were] usually indeed suggested, though informally, by the Governments'.[24]

Veto power in the council and, above all, decision making by consensus within the EFO's committees simply magnified the risk that its technical consideration of international economic and trade issues would stall, as a

[21] Martin David Dubin, 'Transgovernmental Processes in the League of Nations', *International Organization* 37 (1983), 469–93.

[22] See Vladimir D. Pastuhov, *Memorandum on the Composition, Procedure and Functions of Committees of the League of Nations* (Washington, 1943). In practice, the control exercised by the council and the assembly varied over time and according to some authors should not be overestimated: council members – usually foreign ministers or high-ranking diplomats but also assembly delegates who themselves were often officials from the economic ministries – lacked the time and sometimes the interest, often even the competence, to engage in close scrutiny.

[23] As far as the Economic Committee is concerned, each of the great powers (Great Britain, France, Italy and Japan) had one member on the committee, as did various groupings of countries such as the Commonwealth, South America, the Scandinavian countries and East Central Europe according to a principle of indirect representation. See H. R. G. Greaves, *The League Committees and the World Order* (London, 1931), 43–44; Zimmern, 447–48. Most committee members came from the ministries of commerce and the treasuries, but there were also industrialists (on the Economic Committee) and bankers, central bank officials and financiers (on the Financial Committee).

[24] League of Nations Archives (LNA), Salter's Papers, box 123, file 8, note enclosed to a letter to Dwight Morrow, July 1927.

result not only of diverging national interests and intellectual approaches to international trade but also, possibly, of international friction.[25] In these circumstances, it did not take long before committee members shifted their loyalty and accountability from bodies of the League to their home governments, giving national politics priority over the goal of international economic cooperation. Inevitably, this would impair the efficacy and undermine the legitimacy of the EFO's committees, most notably the EC. In fact, during the first half of the 1920s, the EC's agenda focused almost exclusively on technical matters of commercial law, without readily apparent political implications.[26]

The failure of this early mode of governance, which roughly echoed the pattern of wartime inter-allied cooperation,[27] increasingly called for the EFO to explore alternative, more effective approaches. In practice, this meant turning to 'public opinion' as a route to escape deadlock and recover legitimacy.

Global Governance through Nonstate Actors, 1925–1929

By the mid-1920s, the EFO's officials had become fully cognisant of the serious impairment to the work of the Economic Committee resulting from politicisation and were seeking ways to enhance its effectiveness and legitimacy. In his 1925 'Proposal for a World Economic Conference', Arthur Salter was straightforward about how politically intractable trade talks had proved since the 1922 Genoa Conference and the scant prospect that an international conference of government representatives would yield positive results in the near future. Worse, 'it might well do more harm than good'. In view of this, argued Salter, the League had 'certainly been right so far in not convening a general economic conference of any

---

[25] On how Anglo-French – not to mention Franco-German – differences reverberated in the League of Nations see for instance Ruth Henig, 'Britain, France and the League of Nations in the 1920s', in A. J. Sharp and G. Stone (eds.), *Anglo-French Relations in the Twentieth Century: Rivalry and Cooperation* (London, 2000), 139–57.

[26] See Alexander A. Menzies, 'Technical Assistance and the League of Nations', in *The League of Nations in Retrospect* (Berlin, 1983), 295–312. A turning point was the swiftly terminated debate held in 1922 on drafts for three conventions representing the Economic Committee's interpretation of the 'equitable treatment' of commerce: on that occasion the French committee member Daniel Serruys made clear he would endorse none of the drafts. See Private Papers of Alberto Pirelli (PPAP), box 48, file II-1, report on the work of the Economic Committee.

[27] On the structure and working of wartime inter-allied cooperation see Arthur Salter, *Allied Shipping Control: An Experiment in International Administration* (Oxford, 1921); Jean Monnet, *Mémoires* (Paris, 1976), 59–82.

kind', but it 'surely has not done its duty until it has at least tried one method available to it of breaking out of the closed circle, i.e. the organization of a forum of general world opinion which may influence the policies of the Governments'.[28]

This view was consistent with both Salter's and Lord Cecil's early sense that in times when governments were extremely jealous of their sovereignty and fearful that the new international organisation would restrict their freedom of action, public opinion would be crucial to the League of Nations' success or failure.[29] However, that public opinion would be embodied by a multiplicity of nonstate actors is much less obvious. In fact, such a view rested on twin assumptions: that private sector representatives possessed unparalleled knowledge of world economic affairs and that they wielded sufficient influence in domestic politics to bring the policy stance of governments in line with the goal of international cooperation.

The EFO's move reflected a substantially correct reading of current developments in the role of government and the evolving nature of the political process in many countries. Wartime mobilisation had led to a growth in the moral, social and political authority of many business and trade union leaders as a result of their taking on significant responsibilities in reallocating production, expanding output and keeping workers as disciplined as possible.[30] In addition, organising the war effort had entailed a huge, swift expansion of government functions that put the state's administrative apparatus under severe strain, leading to the recruitment of private individuals from the outside to serve on the many newly created bodies.[31] A key determinant of this process was the lack of

---

[28] See Arthur Salter, 'A Proposal for a World Economic Conference', in *The United States of Europe and Other Papers*, (London, 1933), 33–43, 39.

[29] As early as 1919, Salter wrote that it would be 'one of the main tasks' of the nascent institution 'so to manage things as to give every chance for this public opinion to develop, and to time [its] action at different stages with a very close regard to the actual and potential public sentiment of the period'. See Arthur Salter, 'The Organization of the League of Nations', in Arthur Salter, *The United States of Europe and Other Essays* (London, 1933), 14–31. For the views of Lord Cecil – one of the British founders and most wholehearted supporters of the League – on how the Geneva organisation would work see Robert Cecil, *World Opinion and the League of Nations* (London, 1918). On the importance of public opinion in the 1920s, partly as a result of the intense use of propaganda during wartime, see Steiner, *The Lights That Failed* (New York, 2005), 7–8.

[30] See for instance Steiner, *The Lights That Failed*, 6–7.

[31] Remarkable examples are Louis Loucheur and Jean Monnet from France; Alberto Pirelli from Italy; Walter Layton and Sidney Chapman from Great Britain; and Emile Francqui from Belgium. Some new recruits served on a temporary basis, returning to private activity at the war's end, whereas others started a new career altogether.

adequate technical knowledge at the direct disposal of governments. In the 1920s, while the demand for outside expert advice remained steady owing to the complex, technical nature of new governmental functions,[32] the harsh distributional conflict over which social groups should bear the cost of the war and subsequent reconstruction considerably heightened the trend towards 'political devolution', that is, decentralisation of the loci of decision making.[33] Increasingly, this led to a hollowing out of legislative bodies and the transfer of authority to ministerial bureaucracies and other political organisations in close contact with vested interest groups. Political stability was thus achieved by means of what Charles Maier has termed 'corporatist equilibrium'.[34]

In 1925, the proper time to convene an international conference seemed to have arrived. The international political and financial situation had by then greatly improved thanks to the Locarno Treaty and the Dawes Plan for German reparations; the return to gold of the pound had paved the way for restoration of other major currencies; inter-allied war debt negotiations were underway; and world production and trade had almost recovered to prewar levels. Yet despite such progress, reconstruction had proceeded unevenly across Europe, and structural adjustment of the various national economies was far from complete.[35] In that context, high unemployment rates and excess capacity in several industries and commodity markets encouraged a sentiment that some form of international collective action was needed. By the mid-1920s, organised labour, the ILO and the ICC had all welcomed a multilateral initiative to that effect, leading to the convening of the International Economic Conference.[36] The endorsement of Salter's proposal by the French politician Louis Loucheur and its approval by the League of Nations assembly in September

---

[32] See for instance Arthur Fontaine, 'Le fardeau écrasant de l'Etat', *La revue des vivants* 3 (1929), 763–73.

[33] Harold Richard Goring Greaves, *The League Committees and World Order: A Study of the Permanent Expert Committees of the League of Nations as an Instrument of International Government* (London, 1931), 3–6. According to Greaves, political devolution was also the result of construing democracy as a process of government through continuous consultation with those mainly affected by policy measures.

[34] Charles S. Maier, *Recasting Bourgeois Europe: Stabilization in France, Germany, and Italy in the Decade after World War I* (Princeton, 1975), 353.

[35] See Derek Howard Aldcroft, *From Versailles to Wall Street, 1919–1929* (London, 1977), 187 ff.; Ronald Findlay and Kevin H. O'Rourke, *Power and Plenty: Trade, War, and the World Economy in the Second Millennium* (Princeton, 2007), 435 ff.; Feinstein, Temin et al., 52 ff. Harold James, ch. 3, has explored the EFO's handling of trade issues.

[36] See Edgar Milhaud, 'L'organisation économique de la paix', *Recueil des cours* 15 (1926), 277–431, 289–92.

1925 marked a turning point in EFO governance. As Loucheur put it, it inaugurated 'not merely a stage but an epoch' in the organisation's work.

The defining principles of the new mode of governance hinged on large-scale private actor involvement, broader national representation, and as great an insulation from political pressure as could be achieved. To varying degrees, all of this can be seen at work in the composition and procedure of the Preparatory Committee (PC) of the International Economic Conference, the conference itself, and the 1927 reform of the Economic Committee along with its outcome, the Economic Consultative Committee (1928–29).

Established in late 1925 and early 1926 with a view to setting the conference agenda, the PC was made up of thirty-five persons from twenty-one countries as against twelve members from twelve countries in the EC. Furthermore, whereas most EC members came from economic ministries, nearly all members of the PC were business association and trade union leaders, representatives of consumer movements and, to a smaller extent, economists. A few representatives of international organisations such as the EFO, the ILO and the International Institute of Agriculture (IIA) were also present, alongside those of major private organisations including the International Chamber of Commerce, the International Federation of Trade Unions, the International Christian Trade Union and the International Cooperative Alliance.[37] Appointments to the PC were made by the council upon the secretariat's proposal: its members were not official governmental delegates but served in their personal capacity as sources of expert knowledge. Although the procedure was generally the same as that involved in appointments to the EC, several elements signalled a difference. First, it was explicitly aimed at discussions in the PC being 'entirely untrammelled' by political pressures;[38] next, the larger membership made the outcome of debates less predictable; and most important, decisions were taken by majority vote instead of consensus.

Held in Geneva in May 1927, the International Economic Conference involved the participation of 194 delegates and 157 experts from fifty countries, including some non-members of the League of Nations. Private

[37] Actually, the International Cooperative Alliance was not officially invited to the Preparatory Commission, but the Swedish Anders Örne and the Austrian Emmi Freundlich, two eminent leaders of the organisation, took an active part in the commission's work. See William Pascoe Watkins, *The International Co-Operative Alliance, 1895–1970* (London, 1970), 156.

[38] League of Nations Archives (LNA), C.818.1925.II.B and C.807.(1).1925.II.B, Paul Hymans' statement and report, respectively, to the council, December 1925.

actors again predominated, although the conference had a much more official character than the PC, because the choice of delegates was left to governments and recommendations had to be passed unanimously. The conference also set the stage for ever closer cooperation between the EFO and the ICC: all the chairpersons and rapporteurs at the conference had been eminent personalities of the ICC,[39] and the relationship between the two organisations was further reinforced by the election of Alberto Pirelli, long-time Italian member of the EC, to the ICC presidency for the 1927–29 period.

Among the many subjects discussed at the conference, the EFO's reform, although relegated to a secondary role vis-à-vis trade, industrial organisation and agricultural issues, was nevertheless of great importance. The five proposed reform schemas all emphasised institutionalising the practice of consulting with private actors, on the grounds they would bring deeper technical knowledge and enhance the legitimacy and effectiveness of the EFO's work. The most ambitious such plan, proposed by Léon Jouhaux, envisaged creation of a new international economic organisation within the League's framework, based upon the model of the ILO, but not under control of the council or assembly.[40]

Once reform proposals were referred to the council, it fell to the secretariat to work out a plan. In his review of the situation, Salter regarded continued collaboration of private actors, the ICC and the ILO in a form influencing the EFO's general work as a priority. At the same time, he worried about the risks entailed by an entirely new organisation, such as excessive budgetary burdens and a possible conflict of authority with the EFO's existing structure. He thus discarded both Jouhaux's project and the idea of an enlargement of the EC to include business, labour and agricultural representatives. Instead, he put forward a plan for broadened national representation on the EC[41] and creation of the Economic

---

[39] Private Papers of Alberto Pirelli (PPAP), Writings and speeches, report to ICC's Economic Committee on the International Economic Conference, 2 June 1927.

[40] League of Nations, *Rapport et actes de la Conférence économique internationale*, (Geneva, 1927), vol. 1, 185–86. The plan's other proponents were Arthur Pugh, a member of the general council of the British Trade Union Conference from 1920 to 1936; the German Friedrich Baltrusch and the Dutch Serrarens (both Christian union leaders, the latter also secretary general of the International Christian Trade Union); the British statesman Arthur Balfour (now famous as author of the Balfour Declaration); and the Polish former trade minister Hipolit Gliwic. Léon Jouhaux was the secretary general of the French Confédération Générale du Travail from 1909 to 1947 and a representative of labour on the ILO's governing body from 1919 to 1954.

[41] Membership in the EC was eventually increased from twelve to fifteen with one seat reserved for the United States. A new class of 'correspondent members' was created for countries without an official member.

Consultative Committee (ECC), devised as a forum bringing together 'the most competent section of public opinion [...] whence each year new ideas may emerge which are likely to be of particular value as representing the views of the most varied economic circles'.[42]

Consistent with the principles that had inspired the Preparatory Committee, the new ECC was composed of sixty-four members from twenty-six countries, most of them business association and trade union leaders, consumer-movement representatives and agricultural experts. Again, a handful of economists, together with a range of EFO, ICC, ILO and IIA delegates, completed the picture.[43] The ECC was constituted on the basis of a three-year term and was meant to meet once a year. As was the case for the PC, the council made appointments to the ECC in light of technical expertise and personal capacity. The ECC's tasks consisted of monitoring compliance of governmental policy with the conference's recommendations and directing suggestions to the council regarding new research and initiatives by the Economic Committee. Unlike the PC, however, its recommendations were to be made unanimously.

With the establishment of the ECC, the League of Nations' Economic and Financial Organisation could secure access to the information and policy advice in a manner actually affecting its activities. True, the new body had no authority to adopt binding resolutions, and its actions were subject to review by the council. Furthermore, those ECC proposals that succeeded in shaping the EC's agenda, as they actually did to a significant extent, still entered a highly politicised environment where their innovative thrust was likely to be thwarted. Nevertheless, the new committee was relatively insulated from political pressure. Furthermore, expectations concerning its work went much further than securing contact with the real world and access to privileged expert advice. As the ECC's chairman Georges Theunis wrote in convening the committee's first meeting in 1928, not only were ECC members meant to monitor national economic policies and put forward new ideas; they were also meant to commit themselves to using all their weight with national governments and public opinion, both personally and through their

---

[42] League of Nations, *Official Journal*, Assembly records, 9th session (1928), special supplement n. 66, Annex 2, 'Economic work of the League', 57.

[43] The ECC's meetings were attended on invitation by representatives of other international bodies such as the International Management Institute, the Commission Internationale d'Agriculture, the Conseil International Scientifique Agricole, the Joint Standing Committee of Women's International Organisations, and the International Federation of League of Nations Societies.

constituencies, in pressing for policy changes along the lines agreed upon in Geneva.[44] In the EFO's new system of governance, private sector representatives were thus involved as policy advisers and, though informally, as agents of policy change at the national level.

International Cartel Debate and Diversity: From Deadlock to Stalemate, 1927–1929

At the International Economic Conference, the policy debate over how Europe's prosperity and competitiveness could best be restored, not least in the face of the U.S. economy's 'roaring' performance, set the stage for a major confrontation between free traders and protectionists, championed, respectively, by Swedish economist Gustav Cassel and French politician Louis Loucheur. Whereas Cassel blamed European slow growth on practices restraining market competition, such as trade unionism, monopolies and cartels, Loucheur regarded international industrial cartels as a substitute for tariff protection. In his view, such cartels would allow industrial restructuring to take place in an environment sheltered from international competition; once the process was completed and efficiency regained, it would be much easier to resume trade liberalisation talks. Loucheur thus proposed organising European industry into a web of international cartels. Yet the discussions surrounding this plan brought to light profound cleavages cutting across national and class lines and proving much more difficult to bridge than those created by tariff reduction.

A first sharp difference was that between supporters and opponents of the cartel project itself. Among industrialists, Henry de Peyerimhoff, French president of the Comité des Houillères, and the German Clement Lammers, a member of the Reichstag and the Reichsverband der Deutschen Industrie, warmly welcomed international cartels. Lammers in particular played an active part in seeking a compromise that ultimately resulted in a conference recommendation for further consideration of the matter by the EFO. Although they approved of the project in general terms, both Gino Olivetti, secretary general of the Italian Federation of Manufacturers and an ICC delegate, and Ernest Wetter, vice-president of the Union Suisse du Commerce et de l'Industrie, raised concerns that firms using the regulated goods as production inputs might have to bear undue costs. The stance of other industrialists was at best sceptical. For

---

[44] PPAP, International Chamber of Commerce, file I-2, letter to the members of the Economic Consultative Committee, 3 May 1928.

instance, Vilhelm Lundvik, director general of the Federation of Swedish Industries in 1926–41, though conceding that international cartels might help reduce production costs and improve capital efficiency, believed that economic growth would be the result of free markets far more than private regulation. In addition to voicing fears that raw material importers could fall prey to monopolistic abuses, he indicated that he did not expect any positive impact on tariffs from the cartelisation movement.[45] The Norwegian Hjalmar Wessel, managing director of the wood pulp multinational firm Borregaard, was even more insistent in denying that cartels produced general growth effects and submitted a draft resolution calling for the conference to avoid any recommendation favouring cartels.[46] V. A. Magnus Lavonius, the Finnish director-general of the Suomi Life Insurance Co., basically held the same view.[47]

For their part, the trade union representatives were inclined to think of cartels as simply a phase in the capitalist system's evolution, a factor of price and employment stability, and a means to rationalise industry and diffuse technological innovation. Whether French, British, German, Belgian or Dutch, or whether emerging from a Christian or a Socialist tradition, trade unionists were essentially concerned with the effect of cartels on the general public; they thus placed greatest emphasis on corporate governance and questions of regulation. Although revealing a wider spectrum of feelings, representatives of consumers' movements took the same general attitude.[48]

Amongst the economists at the conference, the Chilean professor of political economy Dario Urzua and his Latvian colleague Charles Balodis generally shared Cassel's views. High-ranking civil servants displayed

[45] League of Nations, *Rapports et actes de la Conférence Economique Internationale*, 2nd Sub-committee, vol. 2, 161. For a contemporary review of the connection between international industrial agreements and tariffs see Clemens Lammers and Karl Scholz, 'The Cartel Question at the World Economic Conference', *Annals of the American Academy of Political and Social Science* 134 (1927), 145–50; Louis Domeratzky, 'The International Cartel as an Influence in Tariff Policies', *Annals of the American Academy of Political and Social Science* 141 (1929), 238–42.

[46] League of Nations, *Rapports et actes de la Conférence Economique Internationale*, 2nd Sub-committee, vol. 2, 178.

[47] Ibid., 157.

[48] It was also the case that members of the International Cooperative Alliance – for instance, the Austrian Emmi Freundlich – were pronouncedly more supportive than Jaakko Keto, vice-chairman of the Finnish national diet and director-general of the Central Union of Distributive Societies, or the Swedish politician Anders Örne, director general of the Swedish Post and a member of the executive board of the International Cooperative Alliance.

widely varied opinions. The chief of the Estonian National Economic Council and former president of the Estonian parliament, Jean Toenisson, favoured cartels, provided they were subjected to close monitoring by some state national or international authority. The former Dutch general commissioner of the League of Nations in Austria, Alfred Zimmerman, and the former Czech minister of commerce, Charles Urban, both believed, to the contrary, that private international industrial agreements should be encouraged or at least left free to develop and that any government interference would be ineffectual or even harmful. At the opposite extreme, Gunnar Jahn, director of the Norwegian Central Office of Statistics, was personally aware of the difficulties inherent in the control of cartel price policies and was convinced that cartels only benefitted a limited group of rent-seekers.[49]

Within the field of cartel supporters the issue of whether and how cartels should be regulated was even more contentious. Both the trade union and consumers' representatives regarded such regulation as a *sine qua non* of any cartel policy: an excessive concentration of power in the hands of employers, they feared, would result in exploitation and abuse of workers and the broader public. To avert this, Christian unionists advocated worker representation on cartel boards and pressed for some form of institutional arrangement making for permanent international cooperation between governments and social partners.[50] The blueprint envisaged by socialist trade unions was much more elaborate, involving creation of a legal institutional framework based on national supervising agencies connected to an international bureau (both with powers to carry out investigations and impose sanctions); harmonisation of national legislations; public knowledge of the articles of association and operations of cartels; and representation by workers and consumers on national supervising bodies.[51]

Industrialists and officials were divided along different lines. Some – like Zimmerman and Urban – did not want any regulation, whereas others – for instance, Toenisson, Balodis and the Polish government's expert Roger Battaglia – thought of it as a prerequisite. Still others, like de Peyerimhoff, merely showed little sensitivity to the issue. In addition, some saw regulation as simply amounting to the furnishing of public

---

[49] League of Nations, *Rapports et actes de la Conférence Economique Internationale*, 2nd Sub-committee, vol. 2, 157.

[50] See for instance the Declaration of Christian unionists signed by eight representatives from seven European countries in ibid., vol. 1, 241–42.

[51] See the Declaration signed by eleven delegates from eleven countries in ibid., 240–41.

information on cartels. International oversight was a separate question. Among the industrialists, it was Lammers who laid down the most detailed views in this respect. Although he sympathised with the claim staked by workers and consumers to sit on cartel boards, he pointed to the potential conflict of interest facing the former, and the likely bafflement of the latter, who most times were workers themselves. The state, he believed, could actually protect consumers' interests, but its participation in cartel management was to be avoided. Lammers favoured the adoption of national regulatory frameworks and also allowed for some form of international control, provided that equally effective policing instruments were put in place in each country. Yet international control was not to include an international court with the capacity to intervene in a country's private economic organisation: any complaints concerning monopolistic abuses were to be referred to arbitration courts established on a voluntary basis by the parties to the cartel.[52]

The principle of unanimity made finding points in common within such disparate positions as important as it was difficult. In the final recommendations agreed on at the conference, cartels were recognised as a product of the economic circumstances prevailing after the war, not more than part of the solution to Europe's industrial problems. Likewise, cartels might be good or bad depending on their objectives and actual managerial policies. As to national cartels, no recommendations were made to governments regarding specific legislation, aside from avoiding hostile legal provisions. International legislation was dismissed on the grounds that it could not find any practical realisation. The best means to effectively control cartel behaviour consisted in publicizing information on cartel contracts and operations. To this effect, the EFO was meant to gather and occasionally publish such information.[53]

At the first session of the Economic Consultative Committee in May 1928, the differences that had emerged at the conference stood almost unchanged. These now blended with feelings of general dissatisfaction caused by scant progress of the Economic Committee on all the important issues the conference had brought to its attention. As Daniel Serruys reported, doctrinal disputes among protectionists and free traders had rendered the EC's work difficult. Uneasiness was also caused by governmental action regarding tariffs: as Walter Layton, Arthur Balfour

---

[52] Lammers and Scholz, 'The Cartel Question at the World Economic Conference'.
[53] League of Nations, *Rapports et actes de la Conférence Economique Internationale*, vol. 1, 50–51.

and Anders Örne acknowledged, the general level of protection had stopped rising, but it had shown no tendency yet to decrease. Nor had employment recovered significantly. In brief, as Jouhaux observed, there were good reasons for disappointment.[54]

With the support of union leaders and consumer representatives, Louis Loucheur invited the ECC's members to be more resolute in urging the EC to focus on a limited agenda, at the head of which stood international cartels, but his efforts were largely frustrated by the neglect of most of the consultative committee, which was mainly concerned with trade liberalisation. Regarding international industrial cartels, the ECC's report for 1928 only contains a recommendation that the EC undertake a general study of their nature and legal form and the different national legislations regulating their operations. This was simply a preliminary step towards executing the much broader task assigned the EFO by the International Economic Conference in 1927.

In September 1928, the League of Nations assembly undertook a review of where things stood with the cartel issue. Loucheur now overtly complained that the EFO's reform had reached a standstill in 1927 and that the organisation had not been empowered to the point where it could affect economic conditions. He also blamed the slow progress on industrialists being so concerned with their own interests that reaching an agreement with organised labour had become impossible.[55]

By the time the ECC met for the second time in May 1929, the economic situation had worsened further. Tariffs in Europe were now on the rise, the U.S. Congress was debating the highly protectionist Smoot-Hawley tariff, capital flows across the Atlantic had shrunk, and the initiatives undertaken by the Economic Committee at the ECC's behest – among these, dealing with the problem of coal and sugar overproduction – had produced almost no tangible results. Information gathering and the study of international cartels had begun, but the descriptive way in which such work was being framed did not seem to promise anything meaningful in the short term. A sense of disillusionment thus appears to have spread among ECC members, exacerbating the debates and bringing out differences instead of producing cohesion. As Jouhaux put it, 'the feelings expressed [were] many, and as diverse as the various methods used in the cultivation of the soil. They [had] nearly all given expression

---

[54] LNA, Economic Consultative Committee, 1st session, proceedings, May 1928. Layton was the editor of the Economist from 1922 to 1938.
[55] League of Nations, *Official Journal*, Assembly records, 9th session, 1928.

to a hope unfulfilled, to an impatience arrested, and to a desire to introduce an optimistic note into the discussions of this Committee. In what that optimism should consist, no one appear[ed] to be quite clear'.[56]

The report the ECC eventually submitted to the council on its second session openly acknowledged divisions as to cartel policy. Although industrialists (mainly Loucheur and Lammers) and unionists (Jouhaux, Pugh and Serrarens) had made substantial headway towards a compromise on regulatory arrangements, the great majority of committee members had shown very little interest in the subject. The only recommendations that could reach unanimity were for further study of national cartel legislations and of the effects of cartels on technological diffusion, industrial output, working conditions and prices. In addition, the EC was invited to publish annual reports based on publicly available information about international cartels.[57]

In September 1929, the assembly changed the EFO's agenda, giving priority to an intergovernmental conference aimed at a tariff truce. This did not mean the end of the cartel project, which was revived in the context of Aristide Briand's plan for a European Union, but certainly marked the end (and failure) of the system of governance inaugurated in 1925. Until 1931, private actors continued to play a role, although a much reduced one, in the EFO's activities and consultations, but, as the Great Depression swept across Europe, they disappeared from Geneva, their role being replaced by experts from the ranks of government.

Conclusion

In the second half of the 1920s, after years of stalemate on the most important issue of the agenda of its Economic Committee – establishing a new international trade regime that would secure equitable treatment of commerce among League of Nations members – the League's Economic and Financial Organisation embarked on a new mode of global governance. Indeed, the paralysis resulting from the interference of national politics had de facto transformed the EC into a venue for intergovernmental negotiations – a far cry from its statutory character as an international technical body advising governments on international economic cooperation. By the mid-1920s, this situation, already greatly diminishing the EC's effectiveness, was also seriously undermining its

[56] LNA, Economic Consultative Committee, 2nd session, proceedings, May 1929.
[57] League of Nations, *Rapport du Comité consultatif économique sur sa deuxième session*, 15 May 1929, 18–19.

legitimacy, in the face of widespread perceptions that monetary stabilisation and reconstruction had not restored a healthy world economy.

The EFO's new global governance centred on nonstate actors – mainly representatives of large national and transnational vested interests organisations – as providers of policy advice and as agents of policy change. This was a mutually reinforcing coalition meant to overcome differences between governments and devise and implement policies whose viability was conditional on international collective action.

However, the EFO's officials miscalculated the capacity of nonstate actors to negatively affect the policy formulation process. Indeed, as the international cartel debate clearly demonstrates, different intellectual approaches, class cleavages and conflicting interests prevented agreement both at the International Economic Conference and within the Economic Consultative Committee. Even when a minimum common denominator could be found among ECC members – for instance, on the coal and sugar sectors hit by overcapacity and tariff reduction for a select group of commodities – the Economic Committee, on which governmental pressure was more or less directly exerted, thwarted the effort to take effective action.

In the end, governments managed to retain virtually full control over international economic policy making through their 'representatives' on the Economic Committee, bringing about the defeat of the most ambitious proposals aimed at EFO reform. In this respect, Kahler and Lake are certainly right in maintaining that the years 1914–45 witnessed a 'centralization of political authority at the level of the nation-state'.[58] Still, as seen from Geneva, the second half of the 1920s would perhaps merit a more nuanced depiction.

The League of Nations' secretariat, which had staked its reputation on the successful implementation of international economic cooperation, consistently sought to strike a balance between maintaining the support of member governments and its own interpretation of the EFO's mission. In light of the poor outcomes of the new mode of governance, it is telling that the head of the Economic and Financial Section, Arthur Salter, left his office in 1931, as the League's deputy secretary-general Jean Monnet did in 1923.

Insofar as the EFO's experiment in global governance was based on the assumption that nonstate actors had unrivalled expert knowledge and sufficient political clout to alter governmental policies, it attests to

---

[58] Miles Kahler and David A. Lake, 'Globalization and Governance', in M. Kahler and D. A. Lake (eds.), *Governance in a Global Economy* (Princeton, 2003), 1–30.

the corporatist order of some major European polities in the 1920s – an order it reinforced. On the one hand the experiment implicitly conveyed mistrust in the ability of traditional politics to effectively deal with pressing economic and social issues; on the other hand it explicitly empowered nonstate actors as a more competent and reliable force in policy making.

More generally, the EFO's new approach to governance can be viewed as a sign of the deficiencies and contradictions of the role of government in the 1920s. Why did both governments and legislative bodies continuously rely on outside experts, in effect yielding authority to nonstate actors? Could governments and parliamentary assemblies not develop internally the knowledge they needed so badly and thus retain greater control over policy-advice sources? If we see the 1920s as a decade of contested political authority, this development seems the result of ideological and political uncertainty regarding the extent to which government should take on responsibility for economic and social management. With the onset of the Great Depression the situation changed, substantially and abruptly. Governments assumed broader responsibilities, working to develop adequate administrative capacity and the requisite human capital. Accordingly, as governments came to be seen as the only actors possessing both the legitimacy and means to tackle the crisis, their authority was gradually restored. In this light, it is no surprise that the EFO's experiment in global economic governance was so short-lived. Its duration was brief not only because irreconcilable differences prevented agreement on international economic policies by private sector representatives but also because the Great Depression had led to a more sharply defined map of political authority: one redrawing the boundaries between private and public spheres and placing governments and states on top of the ladder.

Index